# Comparative Regional Protection Frameworks for Refugees

This collection focuses on regional approaches to refugee protection, and specifically upon the norms, and the norm entrepreneurs of those approaches. It considers how recent crises in refugee protection (such as the Syrian and Andaman Sea crises) have highlighted the strengths and limits of regional approaches to refugee protection and the importance of looking closely at the underlying norms, and the identities and activities of the relevant 'norm entrepreneurs' at the regional level. It compares the norms of refugee protection that have evolved in three regions: the EU, Latin America and the South East Asian region, to identify which norms of refugee protection have been 'internalised' in the three regional contexts and to contextualise the processes. The authors demonstrate the need for awareness of the roles of different norm 'entrepreneurs' such as states, international organisations and civil society, in developing and promoting basic norms on refugee protection.

This book was originally published as a special issue of *The International Journal of Human Rights*.

**Susan Kneebone** is a Professorial Fellow in the Melbourne Law School at the University of Melbourne, Australia. Her recent research, funded by ARC grants, focuses on issues around governance of forced migration issues in South East Asia, including human trafficking and labour migration. She is the author of numerous books and articles, including many on the Bali Process and ASEAN processes.

T0347164

# Comparative Regional Protection Frameworks for Refugees

*Edited by*
**Susan Kneebone**

LONDON AND NEW YORK

First published 2017
by Routledge

2 Park Square, Milton Park, Abingdon, Oxfordshire OX14 4RN
52 Vanderbilt Avenue, New York, NY 10017

*Routledge is an imprint of the Taylor & Francis Group, an informa business*

First issued in paperback 2018

*British Library Cataloguing in Publication Data*
A catalogue record for this book is available from the British Library

ISBN 13: 978-1-138-63702-3 (hbk)
ISBN 13: 978-0-367-14255-1 (pbk)

Typeset in Times New Roman
by RefineCatch Limited, Bungay, Suffolk

**Publisher's Note**
The publisher accepts responsibility for any inconsistencies that may have
arisen during the conversion of this book from journal articles to book chapters,
namely the possible inclusion of journal terminology.

**Disclaimer**
Every effort has been made to contact copyright holders for their permission to
reprint material in this book. The publishers would be grateful to hear from any
copyright holder who is not here acknowledged and will undertake to rectify
any errors or omissions in future editions of this book.

# Contents

# Citation Information

The chapters in this book were originally published in *The International Journal of Human Rights*, volume 20, issue 2 (2016). When citing this material, please use the original page numbering for each article, as follows:

**Chapter 1**
*Comparative regional protection frameworks for refugees: norms and norm entrepreneurs*
Susan Kneebone
*The International Journal of Human Rights*, volume 20, issue 2 (2016), pp. 153–172

**Chapter 2**
*ASEAN and its approach to forced migration issues*
Sriprapha Petcharamesree
*The International Journal of Human Rights*, volume 20, issue 2 (2016), pp. 173–190

**Chapter 3**
*Refugee protection and responsibility sharing in Latin America: solidarity programmes and the Mexico Plan of Action*
Stefania Eugenia Barichello
*The International Journal of Human Rights*, volume 20, issue 2 (2016), pp. 191–207

**Chapter 4**
*Human security and external burden-sharing: the European approach to refugee protection between past and present*
Paolo Biondi
*The International Journal of Human Rights*, volume 20, issue 2 (2016), pp. 208–222

**Chapter 5**
*Networks and norm entrepreneurship amongst local civil society actors: advancing refugee protection in the Asia Pacific region*
Alice M. Nah
*The International Journal of Human Rights*, volume 20, issue 2 (2016), pp. 223–240

**Chapter 6**

*The ethics of resettlement: Australia and the Asia-Pacific Region*
Maria O'Sullivan
*The International Journal of Human Rights*, volume 20, issue 2 (2016), pp. 241–263

**Chapter 7**

*Rights, needs or assistance? The role of the UNHCR in refugee protection in the Middle East*
Dallal Stevens
*The International Journal of Human Rights*, volume 20, issue 2 (2016), pp. 264–283

For any permission-related enquiries please visit:
http://www.tandfonline.com/page/help/permissions

# Notes on Contributors

**Stefania Eugenia Barichello** is a PhD candidate in the Institute of Advanced Legal Studies at the School of Advanced Study, University of London, London, UK.

**Paolo Biondi** is a PhD candidate in the Institute of Advanced Legal Studies at the School of Advanced Study, University of London, London, UK.

**Susan Kneebone** is a Professorial Fellow in the Melbourne Law School at the University of Melbourne, Australia.

**Alice M. Nah** is a Lecturer in the Centre for Applied Human Rights at the University of York, York, UK.

**Maria O'Sullivan** is a Senior Lecturer in the Faculty of Law at Monash University, Melbourne, Australia.

**Sriprapha Petcharamesree** is a Lecturer in the Institute of Human Rights and Peace Studies at Mahidol University, Thailand.

**Dallal Stevens** is a Reader in the School of Law at the University of Warwick, Coventry, UK.

Dedicated to the memory of Stefania Eugenia Barichello who passed away before her time on 10th March 2017.

Devoted academic and passionate human rights defender.

# Comparative regional protection frameworks for refugees: norms and norm entrepreneurs

Susan Kneebone

*Faculty of Law, University of Melbourne, Australia*

This article analyses the strengths and limits of regional approaches to refugee protection. It compares three regions; namely the EU, Latin America and the Southeast Asian (SEA) region. It refers to two refugee protection crises to highlight the importance of regional approaches to refugee protection: namely the Rohingya "boat people" crisis which unfolded in the Indian Ocean in May 2015 and the advance of Syrian refugees towards Europe which escalated from the same period. It identifies the norms of refugee protection which have been "internalised" in the three regional contexts and contextualises the regional processes. It argues for the importance of looking closely at the underlying norms, and the identities and activities of the relevant "norm entrepreneurs" at the regional level. It concludes that regional solutions for refugee protection will be most effective when the norms have been solidly embedded in legal systems and institutions.

The focus of this collection is generally on regional approaches to refugee protection, and specifically upon the norms, and the norm entrepreneurs of those approaches. In 2015 two refugee protection crises highlighted the importance of regional approaches to refugee protection: namely the Rohingya 'boat people' crisis which unfolded in the Indian Ocean in May 2015 and the advance of Syrian refugees towards Europe which escalated from the same period. In each case it was the dissemination of shocking images in the global media which raised attention to the crisis: in the situation of the Rohingya it was the discovery of 26 bodies in a mass grave of smuggled Rohingya in a trafficking camp in southern Thailand in early May,[1] whereas in the case of Syrian refugees it was the single image on 2 September 2015 of the body of a young Syrian boy named Eylan. In fact both crises have been simmering for some time and arose from protracted, unresolved situations involving groups from different religious and ethnic backgrounds. The Syrian crisis is an outcome of the conflict in Syria which is now in its fifth year, and which has displaced half of the country's population of 22 million people. The Rohingya situation is complex and long-standing, but was precipitated by the actions of people smugglers who abandoned their human cargo at sea.

Each crisis has highlighted the strengths and limits of regional approaches to refugee protection and the importance of looking closely at the underlying norms, and the identities and activities of the relevant 'norm entrepreneurs' at the regional level. For example, in 2009 the Rohingya situation was regarded as a 'mini-crisis', which led to the reinvigoration of the regional Bali Process, led by Australia. Its official title is the *Conference on People Smuggling, Trafficking in Persons and Related Transnational Crime*.[2] Yet, the Rohingya situation was not resolved by that or any similar regional process. In the context of the current Syrian crisis, the spotlight now is on the mechanisms of refugee protection which the European Union (EU) has developed. The response of these mechanisms to this crisis will provide an insight into their effectiveness.

The purpose of the articles which make up this this collection are to identify the key actors in promoting refugee protection norms and their agenda-setting or 'steering' modes in the regional context; and to evaluate dominant mechanisms and discourses on regional refugee protection. Some issues considered by the articles in this special issue are whether states are the main actors in norm development at the regional level; and how international law obligations (and refugee protection norms) are conceived by states and organisations? This introduction focuses in particular on the Southeast Asian (SEA) region, because the overall refugee population in the area represents a substantial proportion of the number of refugees and displaced persons globally and yet knowledge about this region is lacking. Further, in terms of regional engagement, the situation in SEA appears to be far less advanced than in other regions which are discussed in this collection. I draw on lessons from other regions to suggest ways to promote refugee protection at the regional level in SEA, and to make some observations about the current EU situation.

The discussion is structured around three headings or clusters of issues; first, norms and refugee protection, second, norm emergence\entrepreneurs and mechanisms at the regional level, and third, whether regional fora can promote norm internalisation.

## Norms and refugee protection

[R]ealists take a minimalist view of law as binding rules to which states have explicitly consented in treaties and tacitly consented in customary law ... [L]iberals have an enlarged view of international law, as encompassing core community values. Finally, constructivists see international law as a discourse of identity representation and norm enactment.[3]

In this section I compare the norms of refugee protection that have evolved in three regions: the EU, Latin America and the SEA region. For this purpose I place myself within the constructivist paradigm as described in the above quote. I recognise the failure of international refugee law to adequately prescribe a 'right' to asylum, or 'durable solutions', which are commonly described as repatriation (or return), integration and resettlement. Whilst the Refugee Convention[4] can be described as an instrument of human rights protection, which confers rights on asylum seekers and refugees according to their level of attachment to the host country, thus creating a hierarchy of human rights, it stops short of providing a right to territorial asylum. It did however enshrine the right of *non-refoulement*, from which the notion of 'durable solutions' has developed.

The value of the constructivist paradigm is that it brings a focus on the ethical, political and legal norms[5] of the international refugee protection regime and corrects the perceived deficiencies of the Refugee Convention. Arguably, the two core norms of this regime are the right to asylum (freedom from *refoulement*) and burden sharing.[6] As Betts explains,[7] the right to a durable solution is an important element of international refugee protection. These components are underpinned by the notion of a shared international responsibility for ensuring protection to refugees, which can be based either upon specific terms of the

Refugee Convention[8] or upon general principles of state responsibility and international cooperation as embodied in the United Nations Charter.[9] Within a regional context, it has been suggested that *regional* shared responsibility may facilitate protection outcomes by cutting across conservative individual state preferences, through promoting cooperation in protection outcomes. The presumed strength of regional approaches to refugee protection is that they lead to harmonisation of refugee protection norms, and to regional responsibility sharing.[10]

In this section I explain and compare the norms of refugee protection that have evolved in three regions: the EU, Latin America and the SEA region. That is, using the trichotomy which Martha Finnemore and Kathryn Sikkink have developed[11] (namely, emergence, acceptance and internalisation – see Alice Nah in this collection), I identify the norms of refugee protection which have been 'internalised' in the three regional contexts and contextualise the processes. As Paulo Biondi's article in this collection explains, although the EU has focussed upon the right to asylum, its approach to durable solutions illustrates a failure to develop a norm of responsibility sharing. The EU focus on border control and security is in fact mirrored in the SEA region, despite the fact that the EU system is grounded in human rights, whilst in SEA the language of human rights is largely absent. By contrast, in Latin America there appears to be a greater acceptance of the norms of refugee protection and responsibility sharing, through the language of 'solidarity', as Stefania Barichello in her contribution to this collection explains.

### The EU and Europe

In the European context there is a well-developed scheme of regional cooperation norms and institutions which is often held up as a model of regional cooperation\protection. The EU response to asylum seekers has developed since the 1990s with the making of the Dublin Convention which is now in its fourth incarnation as the Dublin III Regulation.[12] The 'Dublin system', which allocates responsibility for the determination of an asylum application to the first country of arrival in the EU, is based upon the concept of 'safe country', which in turn is based upon the lack of a right to asylum.[13] In practical terms, the lack of internal borders within the EU has facilitated the onward movement of asylum seekers to countries to the north of Europe which offer more opportunities than the (typically) Mediterranean countries of first arrival. The concept of 'safe country' has however enabled a number of challenges to attempted returns of asylum seekers to putative safe countries, such as Greece, to succeed.[14]

From 2004 the EU has been promoting harmonisation of refugee protection norms by building a Common European Asylum System (CEAS) through a series of directives dealing with reception of asylum seekers, procedures for the grant and withdrawal of refugee status, temporary protection, and returns. The EU Qualification Directive 2011[15] builds upon the Refugee Convention by incorporating principles which have developed in refugee law jurisprudence, as well as human rights principles. However, on some issues, such as the concept that refugee protection can be provided by non-state actors, the 2011 Qualification Directive has been criticised for adopting a 'lowest common denominator' approach.

The coherency of the CEAS is also challenged by the fact that there are two courts which have oversight of compliance with the CEAS, each of which has developed divergent approaches. As Madeline Garlick concludes, the approach of the European courts which have oversight of compliance with the CEAS and human rights:

... reveals two distinct strands: one in which significant weight has been accorded to the position and rights of the asylum-seeker, and the obligation of administrations and courts to ensure that these are respected in Dublin's application; and another which has placed emphasis on the importance of 'mutual trust' among states as a key element of the Common European Asylum System, and the function of Dublin as a convenient arrangement among states for dealing more efficiently with asylum-seekers.[16]

This conclusion points to two features of the Dublin system which have been revealed by the Syrian crisis as weaknesses of the EU approach. First, the notion of 'durable solution' in the EU is based not on refugee resettlement but on access to territory and asylum.[17] Second, the 'mutual trust' among states has failed in the absence of binding commitments from states to agree on resettling refugees. That is, the Syrian refugee crisis is testing the 'solidarity' of EU members on this issue. In terms of development of a norm of responsibility sharing, the EU system has been shown to be lacking as, increasingly, states are polarised in their responses, and public debate on the issue is hostile to the new arrivals.[18]

The 'normative deficit' of the Dublin system[19] is mirrored by the EU's 'externalised burden-sharing model'. As Biondi in this collection describes the EU norm on responsibility sharing, the EU has developed this by promoting protection of refugees in regions of origin.[20] The idea of the 'right to remain' and temporary protection in the region of origin, which developed particularly during the Balkans crisis of the 1990s, is another example of an externalised approach to responsibility sharing. As Biondi explains, the EU's response to the Syrian crisis reflects the 'externalised burden-sharing model'. Biondi argues that this model persists despite some commitments from EU countries to resettlement in 2013. This conclusion is borne out by the recent agreement between the EU and Turkey, which is currently hosting about two million Syrian refugees.[21] Under this agreement the EU will contribute about three billion euros to stem the flow of refugees, in order to improve socio-economic conditions of refugees under temporary protection in Turkey. This is a furtherance of the EU's external border protection policy and another example of 'externalised burden sharing'.

### Development of norms in Latin and Central America

It is useful to make a comparison with how norms developed in Latin and Central America (the Americas), in contrast in particular to SEA, as another colonised region. There are some interesting parallels but also important differences in their histories. In contemporary Latin America, the adjective which summarises the protection norms is 'solidarity', whereas SEA as a region is often characterised as one of 'rejection' of refugee protection norms (see for example, Nah in this collection). Whereas SEA has a refugee 'problem' and crisis, the Americas host 'relatively few' refugees and asylum seekers.[22]

Barichello explains how regional cooperation developed in Latin America through a long legacy of norm development. The background to this is the conflicts leading to mass displacement in the 1970s and 1980s in Central America, arising from land confiscations and disputes, unequal distribution of wealth and restricted enjoyment of political rights.[23] Almost two million people from El Salvador, Guatemala and Nicaragua were displaced during this period. These disputes, which took place against the backdrop of the Cold War, shaped the development of norm responses.

The 1984 Cartagena Declaration on Refugees, adopted at a Colloquium held at Cartagena, Colombia, in November 1984 (the Cartagena Declaration),[24] related to the 'refugee situation' in Central America, but 10 Latin American governments participated in the discussions leading to the declaration. Moreover, the Cartagena Declaration was approved by the 1985 General Assembly of the already extant Organization of American States (OAS) and was the basis of the process arising from the International Conference on Central American Refugees (CIREFCA), Guatemala City, 29–31 May 1989, which produced a Declaration and Concerted Plan of Action in Favour of Central American Refugees, Returnees and Displaced Persons.[25]

CIREFCA was explicitly conceived as a follow up to the Cartagena Declaration.[26] It was a process which ran from 1987 to 1994, intended to promote peace, and to address the root causes of the conflicts. Thus it facilitated durable solutions such as voluntary repatriations through protection principles elaborated in its Plan of Action.[27] It was also a project-driven process, and the projects encouraged self-sufficiency and local integration.[28]

Moreover CIREFCA led to the dissemination of refugee protection norms.[29] The prime purpose of the Cartagena Declaration was to promote the adoption of national laws to implement the 1951 Refugees Convention and 1967 Protocol, 'thus fostering the necessary process of systematic harmonization [sic] of national legislation on refugees'.[30] For that purpose it was recommended that the definition of a refugee for 'use in the region' should complement the 1951 Refugees Convention. It was stated that in addition to the 1951 Refugees Convention definition, legislation should include:

[P]ersons who have fled their country because their lives, safety or freedom have been threatened by generalized [sic] violence, foreign aggression, internal conflicts, massive violations of human rights or other circumstances which have seriously disturbed public order.[31]

Under this definition, refugees are primarily persons whose life, security or liberty is threatened. The inclusion of generalised violence, internal conflicts and massive violations of human rights expands the refugee definition beyond that of the 1969 Organization of African Unity (OAU) Convention,[32] which was a direct inspiration,[33] and picks up the gaps in that definition.

Like the OAU Convention, the 1984 Cartagena Declaration linked the refugee definition to root causes. The declaration also confirms that the granting of asylum is 'humanitarian' in nature, and reiterates the importance and meaning of the principle of *non-refoulement*. The declaration reflects the contemporaneous experiences of refugees by expressing its 'concern' at the problem raised by military attacks on refugee camps and settlements in different parts of the world.[34] Additionally, going beyond the refugee issue, it expresses its 'concern' at the 'situation of displaced persons within their own countries'.[35]

As Barichello explains, since the 1984 Cartagena Declaration Latin American countries have developed mechanisms and concepts that have 'sensibly approached the contemporary refugee problems that exist in the region'.[36] It has become the foundation of refugee policy in the region, incorporated into national legislation by a number of states; it has affirmed the importance of the *non-refoulement* principle, the importance of integration of refugees and the need to eradicate the causes of mass movements of people.[37]

Barichello explains that, in 1994, a process of re-evaluation and revision led to the San Jose Declaration, which reiterated the importance of the 1984 Cartagena Declaration and broadened its scope in order to extend protection to internally displaced people. Furthermore, in 2004 the Mexico Plan of Action (MPA) was also adopted in order to deal with the new crisis of refugees and asylum seekers from Colombia.[38] This was necessitated by the intensification of the armed and socio-political conflict in Colombia from the end of the 1990s, which resulted in between three and four million displaced persons within

Colombia and hundreds of thousands of asylum seekers in other countries in the region (Ecuador, Panama, Venezuela). This led to the 'crowded borders' phenomenon, as Barichello describes it: the massing of displaced persons on either side of the Columbian border with neighbouring countries.

The first mechanism of the MPA is a regional responsibility-sharing programme focussed on the resettlement of refugees and internally displaced persons (IDPs), known as the 'Solidarity Resettlement' programme. The second pillar is the integration of refugees and IDPs in safe communities (the 'Solidarity Cities' programme). The third is the 'Borders of Solidarity' programme, which focuses on the development of the border regions of neighbouring countries to benefit displaced Colombians and their hosts, namely Ecuador, Panama and Venezuela.

Most recently, in 2010, the Brasilia Declaration on the Protection of Refugees and Stateless Persons in the Americas,[39] which strengthens the principle of *non-refoulement* (amongst other measures), was adopted. As these developments illustrate, regional cooperation in Latin America is well developed at the policy level, and it seems that this cooperation is implemented at the national level. For example, Freier identifies five stages of 'liberalisation' in Latin American asylum legislation, including the adoption of a constitutional right to asylum, which defines asylum as an individual human right, and recent reforms in refugee legislation, including provisions for integration of recognised refugees.[40] Thus Latin America has built on the norm of 'political' asylum that predated the 1951 Refugee Convention, and has comprehensively developed refugee protection norms through 'solidarity' measures, which are also supported by the OAS.

### Southeast Asia

The UNHCR's overview of the Asia Pacific region in 2015 states that there are 3.5 million refugees and 1.4 million stateless persons, with the majority of refugees originating from Afghanistan and Myanmar.[41] It is generally agreed that the Asia Pacific region contains 30% of the global refugee population (see Petcharamesree in this collection). Nah's article restates the UNHCR findings, adding also that Malaysia and Thailand are the two major destination and transit countries, whereas Indonesia is largely a country of transit for refugees intending to travel to Australia. The Asia Pacific region essentially contains two subregions: South Asia (which includes Afghanistan, Sri Lanka, India and Bangladesh) and SEA. Thus many refugees originating from South Asia are going to or through SEA. In this discussion I focus on the SEA subregion which has some important regional processes.

According to the September 2014 UNHCR Factsheet from the UNHCR Regional Office,[42] there was a total 'population of concern' of 2.7 million persons in SEA, of which 1.4 million were stateless persons and 523,592 were asylum seekers\refugees. The total population also included over 700,000 IDPs. The geographical coverage of this report covered countries[43] which are also members of the ASEAN Community.[44] The main country of origin of asylum seekers\refugees was Myanmar (500,364). Currently the subregion is hosting about 500,000 Rohingya asylum seekers\refugees, and so the number has doubled since 2014.

The 2015 UNHCR overview of the subregion points out that:

> Only three States are parties to the 1951 Refugee Convention[45] and only one State has signed the 1954 Statelessness Convention. The lack of asylum laws and diversity of national legal frameworks, as well as government practices and protection environments in the region's countries, make achieving regional harmonization challenging.[46]

The UNHCR suggests further that:

> Available protection space for refugees, asylum-seekers and stateless people in the region is fragile and unpredictable, due to a lack of national legal frameworks in most South-East Asian countries. Furthermore, some States have introduced increasingly restrictive policies – such as denying safe disembarkation or access at the airport, and narrowing protection space and access to asylum. There is also an increase in maritime 'push backs' and instances of *refoulement*.[47]

As Sriprapaha Petcharamesree explains in her article, national governments within SEA look upon refugees as 'illegal' or irregular migrants. Under the two regional processes which operate in SEA, namely ASEAN and the Bali Process, refugees are framed within a security\border control paradigm.[48] There is not, as such, a focus on forced migration or refugees except within that paradigm. Both ASEAN[49] and the Bali Process[50] focus on 'securitising' migration through eliminating human smuggling and trafficking. Individual states as well as ASEAN as a regional bloc also focus on skilled labour migration, rather than upon refugees and forced migrants as such. How did this lack of focus on forced migration evolve? The UNHCR refers to a 'fragile' protection space for refugees. Does this mean that refugee protection norms are lacking in a region which typically rejects international law?[51]

Nah explains that the Comprehensive Plan of Action (CPA) for Indo-Chinese Refugees[52] which operated from 1989–1996[53] failed to imbue norms of refugee protection in the region; the region is characterised by a rejection of the protection norms, which were perceived to be 'Eurocentric', and to impose unacceptable burdens on 'developing states'.[54]

As Betts has pointed out, the CPA was devised in the context of a 'specific historical and regional context'. The CPA came about to cope with the human fallout from an ideologically based war. Unlike CIREFCA, which was essentially a 'peace process', the CPA was focussed on preventing mass movements of (boat) people. The CPA was predicated upon two key precepts or norms of refugee protection: first, that countries in the region should offer 'first asylum' to fleeing refugees, second, that resettlement would be provided in third countries of the 'developed' world. These precepts and the context encouraged states in the region to consider that the refugees were the responsibility of the 'developed' world. It is suggested that the international community's willingness to take on the Indochinese burden helped to absolve them from any sense of responsibility or obligation.[55]

However, it should be recalled that a unique feature of the CPA was the involvement of the country of origin (Vietnam) which undertook to promote orderly departures (the Orderly Departure Programme or ODP), in an effort to stem the illegal emigration of Vietnamese people. Furthermore, states in the region gained firsthand experience at processing refugees.

As Betts explains, the CPA demonstrated the interdependence of state interests regionally[56] and so there are probably stronger political and institutional reasons (to be discussed in the next section) which account for the lack of regional norm internalisation arising from the CPA. As Petcharamesree points out, some of the key players in the CPA, Cambodia, Lao PDR and Vietnam, were not part of ASEAN at the time, and neither was Myanmar, which is a major source of refugees in the region (and current chair of ASEAN). Thus these states were not part of the initial debate which might have led to the development of protection norms.[57]

Apart from the CPA, another process, the Asian African Legal Consultative Organisation (AALCO), is relevant. In 1966 AALCO formulated an instrument for the protection of refugee rights, the Bangkok Principles (Principles Concerning Treatment of Refugees as adopted by the Asian-African Legal Consultative Committee at its Eighth Session 1966). These principles, which were reaffirmed in 2001, were contemporaneous with and possibly inspired the OAU Convention.[58] The Bangkok Principles constitute a progressive and respected set of principles on refugee protection within the region.[59] Yet these experiences did not leave a legacy of state-led protection norms.

Within SEA there is a range of state responses to refugees. Whilst Indonesia for example tolerates the existence of refugees, and works with the International Organisation for Migration (IOM) and the UNHCR to provide protection, by contrast, Malaysia (as Nah explains) regards UNHCR refugees as 'illegal migrants'. Thailand, as Petcharamesree argues, has an independent approach: although not a signatory to the Refugee Convention it registers refugees through its Admission Boards, and permits the presence of refugee camps on the Thai-Burma border. As a whole, SEA is characterised as a region where there is lack of a uniform approach\solidarity on refugee issues, but rather a preoccupation on maintaining individual state sovereignty and regional harmony.

### *The recent crisis in the Bay of Bengal and the Andaman Sea*

Petcharamesree points out that the flight of the Rohingya is not new but has been ignored by states in the region for some years. Indeed, it is evident that the failure of SEA to act decisively and collectively on this issue led the Rohingya into the clutches of smugglers and traffickers, as an increasingly marginalised and discriminated group fled. The Rohingya issue shows that the 'irregular migrant' label is one which states in the region use individually and collectively to avoid their obligations to displaced persons within their sphere of responsibility.

Rohingya is the name given to a predominantly Muslim ethnic group that resides in Rakhine State (formerly Arakan) on the west coast of Myanmar. The dominant ethnic group in Rakhine State is the Rakhine Buddhists (60–70%) who regard the Rohingya (30%) as intruders from Bangladesh, although they have lived in Rakhine State for generations. Initially they were encouraged to move to Arakan by the British colonisers. Tensions between the two groups date to at least the end of British colonial rule, and the creation of a socialist state under Ne Win in 1972. Many violent events have been documented since at least 1978. Further, in 1982 the Burmese government revoked their citizenship, thus making them de jure stateless. In addition to removing their nationality, there have been attempts to strip them of their identity, through laws restricting their rights to marry and to bear children, as well as in relation to education. Following widespread communal violence in 2012, many Rohingya fled Rakhine State and Myanmar.

An escalation of departures and push backs by the Thai navy in 2008 led to the revival of the Bali Process in 2009, which Petcharamesree describes as a 'mini-crisis'.[60] In 2012, Surin Pitsuwan, the former ASEAN Secretary-General (2008–20–12) urged ASEAN to act collectively, as it had done during the Indochinese refugee crisis. The crisis of boat people in May 2015 emerged from neglect of the issue. In the same month as the crisis was unfolding, a meeting of Senior Officials under the Bali Process:

[W]elcomed a presentation from UNHCR on irregular maritime movements in the region, noting that they have tripled in the Bay of Bengal since 2012, to 63,000 in 2014, and a large proportion of movers have protection needs. Members agreed that there should be a standing item in future meetings on regional irregular migration trends, as useful context for discussions on specific issues.[61]

At the time, the UNHCR described the movement as 'unregulated and until recently incon-spicuous'.[62] Yet these statements were contemporaneous with the unfolding crisis, which was precipitated by the fact that at 'least 5,000 refugees and migrants from Myanmar and Bangladesh found themselves stranded at sea in May, when the people smugglers and ship crews who had promised to take them to Malaysia abandoned them en masse ... '[63]

As the crisis unfolded, there were denials of responsibility by states in the region (with calls for the 'richer' countries to settle the refugees), and continued push backs of boats car-rying the Rohingya people by Indonesia, Thailand and Malaysia. There were attempts to push the 'blame' for the crisis onto Thailand for failing to solve the trade and 'trafficking' of 'illegal immigrants'\'irregular migrants', and to defend Myanmar from criticism. There was a debate in the Malaysian press as to whether the lives of the Rohingya were 'worth saving'. A couple of 'circuit breakers' entered the arena when it became clear that the inter-national community was not rushing to the rescue. The first was a statement by the Philip-pines government on 18 May 2015 that it would not push back the Rohingya but would shelter up to 3000 people. The second was more symbolic. On 19 May 2015 a group of fishermen from Aceh defied the Indonesian government's push-back policy and rescued a group of 'boat migrants'. A tone of moral high-ground also entered the debate when par-allels were drawn between Australia's push-back policy and the regional response. One commentator referred to the 'pernicious influence' of Australia's 'stop the boats' policy.[64]

The Ministers of Foreign Affairs of Malaysia, Indonesia and Thailand met in Putrajaya, Malaysia on Wednesday 20 May 2015 ahead of an international meeting on 29 May 2015, to discuss the issue of 'irregular movement of people' into Indonesia, Malaysia and Thai-land. It was stated that the purpose of the meeting was for: ' ... finding a solution to the crisis of influx of irregular migrants and its serious impact on the national security of the affected countries'.[65] The joint statement issued following the meeting of 20 May 2015 asserted that these three states had taken 'necessary measures ... on *humanitarian* grounds, beyond their international obligations'[66] as 'the issue cannot be addressed solely by these three countries' . It appealed to ASEAN and to the 'spirit of unity and soli-darity of ASEAN', to play an active role in addressing the issue. It asserted the need to address the 'root causes'; the ministers pledged to uphold their 'responsibilities and obli-gations under international law and in accordance with their respective domestic laws, including the provision of *humanitarian* assistance to ... those 7,000 irregular migrants still at sea'.[67] They agreed to offer them temporary shelter 'provided that the resettlement and repatriation process will be done in one year by the international community'. Malaysia and Indonesia invited other countries in the region 'to join in this endeavour'.

The 17 recommendations in the statement by states following the Special Meeting on Irregular Migration in the Indian Ocean, Bangkok, 29 May 2015,[68] largely endorse those of 20 May 2015. They focus upon preventing irregular migration and responding to the issue of 'human trafficking' and 'people smuggling' rather than lasting solutions. Only the final recommendation (q) which refers to root causes and improving livelihoods in 'at-risk communities' makes allusion to the protection needs of the Rohingya.

The outcome of the 29 May 2015 meeting has been condemned by human rights advo-cates who point to the failure to address root causes, including discrimination and persecu-tion, or to provide asylum procedures and durable solutions.[69] The current situation of the Rohingya refugees supports this critique. The UNHCR estimates that 94,000 refugees and migrants have left Bangladesh and Myanmar by boat since 2014.[70] They are receiving varying treatment – some countries have placed them into refugee camps, others have allowed them to find some work.[71] There is evidence that some of the refugees have dis-appeared from camps in Indonesia.[72] The Rohingya have not been granted 'durable solutions'. For example, Indonesia is making statements that it will adhere to its one-year limit of allowing the refugees to stay. The Indonesian Director General of Immigration said: 'We will give them a year. If there's no certainty on the matter within the year, then with the UNHCR we will return them to their country.'[73] There is some further suggestion that a new wave of migration may be about to start as the monsoon season draws to an end.[74] The responses to the Rohingya confirm the fragility of solidarity on refugee issues arising from the May 2015 meetings.


**Norm emergence\entrepreneurs and mechanisms at the regional level**

In this section the focus turns to the role of norm entrepreneurs in the process of norm emergence, acceptance and internalisation. The articles in this collection identify various organisations within regions as 'norm entrepreneurs', including states (see Petcharamesree and Biondi), non-governmental (including civil society) and international organisations including UNHCR (Nah and Stevens in this collection, respectively), and regional organisations. In principle, states should be strong actors and promoters of refugee protection. In practice that role is often played by the UNHCR and civil society. As the articles in this collection illustrate, the UNHCR's 'complementary' role is often criticised by civil society.

In his article, Biondi describes how the European approach to norm emergence is largely 'state centric', consistent with the principle of territorial asylum embodied in the EU Dublin framework. The EU framework is arguably an aspect of the EU economic and political integration process.[75] The EU and UNHCR have a respectful relationship;[76] as Volker Turk has explained, the UNHCR's supervisory responsibility is recognised in many EU instruments, including the Qualification Directive.[77] More controversially, the UNHCR can claim to have provided the seed for the development of the EU's externalised refugee approach. In 1993, High Commissioner Sadako Osaka formulated 'the right to remain' in the context of mass displacement in the Balkans region, which influenced the development of EU 'safe third country' policy.

Biondi explains how these policies, which are aimed at containing refugees in their region of origin, have been justified by the notion of 'human security', or protection against security threats.[78] As he explains, this concept of 'human security', which is conflated with humanitarian assistance, is another strategy for externalising the EU's burden-sharing responsibilities. But as he also notes, 'human security' can also mutate into a focus on state security. Biondi explores this conflict between notions of human security, state security and burden sharing in the EU context. He points out that EU states are concerned about changes to ethnic composition as well as more 'traditional' security threats posed by asylum seekers.[79] These are points which are strongly confirmed by the current debates around Syrian refugees.

Dallal Stevens in this collection focuses upon the UNHCR's role in the Syrian crisis within the Middle East region. As her contribution illustrates, discussion of the Syrian crisis involves consideration of two regional responses, namely, Europe and the Middle East. In her other writing Stevens has shown how the states in the Middle East region have developed a protection approach despite not being parties to the Refugee Convention. She explains that:

> [M]any Muslim states have resisted signing the Refugee Convention or Protocol because of their ongoing frustration with the international community for the failure to implement numerous UN General Assembly resolutions on the right of return for Palestinian refugees.[80]

As Stevens explains, countries such as Egypt and Jordan are heavily dependent on the UNHCR for both refugee status determination (RSD) and practical advice and assistance. Furthermore, many civil societies and charities fill the gap in refugee protection needs in the region.[81]

In her article in this collection, Stevens is critical of the UNHCR's role as a norm entrepreneur in this context. She critiques the UNHCR's ambiguous 'rights-based' language, which, she argues, does not reflect the reality of assistance or needs of refugees or the norms of international protection. Rather, she says, the UNHCR is focussed on humanitarian protection, on development and development outcomes. Stevens argues that asylum seekers need access to safe territory and freedom from *refoulement*. She is critical of the UNHCR's role in the Middle East as a both a norm entrepreneur and a norm setter.

Both Stevens and Biondi highlight the paradox or dual nature of the UNHCR's refugee protection mandate under its statute – its role as both provider of individual protection and group humanitarian protection.[82] This discussion points to the paradox within the UNHCR as an institution – the fact that it has both an operational focus and a monitoring role. Both Stevens and Biondi discuss the UNHCR's use of the 'good offices' proviso to enlarge its role. A number of commentators have critiqued the UNHCR for its extension into humanitarian work.[83] For example, during the Indochinese War the UNHCR took on a monitoring role for the ODP – for which it has been much critiqued.[84]

In Latin America, as in the EU, the states play a large role in promoting refugee protection, which involves working closely with the UNHCR. As Barichello explains, the MPA was guided by the UNHCR. It arose from intensification of the armed and socio-political conflict in Colombia and the resulting humanitarian crises, which led to three to four million displaced persons within Colombia and hundreds of thousands of asylum seekers in other countries in the region. The OAS is another important entrepreneur within the Latin American region. It includes a number of human rights mechanisms and instruments.[85]

In the SEA region, as Petcharamesree explains, there is a lack of entrepreneurs for refugee rights as they are characterised as irregular migrants. She points out that despite the creation of the ASEAN Community, with its plethora of institutions, in reality the interests of 'national governments predominate'. Within the ASEAN Community, refugees notably are included within the political-security community. Although within ASEAN there is a 'soft law' instrument[86] which promotes the right to seek asylum[87] and human rights,[88] it is notable that during the recent crisis it was individual states rather than ASEAN which took the initiative (despite calls for it to intervene). This is in contrast to the CPA situation which was an ASEAN-led initiative, together with the UNHCR.

Thus the UNHCR plays a larger role in the SEA region due to the lack of national protection mechanisms. It fills the vacuum of 'protection space' created by the fact that few states in the region are parties to the Refugee Convention. In particular it is primarily responsible for RSD in the region, in Malaysia and Indonesia. It also leads the region's policy formulation. In recent years the UNHCR has promoted protection norms via the AALCO and other regional processes.[89] It has focussed on promoting rescue at sea, *non-refoulement* and addressing statelessness. In 2013 the UNHCR and Indonesia convened a meeting outside of the Bali Process which led to the Jakarta Declaration on Irregular Movement of Persons.[90] This declaration recognised the importance of burden sharing and collective responsibility.[91] The UNHCR attempts to fill the gap within the two regional processes: the Bali Process[92] and ASEAN.

Nah observes that there is a negative side to this: 'government officials in Asia tend to see refugees as an "international" or "UNHCR" problem, rather than a domestic problem' . Her article shows that within the SEA region there is rivalry between the UNHCR and civil society for 'entrepreneurship' of the issue. Nah (and Martin Jones) critique the UNHCR's 'protection space' approach. Jones argues that it:

> ... privileges international interests, fora, and UNHCR as the negotiator; devalues the norma-
> tive strength of obligations towards refugees; and, allows the underlying responsibility for the
> provision of refugee protection to drift from the state to UNHCR.[93]

As Nah explains, local civil society actors often work under the protection of the UNHCR – but also 'under their shadow'. The response of states to the recent Rohingya crisis confirms the prevalence of the UNHCR 'protection space' approach, as states in the region continue to regard refugee protection as a 'humanitarian' problem and response.

Nah examines the creation and work of the Asia Pacific Refugee Rights Network (APRRN), a new actor in norm entrepreneurship in the region.[94] She shows how local civil society can pressure states 'from below'; that they have a 'unique location vis à vis states'. Nah argues that working through a formalised network (APRRN) has changed the way in which local civil society actors engage in norm entrepreneurship in several important ways. She argues that it has changed the attributes of actors, helping them develop visibility, capacity and connectedness through the formation of a 'community of practice'; it has changed power relations between them and other actors – in particular, the UNHCR; it has facilitated the development of 'regional imagination' and the practice of 'scale shifting', helping local actors move beyond domestic contexts to engage with state and non-state actors through regional and international fora.

The APRRN is an example of participatory regionalism which is intended to influence states in the region, and to shift their views that refugees are an 'international' and UNHCR problem. It is an important example of solidarity at the 'grassroots' level.

**Can regional fora promote norm internalisation?**

A final question which this collection of articles raises is whether existing regional fora can be effective in promoting norm internalisation of international refugee protection? In the EU today, this issue lies in the balance. The 'normative deficit' of the Dublin system has been noted, and the politicisation of the refugee issue within the EU is well-known. As Biondi explains, the EU approach is premised upon 'externalised burden sharing'. By contrast, in Latin America, as Barichello explains, the regional approach, through the MPA has encouraged news ways of thinking about regional cooperation. As she says, the MPA is an important South–South initiative, [95] and a break from the past. For example, one feature of CIREFCA was the fact that there was strong support from the global North (in particular from the European Commission and the Italian government).[96] Barichello concludes that the Latin American approach reinforces responsibility at the regional level.

In SEA, where the states are the key players, Petcharamesree concludes that there are 'no guarantees' that ASEAN will lead to the adoption of a 'common regional approach' on forced migration issues. As Petcharamesree explains, the ASEAN states are more concerned with issues about migrant workers – both 'high skilled' and 'irregular' migrant workers. The latter issue is the most prominent 'forced migration' issue within ASEAN, but as Petcharamesree explains, they are not included in the ASEAN framework. Even the issue of 'regular' migrant workers has gained little traction within ASEAN despite the existence of formal instruments and institutions, including civil society.[97] This raises an interesting question of whether civil society organisations such as APRRN can influence ASEAN, as some claim.[98] And indeed whether ASEAN itself will take the lead as others suggest they should, particularly on the Rohingya issue.[99] To this point however, ASEAN still adheres to the principle of non-interference in individual state affairs. Until such time as ASEAN as a collective stands up to Myanmar, the Rohingya issue, for example, will not be solved. However, Petcharamesree refers to ASEAN as an institution which has 'an unbreakable paradigm that is dependent and partly threatened by the state'.

The Bali Process is another important regional process which is the backdrop to the article by Maria O'Sullivan in this collection. The Bali Process is an Australia-Indonesia-led process which securitises the issue of forced 'irregular' migration (asylum seekers). It is the vehicle through which the Australian government promotes its policies in the region.[100] Maria O'Sullivan explains that Australian policy reflects a two-tiered system which prioritises the selection of refugees from overseas as part of a managed, 'orderly' resettlement programme, and penalises those who flee their countries of origin and come to Australian shores to apply for asylum. This policy prefers the resettlement of refugees from outside the region; that is, those who have not made 'secondary movements' to SEA as asylum seekers.

In her article O'Sullivan considers the ethics of Australia's approach to resettlement and concludes that it 'is not solely a humanitarian act and is influenced greatly by factors other than refugee need'. She argues that although resettlement is supported by the rhetoric of burden and responsibility sharing, it is used by some resettlement states (such as Australia) to avoid responsibility for onshore arrivals. She argues that by contrast, 'Australia has greater relational [ethical] obligations to refugees' in the region because of its responsibility as a party to the Refugee Convention and its proximity to the region.[101]

The question that O'Sullivan's article raises is: Can the Bali Process become a vehicle of positive change in the region? Can it encourage regional cooperation? There are indications suggesting both negative and positive answers to these questions.

On the negative side it needs to be noted that the July 2011 Arrangement between the Government of Australia and the Government of Malaysia on Transfer and Resettlement, was a bilateral agreement concluded under the Bali Process, providing for the exchange of 800 asylum seekers arriving 'irregularly' by boat in Australian excised territory, or who are 'intercepted in the course of trying to reach Australia by irregular means' (clause 4(1)(a)), with up to 4000 recognised refugees awaiting resettlement in Malaysia. Although promoted as an arrangement which would alleviate Malaysia's protracted refugee problem, it had a 'sting' in that it was a deterrent measure in relation to the 800 asylum seekers who were to be 'exchanged'. Following a challenge to the legality of a decision to implement the arrangement, a majority of 6:1 of the High Court of Australia declared that there was an invalid exercise of power.[102]

Subsequent to the decision, a new Subdivision on Regional Processing inserted in the Migration Act made it clear that in order to enter into a cooperative arrangement with another country in the region, Australia does not expect that the other country will adhere to the full set of rights in the Refugee Convention. Australia thus legitimated a responsibility-shifting rather than responsibility-sharing regime, which is the antithesis to O'Sullivan's argument that Australia has 'greater relational [ethical] obligations to refugees' in the region.

Following the failed arrangement with Malaysia, in 2012 the Australian government commissioned a Report of the Expert Panel on Asylum Seekers (the Houston Report),[103] to canvass the development of a 'regional cooperation framework'. Recommendation 1 includes a statement that the relevant policy principles include 'managing asylum and mixed migration flows across the region'. The report explicitly asserts that Australia's policies towards asylum seekers operate as a 'pull' and seeks to promote 'greater use of regular migration pathways and international protection arrangements'.[104]

However, the response to the recent Rohingya crisis showed the limits of the boat push-back policy which Australia has practised (and arguably encouraged) in the region. Although the Bali Process does not have a specific protection mandate, the UNHCR has successfully, after some setbacks,[105] succeeded in promoting protection. Under the Bali Process there is an encouraging development through the creation of a Regional Support Office (RSO) which is supported by the UNHCR.[106]

However, the protection discourse on refugees in SEA is limited both within ASEAN and the Bali Process. Both the IOM and the UNHCR play significant roles in this context. It is noteworthy that during the recent crisis the IOM played an important role in encouraging the states to cooperate, and to reach agreement on the treatment of the Rohingya people. A statement made by William Swing, Director General of the IOM, ahead of the meeting[107] of 29 May 2015, promotes the idea of managed migration, more avenues for labour migration, as well as 'managing diversity' and balancing 'the paradox between national security and human security'. As Megan Bradley has said, states often prefer to work with the IOM precisely because it does not have a protection role.[108] But on this issue it is important to note that the UNHCR also promotes the grant of work permits to the Rohingya refugees to secure their human rights and development needs.[109] Thus it appears that there is no forum which is promoting regional collective solutions aimed at responsibility sharing as such.

The EU and SEA situations are thus the antithesis of the other. In the European context there is a well-developed scheme of state regional cooperation, uniform norms and institutions, based not on refugee resettlement but on access to asylum. SEA by contrast is characterised by lack of agreement on underlying protection norms, lack of institutions and strong respect for individual state sovereignty. However, at this moment in history each seems unable to respond adequately to the current refugee crises.

## Conclusions

The articles in this special issue demonstrate the need for awareness of the roles of different norm 'entrepreneurs' in developing and promoting basic norms on refugee protection. In the European context, we have seen that some individual states appear to be pitting themselves against the supranational regional entity, the EU. By contrast, in Latin America, the regional cooperation is largely state-led, with support from extra regional institutions (e.g. the OAS) and international organisations (such as the UNHCR). Within SEA the issue of 'entrepreneurship' is more complex and fragmented, pointing to the need for strong leadership.

Within SEA, where states appear to reject ownership of the problem, they are the least likely candidates for successful 'entrepreneurship' of the issue. Nah argues that civil society cooperation working from below is likely to be the most effective entrepreneur in SEA. Other contenders for positions of entrepreneurship are ASEAN, Australia (through the Bali Process), the IOM and the UNHCR. Current efforts are however focussed on local integration through the recognition of labour rights. Durable solutions through resettlement are currently not an option and neither is there any attempt to harmonise the processing of refugees. This leads to several suggestions. Either ASEAN collectively needs to act decisively to tackle the source of the Rohingya issue, and\or Australia needs to 'step up to the mark' and accept its ethical responsibility as O'Sullivan argues, by accepting Rohingya refugees for resettlement. But, as a long-term approach, there needs to be collectivised processing of refugees on a regional basis.

As the articles in this special issue illustrate, regional solutions for refugee protection will be most effective when the norms have been solidly embedded in legal systems and institutions. The Latin American example is a relevant one, as Barichello argues. There, solutions for refugees focus on local integration, resettlement and development in source regions.

As Biondi shows, although the EU appears to be a model of norm development, the current fractured EU debate on refugees suggests that the norms have not been fully developed or equally internalised by all European states. He shows that although the EU has focussed upon the right to asylum, its approach to durable solutions suggests a failure to develop a norm of responsibility sharing, except by externalising the issue. Thus, the EU case shows that imperfect adoption of norms leads to imperfect solutions, as shown by the EU's failure to develop effective refugee resettlement or development programmes in regions of origin.

## Acknowledgements

The articles in this special collection arise from a workshop on Comparative Regional Protection Frameworks for refugees, Norms and Norm Entrepreneurs that was conducted through the Refugee Law Initiative (RLI), School of Advanced Study, University of London on 15 November 2013. The workshop was the occasion for the launch of the Asia Pacific Forced Migration Connection (APFMC) which is supported by the Refugee Research Network, York University, Canada (see http://www. refugeereserach.netwww.refugeereserach.net). I thank David Cantor, Director of the RLI for providing financial and administrative support for the workshop, and the participants at the workshop for their helpful comments. In particular I thank the following: Professor Alexander Betts, Dr Maria-Teresa Gil-Bazo, Dr Martin Jones, Professor Hélène Lambert, Ms Anja Klug and Dr Violeta Lax-Moreno.

Finally, I thank Thomas Harré who has provided considerable and invaluable research and editorial assistance with this collection.

## Disclosure statement

No potential conflict of interest was reported by the author.

## Notes

1. Silvia di Gaetano, 'How to Solve Asia's Refugee Crisis: Steps Can and Should be Taken to Alleviate the Plight of Rohingya', *The Diplomat*, 28 September 2015.
2. See http://www.baliprocess.net/http://www.baliprocess.net/ (accessed 4 January 2016).
3. David Armstrong, Theo Farrell, and Helene Lambert, *International Law and International Relations* (Cambridge: Cambridge University Press, 2007), 107.

4.  Convention Relating to the Status of Refugees, Geneva, 28 July 1951, in force 22 April 1954, 1989 UNTS 137 (Refugee Convention) and the Protocol Relating to the Status of Refugees, New York, 31 January 1967, in force 4 October 1967, 19 UNTS 6223, 6257 (Refugee Protocol).
5.  Armstrong, Farrell and Lambert, *International Law and International Relations*, 102.
6.  Alexander Betts, *Protection by Persuasion: International Cooperation in the Refugee Regime* (Ithaca, NY: Cornell University Press, 2009), 2.
7.  Ibid., 6.
8.  Notably, Refugee Convention, preambular clauses 4, 6 and Art. 35.
9.  United Nations, Charter of the United Nations, 24 October 1945, 1 UNTS XVI, Art1 (3).
10. Susan Kneebone and Felicity Rawlings-Sanaei, eds, *New Regionalism and Asylum Seekers: Challenges Ahead* (Oxford: Berghahn Books, 2007), 1.
11. Martha Finnemore and Kathryn Sikkink, 'International Norm Dynamics and Political Change', *International Organization* 52, no. 4 (1998): 887–917.
12. Regulation (EU) No. 604/2013 of the European Parliament and of the Council of 26 June 2013 establishing the criteria and mechanisms for determining the member state responsible for examining an application for international protection lodged in one of the member states by a third-country national or a stateless person, [2013] OJ L 180/31 ('the 2013 Regulation' or 'Dublin III'). The 'Dublin system' refers to this, and its predecessor Regulation (EC) No. 343/2003 of 18 February 2003 establishing the criteria and mechanisms for determining the member state responsible for examining an asylum application lodged in one of the member states by a third-country national [2003] OJ L 50/1 ('Dublin II'), as well as Regulation (EU) No. 603/2013 of the European Parliament and of the Council of 26 June 2013 on the establishment of 'Eurodac' for the comparison of fingerprints for the effective application of Regulation (EU) No. 604/2013, [2013] OJ L 180/1, and its predecessor Regulation (EC) no. 2725/2000, as well as relevant implementing regulations (Regulation (EU) 118/2014 amending the Dublin Implementing Regulation 1560/2003).
13. Susan Kneebone, 'The Legal and Ethical Implications of Extra-territorial Processing of Asylum Seekers: The Safe Third Country Concept', in *Moving On: Forced Migration and Human Rights*, ed. J. McAdam (Oxford: Hart Publishing, 2008), Chapter 5.
14. For example, *MSS* v. *Belgium and Greece* (European Court of Human Rights), Appn No. 30696/09, 21 January 2011, http://www.unhcr.org/refworld/docid/4d39bc7f2.html (accessed 8 January 2016).
15. EC Qualification Directive, Council Directive (EU) 95/2011 of The European Parliament and of The Council of 13 December 2011 on standards for the qualification of third-country nationals or stateless persons as beneficiaries of international protection, for a uniform status for refugees or for persons eligible for subsidiary protection, and for the content of the protection granted (recast), [2011] OJ L 337/9 (2011 Qualification Directive).
16. Madeline Garlick, 'Protecting Rights and Courting Controversy: Leading Jurisprudence of the European Courts on the EU Dublin Regulation', *Journal of Immigration Asylum and Nationality Law* 29, no. 2 (2015): 192, 210.
17. Joanne van Selm, 'The Europeanization of Refugee Policy', in *New Regionalism and Asylum Seekers: Challenges Ahead*, ed. Susan Kneebone and Felicity Rawlings-Sanaei (Oxford: Berghahn Books, 2007), Chapter 4.
18. Daniel Thym, 'Beyond Dublin – Merkel's Vision of EU Asylum Policy', Odysseus Blog, 26 October 2015, http://eumigrationlawblog.eu/beyond-dublin-merkels-vision-of-eu-asylum-policy/ (accessed 26 December 2015).
19. Ibid., 5. Additionally, the Schengen system has collapsed: Evelien Brouwer, 'Migration Flows and the Reintroduction of Internal Border Controls: Assessing Necessity and Proportionality', Odysseus Blog, 12 November 2015, http://eumigrationlawblog.eu/migration-flows-and-the-reintroduction-of-internal-border-controls-assessing-necessity-and-proportionality/ (accessed 26 December 2015).
20. A. Betts and J.-F. Durieux, 'Convention Plus as a Norm-Setting Exercise', *Journal of Refugee Studies* 20, no. 3 (2007): 509; see also A. Hurwitz, 'Norm-Making in International Refugee Law', *Proceedings of the American Society of International Law* 106 (2012): 430.
21. Jean-Baptiste Farcy, 'EU-Turkey Agreement: Solving the EU Asylum Crisis or Creating a New Calais in Bodrum?', Odysseus Blog, 7 December 2015, http://eumigrationlawblog.eu/

eu-turkey-agreement-solving-the-eu-asylum-crisis-or-creating-a-new-calais-in-bodrum/ (accessed 26 December 2015).

22.	Luisa Feline Freier, 'A Liberal Paradigm Shift? A Critical Appraisal of Recent Trends in Latin American Asylum Legislation', in *Exploring the Boundaries of Refugee Law: Current Protection Challenges*, ed. Jean-Pierre Gauci, Mariagiulia Giuffré, and Evangelia Tsourdi (Leiden/ Boston: Brill Nijhoff, 2015), 118–45 at 119.

23.	Stefania Barichello, 'The Evolving System of Refugee Protection in Latin America', in *Exploring the Boundaries of Refugee Law*, ed. Jean-Pierre Gauci, Mariagiulia Giuffré, and Evangelia Tsourdi, 149–71 at 155.

24.	Regional Refugee Instruments and Related, *Cartagena Declaration on Refugees, Colloquium on the International Protection of Refugees in Central America, Mexico and Panama*, 22 November 1984, http://www.refworld.org/docid/3ae6b36ec.html; OAS/Ser.L/V/II.66,doc.10, rev.1, 190–3.

25.	CIREFCA, *Declaration and Concerted Plan of Action in Favour of Central American Refugees, Returnees and Displaced Persons* , 30 May 1989, CIREFCA 89/13/Rev.1, http:// www.refworld.org/docid/3fbb5d094.html (accessed 2 January 2016).

26.	Alexander Betts, 'Comprehensive Plans of Action: Insights from CIREFCA and the Indochinese CPA', UNHCR, *New Issues in Refugee Research*, Working Paper No. 120 (January 2006), 13; see also Alexander Betts, *Protection by Persuasion: International Cooperation in the Refugee Regime* (Ithaca, NY: Cornell University, 2009), Chapter 3.

27.	Betts, 'Comprehensive Plans of Action', 12.

28.	Ibid.

29.	Ibid., 13.

30.	Cartagena Declaration, paragraph III(1).

31.	Ibid., paragraph III(3).

32.	Organization of African Unity (OAU), *Convention Governing the Specific Aspects of Refugee Problems in Africa (OAU Convention)*, 10 September 1969, 1001 U.N.T.S. 45, http://www. refworld.org/docid/3ae6b36018.html (accessed 2 January 2016).

33.	Susan Kneebone and Felicity Rawlings-Sanaei, 'Introduction: Regionalism as a Response to a Global Challenge', in *New Regionalism and Asylum Seekers: Challenges Ahead*, ed. Susan Kneebone and Felicity Rawlings-Sanaei (Oxford: Berghahn Books, 2007), 8–11.

34.	Cartagena Declaration, paragraph III(7).

35.	Ibid., paragraph III(9).

36.	Stefania Barichello 'Refugee protection and responsibility sharing in Latin America: solidarity programmes and the Mexico Plan of Action', *The International Journal of Human Rights* 20, no. 2 (2016): 191.

37.	Barichello, 'The Evolving System of Refugee Protection in Latin America', 157.

38.	Regional Refugee Instruments & Related, *Mexico Declaration and Plan of Action to Strengthen International Protection of Refugees in Latin America*, 16 November 2004, http://www.refworld.org/docid/424bf6914.html (accessed 8 January 2016).

39.	*Brasilia Declaration on the Protection of Refugees and Stateless Persons in the Americas*, 11 November 2010, http://www.refworld.org/docid/4cdd44582.html (accessed 8 January 2016).

40.	Freier, 'A Liberal Paradigm Shift?', 121, 123, 139–40.

41.	UNHCR, '2015 UNHCR Regional Operations Profile – Asia and the Pacific', 2015, http:// www.unhcr.org/pages/4a02d8ec6.html.

42.	http://www.unhcr.org/519f67fc9.htmlt (accessed 8 January 2016).

43.	Namely, Bangladesh, Brunei Darussalam, Cambodia, Indonesia, Lao PDR, Malaysia, Mongolia, the Philippines, Singapore, Thailand, Timor-Leste and Vietnam.

44.	ASEAN (Association of South East Asia Nations), founded in 1967, originally involved five states (Singapore, Malaysia, Thailand, Philippines and Indonesia) to promote 'common political interests as well as a forum for private business and community-level interactions'. See ASEAN, *The ASEAN Declaration ('Bangkok Declaration')*, Bangkok, Thailand, 8 August 1967, http://www.asean.org/news/item/the-asean-declaration-bangkok-declaration (accessed 25 February 2013). Brunei was added in 1984, Vietnam in 1995, Lao PDR and Mynamar in 1997 and Cambodia in 1999. Thus ASEAN does not include the following countries which are covered by UNHCR's report: Bangladesh, Mongolia and Timor-Leste.

45.	Cambodia, the Philippines and East-Timor.

46.	UNHCR, '2015 UNHCR Regional Operations Profile – Asia and the Pacific'.

47. Ibid.
48. Susan Kneebone, 'ASEAN and the Conceptualisation of Refugee Protection', in *Regional Approaches to the Protection of Asylum Seekers: An International Legal Perspective*, ed. F. Ippolito et al. (Aldershot: Ashgate, 2014), Chapter 13; Susan Kneebone 'The Bali Process and Global Refugee Policy in the Asia-Pacific Region', *Journal of Refugee Studies* 27, no. 4 (2014): 596–618.
49. Kneebone, 'ASEAN and the Conceptualisation of Refugee Protection'.
50. Kneebone, 'The Bali Process and Global Refugee Policy in the Asia-Pacific Region'.
51. Simon Chesterman, 'Asia's Ambivalence about International Law and Institutions: Past, Present, and Futures' (paper presented at the 5th Biennial Asian Society of International Law Conference, Bangkok, 26 November 2015).
52. International Conference on Indo-Chinese Refugees, Geneva, 13–14 June 1989, *Declaration and Comprehensive Plan of Action*, UN Doc. A/CONF. 148/2, 13 June 1989.
53. Kneebone and Rawlings-Sanaei, *New Regionalism and Asylum Seekers*, 11–18.
54. Sara E. Davies, *Legitimising Rejection: International Refugee Law in South East Asia* (Leiden: Martinis Nijhoff Publishers, 2008).
55. Ibid., 225.
56. Betts, 'Comprehensive Plans of Action', 50.
57. As discussed in Kneebone, 'ASEAN and the Conceptualisation of Refugee Protection', 301–5, the debate on the role of human rights in the ASEAN region has been through many iterations.
58. Asian-African Legal Consultative Organization, 'Final Text of the AALCO's 1966 Bangkok Principles on Status and Treatment of Refugees', AALCO's 40th Session, New Delhi, http://www.refworld.org/docid/3de5f2d52.htmlhttp://www.refworld.org/docid/3de5f2d52.html (accessed 2 January 2016).
59. Pia Oberoi, 'Regional Initiatives on Refugee Protection in South Asia', *International Journal of Refugee Law* 11, no. 1 (1999): 193, 195.
60. Kneebone, 'The Bali Process and Global Refugee Policy in the Asia-Pacific Region', 601.
61. Co-Chairs' Statement, Bali Process Ad Hoc Group Senior Officials Meeting, Wellington, New Zealand, 6 May 2015.
62. UNHCR, *Bay of Bengal and Andaman Sea: Proposals for Action*, May 2015, 1.
63. UNHCR South-East Asia, *Mixed Maritime Movements April–June 2015: Highlights*, 1.
64. Mathew Davies, 'The Rohingya and Our Rule-Bending Arrogance', *The Drum*, 18 May 2015.
65. Ministry of Foreign Affairs, Malaysia, Press Statement, http://www.kln.gov.my/web/guest/press-release/-/asset_publisher/t3pS/content/joint-statement:-ministerial-meeting-on-irregular-movement-of-people-in-southeast-asia-english-version-only?redirect=%2Fweb%2Fguest%2Fpress-release (accessed 10 January 2016).
66. Emphasis added.
67. Emphasis added.
68. Summary Statement Ministry of Foreign Affairs of the Kingdom of Thailand, http://www.mfa.go.th/main/en/media-center/14/56880-Summary-Special-Meeting-on-Irregular-Migration-in.html (accessed 10 January 2016).
69. APRRN Statement on Maritime Movements in the Indian Ocean, 12 October 2015. See also Joint NGO Statement Ahead of the Special Meeting on Irregular Migration in the Indian Ocean, Bangkok, 29 May 2015, http://www.savethechildren.org.uk/2015-05/joint-ngo-statement-ahead-special-meeting-irregular-migration-indian-ocean-bangkok-29-may
70. Y. Kojima, 'Rohingya Women in Migration: Lost Voices', United Nations University, http://ourworld.unu.edu/en/rohingya-women-in-migration-lost-voices (accessed 8 January 2016).
71. A. Cornish, 'After Left Stranded at Sea, What Happened to the Rohingya Migrants?', *NPR*, (online edition, 6 January 2016), http://www.npr.org/2016/01/04/461945017/after-left-stranded-at-sea-what-happened-to-the-rohingya-migrants (accessed 8 January 2016).
72. J. Vit, 'Rohingya Refugees Vanish from Indonesia', *Irin News* (online edition, 14 December 2015), http://www.irinnews.org/report/102293/rohingya-refugees-vanish-from-indonesia (accessed 8 January 2016).
73. E. Hall, 'Rohingya and Bangladeshi Asylum Seekers Risk Being Returned if No-one Steps in', *ABC* (online edition, 14 December 2015) http://www.abc.net.au/worldtoday/content/2015/s4371624.htm (accessed 8 January 2016).

74. P. Winn, 'Rohingya Refugee Crisis about to Begin, Again', *Thestar.com* (online edition, 1 January 2016), http://www.thestar.com/news/world/2016/01/01/rohingya-refugee-crisis-about-to-begin-again.html (accessed 8 January 2016).
75. van Selm, 'The Europeanization of Refugee Policy'; Elspeth Guild, 'The Europeanisation of Europe's Asylum Policy', *International Journal of Refugee Law* 18, no. 3–4 (2006): 630.
76. See also van Selm, 'The Europeanization of Refugee Policy', 83 – strong commitment to UNHCR.
77. James Simeon, ed., *The UNHCR and Supervision of International Refugee Law* (Cambridge: Cambridge University Press, 2013), 44–5.
78. See also van Selm, 'The Europeanization of Refugee Policy'.
79. See Elspeth Guild, 'Conflicting Identities and Securitisation in Refugee Law: Lessons from the EU', in *Refugee Protection and the Role of Law: Conflicting Identities*, ed. Susan Kneebone, Dallal Stevens, and Loretta Baldassar (London: Routledge, 2014), Chapter 8.
80. Dallal Stevens, 'Shifting Conceptions of Refugee Identity and Protection: European and Middle Eastern Approaches', in *Refugee Protection and the Role of Law: Conflicting Identities*, ed. Susan Kneebone, Dallal Stevens, and Loretta Baldassar (London: Routledge, 2014), 82, citing Kirsten Zaat, *The Protection of Forced Migrants in Islamic Law* (UNHCR, New Issues in Refugee Research, Research Paper No. 146, 2007).
81. Stevens, 'Shifting Conceptions of Refugee Identity and Protection', 88.
82. See Susan Kneebone, Loretta Baldassar, and Dallal Stevens, 'Conflicting Identities, Protection and the Role of Law', in *Refugee Protection and the Role of Law: Conflicting Identities*, ed. Susan Kneebone, Dallal Stevens, and Loretta Baldassar (London: Routledge, 2014), Chapter 1, at 8.
83. See Davies, *Legitimising Rejection*.
84. Ibid., 110.
85. David J. Cantor and Stefania Barichello, 'Protection of Asylum Seekers under the Inter-American Human Rights System', in *Regional Approaches to the Protection of Asylum Seekers: An International Legal Perspective*, ed. F. Ippolito et al. (Aldershot: Ashgate, 2014), Chapter 12.
86. ASEAN Human Rights Declaration (AHRD), http://jurist.org/paperchase/2012/11/asean-adopts-human-rights-declaration.php (accessed 2 January 2016).
87. Ibid., Art., 16.
88. Kneebone, 'ASEAN and the Conceptualisation of Refugee Protection'.
89. Kneebone, 'The Bali Process and Global Refugee Policy in the Asia-Pacific Region', 607. Since about 2004 the UNHCR has shifted its focus in AALCO consultations from implementing the Refugee Convention to a focus on broader practical protection issues such as rescue at sea, statelessness and support for IDPs. The UN Note on International Protection A/AC.96/989, 7 July 2004 is the last document I could find which called on governments to enact national asylum laws.
90. *Jakarta Declaration on Irregular Movement of Persons*, Jakarta, 20 August 2013. Notably this was subsequently incorporated into the Bali Process – see Co-Chairs' Statement, Bali Process Ad Hoc Group Senior Officials Meeting, Canberra, Australia, 6 August 2014 (Attachment B).
91. Ibid., [8].
92. Kneebone, 'The Bali Process and Global Refugee Policy in the Asia-Pacific Region', 606–10.
93. Martin Jones, 'Moving beyond Protection Space: Developing a Law of Asylum in South East Asia', in *Refugee Protection and the Role of Law: Conflicting Identities*, ed. Susan Kneebone, Dallal Stevens, and Loretta Baldassar (London: Routledge, 2014), 257.
94. See also Kneebone, 'The Bali Process and Global Refugee Policy in the Asia-Pacific Region', 610–13.
95. Tristan Harley, 'Regional Cooperation and Refugee Protection in Latin America: A "South-South" Approach', *International Journal of Refugee Law* no. 26 (2014): 22–47.
96. Betts, 'Comprehensive Plans of Action'.
97. Susan Kneebone, 'ASEAN Norms and Setting the Agenda for the Rights of Migrant Workers', in *Human Rights in the Asia Pacific Region*, ed. Hitoshi Nasu and Ben Saul (London: Routledge, 2011), Chapter 8.
98. Maria-Gabriela Manea, 'The Claims of the ASEAN to Human Rights and Democracy: What Role for Regional Civil Society?', *ASIEN* 136 (2015): S73–97.

99. Elliot Dolan-Evans, 'The Plight of the Rohingya', Australian Institute of International Affairs, 8 January 2016, http://www.internationalaffairs.org.au/australian_outlook/the-plight-of-the-rohingya/ (accessed 8 January 2016).

100. See Kneebone, 'The Bali Process and Global Refugee Policy in the Asia-Pacific Region'.

101. In a note of irony, the link between Australia and the region is shown by the fact that the Thai official leading the investigation into trafficking of Rohingya mentioned at the outset in this article has sought asylum in Australia; see Mark Davis, 'Top Thai Policeman Seeks Political Asylum in Australia, Fears for His Life', *ABC* (online edition, 10 December 2015), http://www.abc.net.au/news/2015-12-10/top-thai-cop-seeks-political-asylum-in-australia-fears-for-his-life/7018018 (accessed 10 January 2016).

102. *Plaintiffs M70/2011 and M106 of 2011* v. *Minister for Immigration and Citizenship* [2011] HCA 32 (31 August 2011).

103. Australian Government, *Report of the Expert Panel on Asylum Seekers*, August 2012. http://apo.org.au/files/Resource/expert_panel_on_asylum_seekers_full_report_0.pdf (accessed 10 January 2016).

104. Ibid., 11.

105. Kneebone, 'The Bali Process and Global Refugee Policy in the Asia-Pacific Region'.

106. For example, in January 2015, the RSO with the IOM and the UNHCR conducted a training workshop and developed a curriculum on good practices for *addressing* irregular movements by sea – see RSO Newsletter, Edition Eight – February 2015, 2–3, http://www.baliprocess.net/files/RSO%20Newsletter%20-%20Edition%20Eight.pdf (accessed 26 December 2015). Although most of the activities reported through the RSO can be characterised as related to preventing irregular migration, a UNHCR official in private conversation in August 2015 assured me that it is taking a 'protection' focus. Recently the RSO has developed guidelines on identification and protection of victims of trafficking – see RSO Newsletter, June 2015 Edition, http://www.baliprocess.net/files/RSO%20Newsletter%20-%20Edition%20Ten.pdf (accessed 26 December 2015). The new set of protection policy guides are available at: http://www.baliprocess.net/regional-support-office/policy-guides-on-identification-and-protection-of-victims-of-trafficking (accessed 7 January 2016).

107. William Lacy Swing, Special Meeting on Irregular Migration in the Indian Ocean, 3 June 2015, Bangkok http://www.iom.int/speeches-and-talks/special-meeting-irregular-migration-indian-ocean (accessed 25 June 2015).

108. Megan Bradley, 'IOM: What Role in the Global Forced Migration Regime?' (paper presented to Conference on Power and Influence in the Global Refugee Regime held at Carleton University, Canada, 24 September 2015).

109. UNHCR, *Bay of Bengal and Andaman Sea: Proposals for Action*, May 2015, 5.

# ASEAN and its approach to forced migration issues

Sriprapha Petcharamesree

*Institute of Human Rights and Peace Studies, Mahidol University, Thailand*

The issue of forced migration has been a difficult challenge for ASEAN to address. Despite the number of international, regional and national frameworks in place, it is clear that within the international community, emigration is regarded as a right but immigration is seen as a matter of national sovereignty and security. Irregular migrants, especially migrant workers, asylum seekers and refugees, are not only forced to leave their own state but they are vulnerable to the whims of their host state, because they are considered to be secondary to citizens and national interests. The purpose of this article is to examine forced migration in the ASEAN context and how ASEAN member states have perceived and dealt with the issues so far. It also looks critically at how ASEAN as a group has been approaching forced migration and whether the establishment of the ASEAN human rights regime has contributed to changing ASEAN's approach to forced migration. ASEAN has some policies and frameworks in place for the protection of immigrants, including for those who are forced, but are assumed to be voluntary. Although ASEAN has a number of regional frameworks which could be applied to protect the rights of those forced to migrate, it is regrettable that the overall policies and laws on migration are left to the will of national governments which, in many ways, may not comply with international human rights standards. Moreover, while the existence of the ASEAN human rights regime is significant, there are no guarantees that it will lead to the adoption of a common regional approach to forced migration. The fact that ASEAN has been upholding very strong working principles – respect of state sovereignty, non-interference in the international affairs of member states, consultation and consensus – weakens the existing ASEAN human rights system. In addition, although ASEAN is one organisation, it is made up of ten member states, each driven by their prevailing national approach to the issues. A regional approach like the one applied two decades ago, would be difficult to reach now, as the member states do not yet see forced movements and forced migration as a 'crisis'. While ASEAN does react to issues, it is always reluctant to act before the issue becomes a 'crisis'. However, even if ASEAN reacts, it might not be in support of the interests of those who are forced to leave their country.

## 1. Introduction

The Association of Southeast Asian Nations (ASEAN)[1] which comprises ten member states in Southeast Asia, is currently home to more than 625 million people[2] with a work force of 285 million.[3] In 2011 the population was 604 million, of which a little less than half (263 million) were of working age.[4] Using estimates based on bilateral migrant stocks, in 2011 ASEAN countries contributed 12.8 million or 6% of the total 216 million international migrants of the world, 3.9 million or 30% of which are migrants within the ASEAN region.[5] The proportion of these movements within the ASEAN region is rapidly rising. International migration has become an integral component of development in many countries, including countries in Southeast Asia. The main labour destination countries in the Southeast Asian region are Malaysia, Singapore and Thailand. Cambodia, Indonesia, Philippines and Vietnam are the main origin, or labour sending countries. The biggest flows are among those countries that share borders, such as Cambodia and Thailand, and Malaysia, Indonesia and the Philippines.[6]

Most studies about migration in the ASEAN region focus on labour migration rather than 'forced migration' (although as explained below many labour migrants are arguably 'forced'). According to the International Labour Organisation (ILO), migration trends in the ASEAN region tend to follow the path of economic opportunity, which explains the focus on economic migration in the ASEAN region.[7] Another form of migration, well-recognised and promoted by ASEAN, is highly-skilled labour or professional movement. To date, ASEAN has signed nine agreements on 'free' movement of highly-skilled workers.

As many ASEAN member states rely on the labour and remittances of migrant workers, both as sending and receiving countries, most attention is given to the approach to labour migration within ASEAN. However, as the ILO has recently clearly noted, issues such as statelessness, discrimination, violence and conflicts in some countries are also causes of migration in the region. In addition, environmental migration and displacement through other causes are becoming increasingly common in ASEAN.[8] The ILO further explains that:

> irregular and mixed migratory flows are also key trends in the region. Irregular migration is the cross border flow of people who enter a country without that country's legal permission to do so. Mixed migratory flows are complex population movements including both voluntary and forced ones. The most common forms of irregular migration in the region are irregular labour migration and trafficking for labour and/or sexual exploitation.[9]

Although a number of countries in ASEAN have established labour export and migrant or 'foreign' worker 'import' policies, many ASEAN member states lack coherent long-term and systematic migration policies. According to an IOM study, Singapore:

> has the most pro-active migration policy in the region, in that it projects the type of economy it wishes to achieve in the future and, from that projection, determines the number of foreign workers it will require by skill category. It then implements the programme to attract those migrants and limit the number of unneeded migrants. In comparison to Singapore, it may be argued that migration policy in most other countries reacts to the situation of migration rather than guiding it.[10]

It is true that to date in most of the ASEAN countries, particularly those receiving migrants, migration policies are ad hoc and inadequate.

Due to the lack of proactive migration policies, most receiving countries in ASEAN are now facing the problem of irregular migrants entering the countries through illegal channels, including via smuggling and trafficking routes. This has very serious impacts on migrants themselves, especially those working in informal sectors such as garment making, agriculture and electronics, which are often conducted out of sight and beyond the law. Migrants who illegally enter these countries, or who subsequently become illegal, face different challenges including detention, deportation, exploitation and discrimination. An IOM study rightly points out that 'a truly integrated labour market would be one in which laws, regulations and labour related institutions are unified; however, the region is very far from achieving such a situation'.[11] There is therefore a need not only for an integrated regional labour policy but also an appropriate regional regime to protect labour rights and the rights of migrant workers.

As mentioned earlier, ASEAN's approach on labour migration has not been consistent or adequate, despite the fact that many sending and receiving ASEAN member states are relying on migrant workers. The approach to forced migration within ASEAN is even more problematic; indeed it is questioned whether ASEAN itself has any notable policy or approach at all. For the most part, discussions about migration have so far focused on irregular migration and the issue of 'documented' versus 'undocumented migrants', with no concrete regional measures in place.

The purpose of this article is to examine forced migration in ASEAN and how ASEAN member states have perceived and dealt with the issues so far. It also looks critically at how ASEAN as a group has been approaching forced migration, and whether the establishment of the ASEAN human rights regime has contributed to changing ASEAN's approach to forced migration. As such, the article will first give an overview of forced migration issues in the ASEAN region, before looking at how forced migration has been perceived and dealt with to date. The next section will examine if ASEAN has an approach to forced migration and if so, what it looks like. Finally, the article will examine the role of the ASEAN human rights mechanisms in tackling and approaching forced migration and discuss whether a human rights based approach to migration is likely to be accepted.

## 2. Forced migration in the ASEAN region

The issue of forced migration, or even migration in a broader sense, is not as simple as it might appear. The term 'forced migration' refers to the movement of people 'in which an element of coercion predominates'.[12] The Hague Process on Refugees and Migration Foundation (THP Foundation) Handbook elaborates further that:

> [f]orced migration can be conflict-induced, caused by persecution, torture or other human rights violations, poverty, natural or manmade disasters (non-exhaustive listing). As repeatedly stated by UNHCR, the distinction between voluntary and forced migration continues to be of relevance. It still constitutes an essential element in the distinction of asylum and immigration policy and the persons they respectively concern. Migration as a general phenomenon relates to a variety of situations engaging forced and voluntary decisions. Elements of choice and coercion can be overlapping but in the case of refugees and other displaced persons, compelling factors are decisive.[13]

The Handbook adds that:

> the same migration routes are sometimes travelled by persons with different protection needs. The expression mixed migration is used in this context to refer to complex movements involving at the same time asylum seekers, refugees, displaced persons as well as migrants in general.[14]

The situation as explained by the Handbook reflects the current situation of migration in the ASEAN region. People fleeing from fighting, persecution, armed conflicts (and religious conflicts) all fall into the category of forced migrants. There are also many others who are forced to leave their country of origin due to poverty and development projects initiated and imposed by the government, which in many cases result in the loss of livelihood. The lack and/or deprivation of citizenship, such as is present in the cases of the Rohingya in Northern Arakan State, Myanmar, and the Hill Tribe peoples in Northern Thailand, must be mentioned as well. It is sometimes pointed out that there are approximately three to four million irregular immigrants in Thailand who are in the country voluntarily. In fact, many studies have revealed that a number of them could be considered 'forced migrants'.[15] Many of these migrants could have qualified for refugee status, which would denote the forced nature of their migration, but they have not been recognised as such. Therefore, they have registered themselves as migrant workers, as one of the few options available to them to ensure their survival. The distinction between forced and voluntary migration in the ASEAN region can thus be blurred, and it can be difficult to draw a line between the two categories.

Forced migrants in the ASEAN region mostly cross borders by land. However, an increasing number are now moving by sea, reminding us of the 'boat people' from Vietnam in the 1970s. Nevertheless, the present situation is different, as unlike during that crisis there are no ongoing, officially recognised interstate wars or major conflicts in the region. Furthermore, countries in the region are not granting asylum on the basis of 'country of first asylum', in exchange for a guarantee of resettlement in the West, as was the case when the Vietnamese people were fleeing as refugees. Rather, today the international community and the traditional countries of resettlement are facing 'refugee fatigue'. Resettlement is currently more difficult to obtain than over two decades ago. Moreover, comparison with the crisis in the Middle East, Syria and Libya after the Arab Spring makes the problem of forced migration in the ASEAN region seem insignificant, in terms of its magnitude and urgency, when compared with the large-scale influx of refugees in the Middle East and the serious human rights situation which this has created.

According to the United Nations High Commissioner for Refugees (UNHCR) in its 2014 Regional Operations Profile,

> a number of States implement detention, border-control, and restrictive maritime and other policies to manage irregular migration and ensure national security, which at times are detrimental to international protection. Furthermore, people-smuggling and human-trafficking networks in the sub-region have flourished, along with an increase in irregular maritime movements and a loss of life at sea.[16]

The UNHCR report provided an update on the inter-communal conflicts in mid to late 2012 in Myanmar's Rakhine State, which resulted in large-scale internal displacement and undeniably caused a growing number of refugees from Rakhine to depart to or transit through various countries in the region.[17] Malaysia and Thailand are considered as net receiving countries of forced migration due to their geographical position. Increasingly, Indonesia also receives refugees and asylum seekers from countries both within and beyond the ASEAN region. The highest number of refugees and asylum seekers are found in Thailand, although a very small number of them are recognised as such.

When it comes to stateless persons, the UNHCR points out that 'only one State in the sub-region has signed the 1954 Convention relating to the Status of Stateless Persons'.[18] That one country is the Philippines. In 2012, it adopted combined refugee status and stateless determination procedures. It also provides a transit centre for those refugees who are in need of temporary relocation outside the country of asylum pending possible resettlement.

Dr Wibisono, before he became the UN Special Rapporteur on Human Rights Situation in Syria, commented:

It is a disturbing fact to admit that only few people uproot themselves by choice. Most are compelled to become migrants, refugees, or exiles by forces beyond their control, by poverty, repression, or war. They set off with their belongings they can carry, making their way as best they can, aboard rickety boats, strapped onto trains, squeezed into trucks, or on foot; they travel alone, with families, or in groups. Some know where they are going, confident that a better life awaits them, others are just fleeing, relieved to be alive, many never make it.[19]

What was said about the reality of migration by Wibisono is also true for Southeast Asia. Another fact is that the situation of forced migration in ASEAN is always a sensitive issue to discuss and deal with among ASEAN member states. It is therefore important to look at the ASEAN member states' perceptions of forced migration.

## 3. The perception of and responses to forced migration by ASEAN member states

The UNHCR made the following comments about the asylum systems of Southeast Asian countries:

> Most countries in South-East Asia do not have any legislation regulating the rights of asylum-seekers and refugees, and UNHCR conducts refugee status determination in the absence of a national asylum system. Three countries in South-East Asia have national asylum systems at varying levels of development. One country has limited processing for certain groups under an 'admissions board' process. A number of States without national asylum systems generally consider refugees and asylum-seekers to be illegal migrants, who as such are susceptible to detention, expulsion, *refoulement* and other serious protection risks.[20]

The brief discussions which follow reflect the perceptions and responses to forced migration in Thailand, Malaysia and Indonesia.

### 3.1 *Thailand*

In June 2013, there were nearly 82,000 registered refugees and some 13,000 asylum seekers in Thailand. Most refugees are ethnic minorities from Myanmar, mainly Karen and Karenni, who live in nine camps in four provinces along the Thai-Myanmar border. Refugees in Thailand have been fleeing conflict and crossing Myanmar's eastern border jungles for the safety of Thailand for nearly 30 years. Inside Thailand, they find refuge in nine government-run camps along the border, where Myanmar refugees and asylum seekers receive basic food, shelter, medical care and schooling. The Thai government runs all camps, with most assistance provided by non-governmental organisations (NGOs), while the UNHCR focuses on protection activities and programmes to ensure that refugees live in safety and relative security within the camps.[21]

As of January 2014, the total population of concern identified by the UNHCR numbered 647,624 persons, out of whom 136,499 were refugees, 4712 asylum seekers and 506,197 stateless persons. The remaining 216 persons were put under the 'various' category. Refugees and asylum seekers of more than 40 nationalities are travelling to Thailand in increasing numbers. Many live in Bangkok and the surrounding urban areas with no legal means to sustain their livelihoods. Close to 200 are held in immigration detention centres. Those not detained risk arrest and detention, as well as deportation, if found without valid visas. Additionally, Rohingya people fleeing communal violence in Myanmar's Rakhine State have been allowed to stay temporarily in Thailand.[22]

Despite the existence of refugees and asylum seekers in the country, Thailand is not party to the 1951 Convention or the 1967 Protocol Relating to the Status of Refugees and it does not have any national legislation to govern the admission of asylum seekers. Nevertheless,

Thailand is the one country with the 'admission board' that the UNHCR referred to. The Thai government set up several 'Provincial Admissions Boards' in refugee-hosting provinces. The role of these boards was to undertake screening of asylum seekers from Myanmar prior to official government registration in the camps. However, the screening process has not been regular, and has not functioned since 2006. Nevertheless, according to the UNHCR report, in 2012 the Thai government initiated a fast-track procedure that provides access to the board for unregistered camp residents – if they are immediate family members of registered individuals already resettled or in the process of being resettled – to facilitate their eventual resettlement and reunion with family members.

### 3.2 *Malaysia*

Like Thailand, Malaysia is not a party to the 1951 Refugee Convention or its 1967 Protocol and lacks a formal legislative and administrative framework to address refugee matters. It is also known that the Malaysian government regularly implements strict policies to deter undocumented migrants from entering its territory. Since refugees and asylum seekers are not distinguished from undocumented migrants under Malaysian law, they are vulnerable to the same penalties applicable to undocumented migrants, including arrest, detention and deportation.[23] According to the UNHCR, over 100,000 asylum seekers and refugees in Malaysia reside in urban areas. The majority, 90%, come from Myanmar, and the other 10% are from Afghanistan, Iraq, Somalia and Sri Lanka. Approximately 40,000 people residing in Malaysia are considered stateless. The majority are ethnic Tamils formerly from India.[24] As stated in the UNHCR report, there were 234,920 asylum seekers, refugees, people in refugee-like situations, stateless people and others of concern in Malaysia at the end of 2013. The UNHCR forecasts that the number might increase to 250,390 by December 2015.[25] Half of that number are stateless persons and others of concern from the Philippines, while the other half are mainly from Myanmar, with approximately 5000 from various other countries.[26]

### 3.3 *Indonesia*

By April 2014, more than 10,567 asylum seekers and refugees were registered with the UNHCR in Indonesia.[27] In contrast to Malaysia where asylum seekers can easily find employment in the construction industry or on plantations – even though it is against the law to employ asylum seekers without proper working permits – Indonesia does not offer such options, as it can hardly cope with the high rates of unemployment and underemployment of its own citizens.[28] According to Missbach, until 2013 Indonesian officials were proactive in dealing with the thousands of asylum seekers who were trying to leave Indonesia by boat. Since 2014 however, officials have taken far fewer enforcement actions against asylum seekers. Recent statistics on asylum seeker interceptions show that most recent cases involving asylum seekers involve the asylum seeker voluntarily surrendering to Indonesian authorities.[29]

Like Malaysia and Thailand, Indonesia has not yet ratified the 1951 Refugee Convention and does not have legislation dealing with asylum seekers. As such, many asylum seeker issues in Indonesia get handled on an ad hoc basis.[30] Indonesia will need to have more a durable policy as:

> only a few asylum-seeker boats have arrived on Australian territory since the government of Australian Prime Minister Tony Abbott implemented its new border policies in September

2013. The 'success' of this new approach, which relies mainly on forced returns and outsourced processing of refugee claims in Nauru and Papua New-Guinea, raises the question as to what implications these new scare tactics may have on the neighboring transit countries. After all, Indonesia has been the departure point for the maritime passages of thousands of asylum seekers.[31]

One could conclude that the laws in place to address these issues in Thailand, Malaysia and Indonesia are mainly immigration focused, meaning that in many cases, those who cross the borders without proper documentation are considered 'illegal migrants'. As such, they are to be pushed back, detained or criminalised. In spite of this general situation, Thailand, Malaysia, and to a certain extent Indonesia and the Philippines, have been assisting forced migrants on humanitarian grounds. Hundreds of thousands of people who were forced by the situation in Myanmar to leave their homes were allowed to live in 'temporary shelters' along the Thai-Myanmar borders. A number of them became migrant workers and/ or 'urban refugees'. Although the number of these people is lower than in Thailand and there is no official 'shelter', Malaysia has given the UNHCR permission to register and conduct refugee status determinations for those applying for refugee status. Indonesia also allows the UNHCR to register and determine the refugee status of those arriving in its territory, although the process has been slow. In Thailand, as stated earlier, refugee status determination is either limited or restricted.

## 4. ASEAN's approach to forced migration

The influx of refugees from Indochina from the mid-1970s to early 1980s pushed the international community and ASEAN to find approaches to solve the problem. This initiative, known as the Comprehensive Plan of Action (CPA), was an agreement brokered by ASEAN with the UNHCR and resettlement states in the West, in response to ASEAN member states' concerns. At that time member states were providing refuge as countries of 'first asylum'. It is important to remember that:

> more than three million people left their homes in Vietnam, Laos and Cambodia, many with their lives in obvious peril and others fleeing fear, hunger and uncertainty. Some came seeking to rejoin relatives overseas or to start a new life of new opportunity. Others waited only for a chance to go home again in peace ... Most of these have been resettled in other countries, including 1.4 million in the United States, 260,000 in China, 200,000 in Canada, 185,000 in Australia, and 130,000 in France. Roughly half a million people have returned home.[32]

Robinson notes though, that 'what these figures do not count are the unregistered movements back and forth across borders nor the tens of thousands who suffered and died along the way as a result of piracy, pushbacks, drowning, banditry and abuse'.[33]

At the conclusion of the CPA, the Indochinese camps in Southeast Asia were all closed. The CPA brought an end to the exodus of Laotian and Vietnamese asylum seekers and provided the means for the continued resettlement of refugees and special immigrants, as well as the safe return of those found not to meet international refugee protection criteria.[34] Keane Shum commended the CPA because:

> [m]ore than two decades ago, the international community, with the full and eager cooperation of the Association of Southeast Asian Nations (ASEAN), embarked on a game-changing approach to burden-sharing in the refugee context. Whatever its flaws, the Comprehensive Plan of Action (CPA) undeniably achieved its goal of ending the Indochinese refugee crisis

... By 1998, the CPA was over and only small pockets of Indochinese refugees remained from the refugee crisis that had gripped Southeast Asia for almost a generation.[35]

Currently, although the scale of 'people fleeing' may be smaller, the ASEAN region is again at the forefront of the discussions on migration as hundreds of thousands of people are forced to leave their country of origin in search of protection and a new life. In spite of some criticisms of the CPA as a model for future multilateral and multifaceted approaches to managing forced migration, some suggest that a second CPA must be considered in order to deal with the current forced migration situation.

However, the contexts of ASEAN and the situation of forced migration in Southeast Asia have changed. At the time of the CPA, the three countries of origin of asylum seekers – namely Cambodia, Lao PDR and Vietnam – had not yet joined ASEAN. Vietnam joined ASEAN as a full member in 1995, followed by Lao PDR in 1997 and Cambodia in 1999. Moreover, Myanmar, which is now the major source country of forced migrants in the region, joined ASEAN in 1997. The regional political situation has also changed since the CPA. Communism is no longer considered a threat to the political security of the region, as the two Communist-Socialist states (Lao PDR and Vietnam) are now members of ASEAN. It is no longer political ideologies that separate ASEAN member states. The ASEAN countries are now moving towards integration to forge an ASEAN Economic Community. As explained above, it is the economic impetus that brings them together. Moreover, the ASEAN region has been gaining economic strength, which encourages the international community to cooperate with ASEAN. Moreover, ASEAN deals with many international states; by contrast, during the CPA period, the United States was the most influential power.

In addition, there is no declared conventional war as there was in Indochina between the 1950s and 1970s. The armed and ethnic conflicts that are occurring in some of the ASEAN states are not officially considered to be conflicts. Therefore, it is considered too controversial and problematic for ASEAN to recognise those forced to migrate as a result of fighting, discrimination, human rights violations and ethnic and religious conflicts as refugees. Recognising the refugee status of any group, as a fact and according to law, is recognition of persecution committed by the state concerned, something that ASEAN and its member states have been reluctant to do. Moreover, the advent of international treaties, in particular the Palermo Protocol to Prevent, Suppress and Punish Trafficking in Persons, Especially Women and Children,[36] and, to a certain extent, the United Nations Convention against Transnational Organized Crime,[37] have made ASEAN member states more open to dealing with forced migration from a trafficking and international crime perspective.

Although there is no longer a CPA, a new approach to forced migration in the ASEAN region has not yet been developed or implemented. Furthermore, the absence of a large-scale exodus, such as the one seen during the Indochina period, gives the false impression among ASEAN members that forced migration is not a significant problem. As such, ASEAN members do not yet see a point where they need to act as a group, which has been seen on various other occasions:

In August 2012, Dr Surin Pitsuwan, the then ASEAN Secretary General, urged all ASEAN foreign ministers to meet and address the Rohingya issue. The ASEAN chair, headed by Cambodian Foreign Minister Hor Nam Hong, called a meeting of the foreign ministers. However, Myanmar refused to attend the meeting and said the situation was under control. Dr Pitsuwan warned that 'the conflict poses strategic and security challenges that could destabilize Southeast Asia',[38] and, referring to the displaced Rohingya:

they are now under tremendous pressure, pain and suffering. If the international community, including ASEAN, are not able to relieve that pressure and pain, conceivably, [the 1.5 million displaced Rohingya] could become radicalized and the entire region could be destabilized, including the Malacca Straits …

If they became radicalized, Dr Pitsuwan further said, the area risked becoming a zone of violence that could damage cooperation in ASEAN and East Asia. He added: 'I think it has wider strategic and security implications'.[39]

Even from a humanitarian basis, ASEAN could not find a common approach to address the Rohingya issue. In 2013, the Brunei Representative to the ASEAN Intergovernmental Commission on Human Rights (AICHR),[40] the Chair of the AICHR, received communications from different NGOs about the plight of, and human rights violations against, the Rohingya. As a result, he decided to raise the issue as a discussion point so that the AICHR had an opportunity to respond to the complaints, although this was behind closed doors. His attempt, which was supported by two representatives, failed completely as it was strongly opposed by some other representatives, who considered it to be an internal issue that should be dealt with at the national level.

In fact, the issues of forced migration have never been properly discussed or addressed in ASEAN by the member states. ASEAN does, however, discuss the free movement of skilled labour and professionals. The skills recognition framework is found in the Mutual Recognition Agreements (MRA). As of 2012, ASEAN had nine MRAs. The engineering MRA was signed on 9 December 2005; nursing on 8 December 2006; architects and surveyors on 19 November 2007; doctors, dentists and accountants on 26 February 2009; and tourism professionals in 2012. Although ASEAN has a common policy and arrangements for labour mobility, such a policy and arrangements only apply to high-skilled labour and professions. Low, semi-skilled and non-skilled labour have been dealt with by another framework of arrangements. This will be explained in the next section.

Through the Indochinese wars of the 1970s and 1980s, ASEAN adopted a common approach, which was encouraged by the international community because the situation had reached a 'crisis' level. Shum suggests that:

the CPA taught us that when [South-East Asia] acts after a crisis breaks out, the region cooperates with each other and the international community out of necessity, but at a great cost to refugee protection once the crisis has passed.[41]

Since the current situation in the region is not considered to be 'a crisis' by ASEAN or its member states, there is no perceived necessity to act or to cooperate. As such, it is those in need of protection who bear the cost and continue to suffer from human rights violations. In order to address this problem, the often 'competing political forces within ASEAN and between ASEAN and developed world would need to coalesce around a new framework in a spirit of cooperation rarely seen in SEA'.[42]

## 5. The ASEAN human rights regime and the ASEAN approach to forced migration

As will be explained below, although ASEAN has shown commitment to human rights and international law, the political will to address forced migration is not yet present. ASEAN is more concerned with upholding its working principles based on the respect of state sovereignty and non-interference in the internal affairs of the member states, as well as consultation, consensus and non-confrontation. Addressing an issue against the wishes of one member state is seen to be breaking ASEAN's norms and procedures. This section will discuss ASEAN's human rights framework, which consists of declarations, commissions and regional processes. Importantly, the Preamble to the ASEAN Charter refers to adherence to 'the principles of democracy, the rule of law and good governance, [and] respect for and protection of' such rights and freedoms.[43]

### 5.1 *The ASEAN Declaration Against Trafficking in Persons, Particularly Women and Children (2004)*

This declaration recognises the seriousness of the issues, the regional nature of the problem, and ASEAN's commitment to deal with them.[44] However, the declaration only requires member states to take measures 'to the extent permitted by their respective domestic laws'.[45] In terms of implementation, ASEAN does not make much progress towards addressing the problem. Even though the ASEAN Ad-Hoc Inter-Agency Working Group was established in 2006, ASEAN's efforts seem to be limited to the areas of information exchange, training of responsible officials and law enforcement agencies, and workshops. In addition, although the issue of human trafficking was included in the Political and Security Community Blueprint adopted by ASEAN in 2009, 'ASEAN States continue to treat the problem of human trafficking as an ordinary crime not as a security problem that poses existential threat that requires extraordinary measures'.[46] It is also to be noted that the issue of trafficking in persons has not been considered within the wider context of migration generally.

The regional and sub-regional arrangements regarding trafficking in persons are important for the protection of the rights of migrants, since a large number of workers are irregular migrants who use smugglers and are vulnerable to trafficking. The fact that Malaysia and Thailand were downgraded from the Tier 2 Watch List to Tier 3 by the US State Department in the annual Trafficking in Person Reports (TIP) in June 2014 suggests the seriousness of the problem within the broader migration process.

### 5.2 *ASEAN Declaration on the Protection and Promotion of the Rights of Migrant Workers*

The issue of labour migration has also been a concern in Southeast Asia. In 2007, with the encouragement of the Philippines, ASEAN adopted the ASEAN Declaration on the Protection and Promotion of the Rights of Migrant Workers.[47] The declaration articulated a rights-based approach to migration. However, this rights-based approach was undermined by the member states' recognition of 'the sovereignty of states in determining their own migration policy relating to migrant workers, including determining entry into their territory and under which conditions migrant workers may remain' in the Preamble. This Preamble weakens the whole declaration, as it curtails any possibility for any regional approach to migration and migrant workers since each state still has full authority to deal with migrant workers, in spite of the recognition for the need to address 'cases of abuse and violation against migrant workers whenever such cases occur'.[48] The Preamble is further strengthened by the General Principles, which essentially stipulate that the treatment of migrant workers will be in accordance with the laws, regulations and policies of respective ASEAN member countries. The declaration is not to be interpreted as 'implying the regularization of the situation of migrant workers who are undocumented'.[49] The declaration does not provide for irregular migrant workers in the ASEAN region. It therefore fails to provide a common approach to labour migration, and for low and semi-skilled labour migrants in particular, which includes those who are forced to migrate out of necessity.

In 2007 ASEAN set up the ASEAN Committee on the Implementation of the ASEAN Declaration on the Protection and Promotion of the Rights of Migrant Workers (ACMW) to oversee the implementation of the declaration. The ACMW's role is to conduct the annual ASEAN Forum on Migrant Workers, develop an ASEAN instrument on migrant workers' rights, prepare pre-departure information for ASEAN migrant workers, collaborate with relevant international organisations on 'Safe Migration' campaigns and pre-departure literature for migrants, as well as strengthen the dialogue between the ACMW and those working on human smuggling and trafficking. The ACMW has been making very slow progress in fulfilling its mandates due to the sensitivity of the issue and the lack of consensus among its members.

Another policy platform in ASEAN regarding migrant workers is the Socio-Cultural Community Blueprint. This document falls under the ASEAN 'social justice and rights' pillar, and includes strategies and activities relating to the rights of migrant workers. However, one has to admit that the issues of migrant workers are considered to be sensitive by most of the countries in the region. This sensitivity is felt in most, if not all, documents, including the blueprints.

## 5.3   *ASEAN Commission on the Promotion and Protection of the Rights of Women and Children (ACWC)*

The establishment of the ACWC in April 2010 was strengthened by the adoption of the Hanoi Declaration on the Enhancement of Welfare and Development of ASEAN Women and Children,[50] which was adopted by ASEAN leaders in October 2010. By affirming different ASEAN declarations on children, this declaration aims to strengthen ASEAN's commitment to ensuring that women and children benefit fully from ASEAN's process of integration and community building. The 2010 Hanoi Declaration, which focuses on the welfare and well-being of children, has a few provisions that promote 'closer cooperation in promoting and protecting the rights of women and children especially those living under disadvantaged and vulnerable conditions including those in disaster and conflict affected areas'.[51] However, it still remains to be seen how much ASEAN has done as a region to promote and protect the rights of children forced to migrate alone or with their care givers. The declaration, if interpreted broadly, may also include children who are on the move.

Although the ACWC's Terms of Reference (TOR) are slightly more advanced than that of the ASEAN Intergovernmental Commission on Human Rights (AICHR), the protection mandates are still hindered by similar principles of non-interference in the internal affairs of the member states and delayed by the principles of consultation and consensus. ACWC's 2012–2016 Work Plan contains specific thematic areas and activities, including the promotion and protection of child migrants through the child protection system, which creates a comprehensive and integrative approach for children in need of special protection. This child protection system covers victims of abuse and neglect, trafficked children, child labourers, children affected by statelessness, undocumented migrant children, children in the juvenile justice system, children in conflict with the law, and children affected by HIV/AIDS, natural disasters and conflicts. It has to be noted though, that the issues of child refugees and asylum seekers, as well as unaccompanied and separated children, have not been properly discussed.

### 5.4 *ASEAN Intergovernmental Commission on Human Rights (AICHR)*

The establishment of the ASEAN Intergovernmental Commission on Human Rights (AICHR) in 2009 represented a step towards the protection and promotion of human rights.The AICHR is intended to assist ASEAN in conforming to the 'purposes and principles of the ASEAN Charter relating to the promotion and protection of human rights and fundamental freedoms'.

The AICHR is thus an ASEAN charter-based body, with the mandate to promote and protect the human rights of all ASEAN peoples. As an overarching body in ASEAN, the AICHR not only deals with all categories of human rights but also has obligations to promote and protect the human rights of all groups within the ASEAN population, including labour and migrant workers. Criticisms have been made against the AICHR, as the body does not have an explicit mandate to perform a protection duty. Although the criticisms have a factual basis, the AICHR could, if the representatives so desired, interpret their mandates and functions expansively and creatively. For example, the AICHR could encourage ASEAN member states to consider acceding to and ratifying international human rights instruments.[52] The AICHR could also seek to obtain information from the member states on the protection and promotion of human rights,[53] which could include the rights of workers, including (forced) migrants. The AICHR could also conduct thematic studies relating to human rights in ASEAN.[54] So far, the AICHR has identified a number of issues for thematic studies, including issues of migration led by the Indonesian Representative, the right to education, women and children in armed conflicts and natural disasters. These thematic studies could potentially cover the issues of migration, including forced migration. In addition, the issue of statelessness has already found its way onto the AICHR agenda, even though the member states have been a bit reluctant. Although the activities organised so far have mainly focused on awareness raising, in the long term this may lead to sensitisation and more concrete actions being taken by the AICHR.

### 5.5 *ASEAN Human Rights Declaration (AHRD)*

The adoption of the ASEAN Human Rights Declaration (AHRD)[55] is another milestone for ASEAN. Although some provisions of the AHRD are below international standards and it does not contain any specific provisions on the rights of refugees, the general principles make it clear that:

- 'Every person is entitled to the rights and freedoms set forth herein, without distinction of any kind, such as race, gender, age, language, religion, political or other opinion, national or social origin, economic status, birth, disability or other status'[56];
- 'Every person has the right of recognition everywhere as a person before the law'[57];
- 'Every person is equal before the law'[58];
- 'Every person is entitled without discrimination to equal protection of the law'[59] and;
- 'The rights of women, children, the elderly, persons with disabilities, migrant workers, and vulnerable and marginalised groups are an inalienable, integral and indivisible part of human rights and fundamental freedoms'.[60]

The reference to every person in most of the provisions could be positively interpreted to contribute to the promotion and protection of the rights of refugees and asylum seekers. However, the general practice of the ASEAN member states is to interpret the provisions narrowly.

Although Article 16 of the AHRD recognises 'the right to seek and receive asylum in another State', the same provision makes it clear that asylum is to be granted 'in accordance with the laws of such state and applicable international agreements'.[61] In addition, Article 15 of the AHRD recognises 'the right to freedom of movement and residence within the borders of each State'.[62] Every person has the right to leave any country including his or her own, and to return to his or her country. However, the recognition of the right to freedom of movement and to leave one's own country does not guarantee the right to cross or to enter another country in the region, as the movement of people is still restricted in the ASEAN region. It must also be noted that the AHRD recognises the right to nationality.[63] However, Article 34 of the AHRD says very clearly that the member states 'may determine the extent to which they would guarantee the economic and social rights found in this Declaration to non-nationals, with due regard to human rights and the organisation and resources of their respective national economies'.[64] Therefore, the protection and promotion of the rights of those forced to migrate is left to the mercy and discretion of the national governments.

## 5.6   *The Bali Process*

At the wider Asia-Pacific level, there is a framework that could be used to address the issue of migration, namely the Bali Process[65] which is co-chaired by Australia and Indonesia, and which the ASEAN Secretariat sometimes attends as an Observer. The Bali Process commemorated the tenth anniversary of its establishment in 2012. All ASEAN member states are members of the Bali Process. The Bali Process was initiated due to the common concerns of irregular migration in the region, especially people smuggling and trafficking in persons, and the need for regional solutions to these issues.

Although the core objectives of the Bali Process are to address the issues of people smuggling and trafficking and to detect and prevent illegal movements, it also aims at assisting countries to:

> adopt best practices in asylum management, in accordance with the principles of the Refugees Convention, and advancing the implementation of an inclusive non-binding regional cooperation framework under which interested parties can cooperate more effectively to reduce irregular movement through the region.[66]

Until 2009, the Bali Process focused mainly on transnational crime, including people smuggling and trafficking in persons. However, in 2009 the Bali Process made tangible progress as a result of the wave of refugees travelling by sea from Afghanistan, Sri Lanka and Myanmar, which became a 'mini-crisis' in the region. The UNHCR began to see the results of its persistent efforts from 2009 onward, as the protection of refugees was included, and has remained, on the agenda of the Bali Process.[67] The 'mini crisis' in Southeast Asia led the Bali Process to find 'regional responses to current situations concerning the irregular movement of people in the Asia-Pacific region'.[68] The Ad Hoc Group (AHG)[69] in its second meeting held in June 2010 agreed to 'a proposal for the UNHCR to host a workshop on regional cooperation on refugees and irregular movement'.[70] It was during the workshop organised in Manila in November 2010 that the UNHCR presented a proposal called the 'Regional Cooperation Framework' (RCF) containing 'a set of common understandings for dealing with irregular movement and asylum seekers in a protection sensitive manner'.[71] The move is important because country members of the Bali Process recognise that the issues of irregular migration require regional solutions and that the issues of refugee protection are a common concern in the region. The RCF was recommended by the AHG senior officials and was finally endorsed by the Bali Process ministers in their fourth Regional Ministerial Conference on People Smuggling, Trafficking in Persons and Related Transnational Crime held in Bali between 29 and 30 March 2011.

Although the RCF was adopted with an expanded agenda and activities, the arrangements agreed by the ministers emphasise border control and migration management. While human life and dignity are to be observed, there is no guarantee that members will enshrine the concepts, especially when it comes to irregular migrants and asylum seekers, because most of the members and participants of the Bali Process are not parties to the 1951 UN Convention Relating to the Status of Refugees or its 1967 Protocol. Moreover, the future activities proposed by the RCF do not seem to be concrete as most are subject to further negotiations and depend on agreements being made either bilaterally or multilaterally. It is also important to note that the RCF is not a binding document. Its implementation depends on the political will of its members. The establishment of the Regional Support Office (RSO) based in Bangkok and co-managed by Australia and Indonesia was considered as a step towards a more concrete implementation of the RCF. The RSO is mandated to implement activities under the RFC and act as a focal point for members for:

- facilitating information sharing on refugee protection and international migration;
- supporting capacity building and exchange of best practices; and
- encouraging pooling of common technical resources;

Offering logistical, administrative, operational and coordination support for joint projects,[72] the RSO is an open structure which can take on assignments proposed by government officials and other contributions from Bali Process member states. New projects submitted by members will be considered by the RSO, in consultation with UNHCR, IOM and the Bali Process Steering Group, and under the oversight of the Bali Process Co-Chairs. According to the RSO, its purpose is to operate under the oversight and direction of the Bali Process Co-Chairs, the governments of Australia and Indonesia. In addition, it also operates in consultation with UNHCR and IOM. Its day-to-day operations are managed by co-managers from both the Australian and Indonesian governments.[73]

Although the RSO has been managed by the co-managers, the funding comes mainly from the government of Australia. Moreover, since the RSO exists to 'facilitate, support, encourage and offer logistic support as stated in its mandate', the RSO may not have decision-making power in policy decisions. In addition, to date, the Bali Process has been 'state centric', the participation of other key stakeholders has been minimal.

## 6. Conclusion

The issue of forced migration has been a difficult challenge for ASEAN to address. The mini-crisis of 2009 and the issue of Rohingya refugees have not so far been considered serious enough to push ASEAN towards a common approach. Despite the number of international, regional and national frameworks in place, it is clear that within the international society, emigration is regarded as a right but immigration is seen as a matter of national sovereignty and security. There is an imbalance in power when individual security is locked into an unbreakable paradigm that is partly dependent on and partly threatened by the state. This imbalance results in manipulation by the state. Irregular migrants, especially migrant workers, asylum seekers and refugees, are not only forced to leave their own state but they are vulnerable to state whims because they are considered to be secondary to citizens and national interests.

ASEAN does have some policies and frameworks in place for the protection of immigrants, including those who are forced but are assumed to be voluntary. However, ASEAN's human rights system is still weak, as it does not have a human rights court and the commissions do not have mandates to receive complaints or conduct investigations. This is because of ASEAN's very strong working principles – respect of state sovereignty, non-interference in the international affairs of member states, consultation and consensus. What is more regrettable is the fact that the overall policies and laws on migration are left to the will of national governments which, in many ways, may not comply with international human rights standards. Moreover, while the existence of the ASEAN human rights regime is significant, there are no guarantees that it will lead to the adoption of a common regional approach to forced migration. While ASEAN is one organisation, it is made up of ten member states, who are each driven by their prevailing national approach to the issues. A regional approach like the one applied two decades ago, would be difficult to reach now, as the member states do not yet see forced movements and forced migration as a 'crisis'. While ASEAN reacts to issues, it is always reluctant to act before an issue becomes a 'crisis'. However, even if ASEAN reacts, it might not react in the interests of the protection of those who are forced to leave their countries.

## Acknowledgements

The author would like to thank Professor Susan Kneebone, Faculty of Law, Monash University for her kind invitation to the launch of the Asia Pacific Forced Migration Connection (APFMC) on 8 August 2014 at Monash University, Melbourne. I am particularly thankful for all support provided for my trip. Built upon my presentation made during the launch, I was honoured to be requested by Professor Kneebone to develop this article. I really appreciate her assistance in editing my paper. My appreciation is also extended to her PhD student Thomas Harré who kindly went through this article as well. I am taking full responsibilities of any errors, if any.

## Notes

1. The Association of Southeast Asian Nations, or ASEAN, was established on 8 August 1967 in Bangkok, Thailand, with the signing of the ASEAN Declaration (Bangkok Declaration) by the founding members of ASEAN, namely Indonesia, Malaysia, Philippines, Singapore and Thailand. Brunei Darussalam then joined on 7 January 1984, Viet Nam on 28 July 1995, Lao PDR and Myanmar on 23 July 1997, and Cambodia on 30 April 1999, making up what is today the ten member states of ASEAN. The ten ASEAN member states (AMS) ratified the ASEAN Charter which entered into force on 15 December 2008. With the entry into force of the ASEAN Charter, ASEAN will henceforth operate under a new legal framework and establish a number of new organs to boost its community-building process. Available at http://www.asean.org/asean/about-asean.
2. As of August 2014, the total population of ASEAN was 625,096 million, http://www.asean.org/images/resources/Statistics/2014/SelectedKeyIndicatorAsOfApril/UpdatedAug/Summary%20table_as%20of%20August%2014.pdf.

3. ASEAN, http://www.asean.org/communities/asean-socio-cultural-community/category/asean-labour-ministers-meeting.
4. Aniceto Orbeta Jr and Kathrina Gonzales, *Managing International Labor Migration in ASEAN: Themes from a Six-Country Study* (Philippines: Philippine Institute for Development Studies, 2013), http://www.eaber.org/node/23422, 1.
5. Ibid.
6. Ibid., 3.
7. International Organisation for Migration (IOM), 'Migration Dynamics in ASEAN: Trends, Challenges and Priorities' (PowerPoint presentation at the International Conference 'On the Move: Critical Migration Themes in ASEAN', 17 December, Chulalongkorn University, Thailand), http://www.arcmthailand.com/documents/documentcenter/1701_PPP%20Chula%20Conference_Claudia%2015%20dec%2012.pdf.
8. Ibid.
9. Ibid.
10. IOM, *Situation Report on International Migration in East and Southeast Asia: Regional Thematic Working Group on International Migration including Human Trafficking* (Bangkok: IOM, 2008), 119.
11. Ibid.
12. The Hague Process on Refugees and Migration, *People on the Move: Handbook of Selected Terms and Concepts* (The Hague/Paris: UNESCO Section on International Migration and Multicultural Policies, 2008), 29.
13. Ibid.
14. Ibid.
15. See for example Sriprapha Petcharamesree et al., *The Study on Labour Migration and Possible Protection Mechanim(s) in ASEAN* (Bangkok: Law Reform Commission of Thailand, June 2014); Equal Rights Trust and Institute of Human Rights and Peace Studies, Mahidol University, *Equal Only in Name, The Human Rights of Stateless Rohingya in Malaysia and The Human Rights of Stateless Rohingya in Thailand* (London: Equal Rights Trust and Institute of Human Rights and Peace Studies, Mahidol University, October 2014).
16. UNHCR Regional Operations Profile-SEA, http://www.unhcr.org/pages/4b17be9b6.html.
17. Ibid.
18. Ibid.
19. Makarim Wibisono, 'ASEAN's Approach to Migration Challenges Amidst the Region's Multiculturalism', *Geneva Interfaith Intercultural Alliance*, http://www.giia.ch/joomla/index.php/conferences/un-september-2011/main-presentations/25-government-a-migration/43-aseans-approach-to-migration-challenges-amidst-the-regions-multiculturalism.
20. UNHCR, '2015 UNHCR Subregional Operations Profile – South-East Asia', http://www.unhcr.org/pages/49e487c66.html.
21. UNHCR, 'Refugees in Thailand', https://www.unhcr.or.th/refugee/thailand.
22. UNHCR, '2015 UNHCR Country Operations Profile – Thailand', http://www.unhcr.org/pages/49e489646.html.
23. UNHCR, '2014 UNHCR Country Operations Profile – Malaysia', http://www.unhcr.org/pages/49e4884c6.html.
24. Ibid.
25. Ibid.
26. Ibid.
27. Antje Missbach, 'Asylum Seekers Stuck in Indonesia', *Jakarta Post* (online edition), 4 April 2014), http://www.thejakartapost.com/news/2014/04/04/asylum-seekers-stuck-indonesia.html.
28. Ibid.
29. Ibid.
30. Ibid.
31. Ibid.
32. W. Courtland Robinson, *Terms of Refuge: The Indochinese Exodus and the International Response* (London: Zed Books, 1998), 2.
33. Ibid.
34. Ibid.

35. Keane Shum, 'A New Comprehensive Plan of Action: Addressing the Refugee Protection Gap in Southeast Asia through Local and Regional Integration', *Oxford Monitor of Forced Migration* 1, no. 1 (2011): 60–1.

36. Protocol to Prevent, Suppress and Punish Trafficking in Persons, Especially Women and Children, supplementing the United Nations Convention against Transnational Organized Crime, opened for signature 15 November 2000, completed 25 December 2003. 2237 UNTS 319.

37. United Nations Convention against Transnational Organized Crime, opened for signature 15 November 2000, completed 29 September 2003. 2225 UNTS 209.

38. Yohanna Ririhena, 'ASEAN Chief: Rohingya Issue Could Destabilize the Region', *The Jakarta Post*, Jakarta (online edition), 30 October 2012, http://www.thejakartapost.com/news/2012/10/30/asean-chief-rohingya-issue-could-destabilize-region.html, 1.

39. Ibid.

40. The AICHR was created under Article 14 of the ASEAN Charter.

41. Shum, 'A New Comprehensive Plan of Action', 76.

42. Ibid.

43. ASEAN Charter, Preamble.

44. The 2004 Declaration was preceded by: ASEAN, *ASEAN Declaration on Transnational Crime* (Manila: The Philippines, 20 December 1997), http://www.asean.org/communities/asean-political-security-community/item/asean-declaration-on-transnational-crime-manila-20-december-1997; ASEAN, *ASEAN Plan of Action to Combat Transnational Crime*, endorsed by the 2nd ASEAN Ministerial Meeting on Transnational Crime (AMMTC), Yangon, Myanmar, 23 June 1999, http://www.asean.org/communities/asean-political-security-community/item/joint-communique-of-the-second-asean-ministerial-meeting-on-transnational-crime-ammtc-yangon-23-june-1999.

45. 2004 ASEAN Declaration against Trafficking in Persons, Particularly Women and Children, adopted in Vientiane, Lao PDR on 29 November 2004 by Heads of State/Government at the 10th ASEAN Summit, Preamble.

46. Rizal Sukma, 'Different Treatment: Women Trafficking in the Securitization of Transnational Crimes' (paper presented at the 2nd NTS Convention, Beijing, 9–11 November 2008), http://www.rsis-ntsasia.org/activities/conventions/2008-beijing/rizal.pdf.

47. ASEAN, Declaration on the Protection and Promotion of the Rights of Migrant Workers, Philippines, 2007, http://www.aseansec.org/19264.htm.

48. Ibid., Preamble.

49. Ibid., General Principles, [4].

50. See ASEAN, 'Ha Noi Declaration on the Enhancement of Welfare and Development of ASEAN Women and Children', http://www.asean.org/news/item/ha-noi-declaration-on-the-enhancement-of-welfare-and-development-of-asean-women-and-children.

51. Ibid., [2].

52. ASEAN Intergovernmental Commission on Human Rights, 'Terms of Reference', http://aichr.org/documents/, [4.5].

53. Ibid., [4.10].

54. Ibid., [4.12].

55. http://www.mfa.go.th/asean/contents/files/other-20121217-165728-100439.pdf.

56. ASEAN Human Rights Declaration (AHRD), Adopted in Phnom Penh, Cambodia by the Heads of State/Government of ASEAN Member States, 18 November 2012. Article 2.

57. AHRD, Article 3.

58. Ibid.

59. Ibid.

60. AHRD, Article 4.

61. AHRD, Article 16.

62. AHRC, Article 15.

63. AHRD, Article 18.

64. AHRD, Article 34.

65. See Bali Process, http://www.baliprocess.net/.

66. The Bali Process, *Ad Hoc Group*, http://www.baliprocess.net/ad-hoc-group.

67. Savitri Taylor, 'Regional Cooperation and the Malaysian Solution', *Inside Story* (online edition), 9 May 2011, http://inside.org.au.

68. Ibid.

69. The AHG 'mechanism' was created at the Third Bali Process meeting in April 2009, 'to bring together key source, transit and destination countries as well as relevant international organisations' to develop regional responses to current irregular migration challenges affecting the Asia-Pacific region.

70. See Bali Process, 'Bali Process Senior Officials Meeting, Bali, Indonesia, 10 March 2011 Co-Chairs' Statement', https://www.iom.int/jahia/webdav/shared/shared/mainsite/microsites/rcps/baliprocess/SOM-Final-Co-Chairs-Statement-10-3-2011.pdf.

71. Ibid.

72. See Bali Process, Regional Support Office Information Sheet, http://www.baliprocess.net/files/RSO/RSO%20Information%20Sheet_Overview_30%20Apr%202013.pdf.

73. Ibid.

# Refugee protection and responsibility sharing in Latin America: solidarity programmes and the Mexico Plan of Action

Stefania Eugenia Barichello

*Refugee Law Initiative and Institute of Commonwealth Studies, School of Advanced Study, University of London, London, UK*

The aim of this article is to analyse the three solidarity programmes in the Mexico Plan of Action (MPA) – the responsibility sharing programme for regional resettlement, the integration of refugees into safe communities, and the development of border regions. The MPA is a step forward in strengthening the protection of human rights and the affirmation of the universality of human dignity. The MPA's objectives and programmes promote responsibility both at the regional level, through the notions of international solidarity and shared responsibility, and at the international level, as cooperation at a regional level could encourage similar initiatives in other regions.

## 1. Introduction

Latin America[1] has developed a particular regional policy approach aimed towards providing better protection for refugees through the application of various normative and institutional developments. Aside from the regional instruments that have established the unique instrument of political asylum,[2] since the 1984 Cartagena Declaration[3] Latin American countries have developed mechanisms and concepts that have sensibly approached the contemporary refugee problems that exist in the region. Initially designed as an answer to the problems of the late 1970s and early 1980s in Central America, the 1984 Cartagena Declaration has also influenced Latin American countries. The 1984 declaration goes beyond the definition of 'refugee' that appears in the 1951 Geneva Convention,[4] as it includes people that have left their country of origin because of war, massive violations of human rights or because of similar causes that severely disturb public order.

In 1994, a process of re-evaluation and revision led to the San Jose Declaration, which reiterated the importance of the 1984 declaration and broadened its scope in order to extend protection to internally displaced people. Furthermore, in 2004 the Mexico Plan of Action (MPA) was also adopted in order to deal with the new crisis of refugees and asylum seekers from Colombia.[5] Indeed, one of the principal factors in this decision was the intensification of the armed and socio-political conflict in Colombia and the resulting humanitarian crisis, which resulted in between three and four million displaced persons within Colombia and hundreds of thousands of asylum seekers in other countries in the region.

The 'crowded borders' phenomenon[6] due to the Colombian armed conflict was one of the key concerns of regional states. As such, the MPA takes the form of a regional plan to ensure protection and 'durable solutions' for refugees in Latin America.[7] One of its main points is the adoption of three 'solidarity' programmes to facilitate durable solutions for refugees (predominantly from Colombia) in countries in the region.[8]

Despite the novelty and affirmed practical importance of the MPA, academic research on this topic is lacking. The existing documentation relating to this framework consists predominantly of policy documents created by the United Nations High Commissioner for Refugees (UNHCR) – which pushed for the adoption of the MPA. Whilst these are useful sources, they contain little analysis of the MPA on its own terms or in relation to its wider implications for refugee law and scholarship in Latin America and beyond. A few studies have been published that look briefly at the MPA in policy terms,[9] but only a limited number of articles explore the three 'solidarity programmes'.[10]

Thus, the aim of this article is to analyse the solidarity programmes within the wider context of the MPA, as well as to discuss the main proposals of these programmes and their achievements. For this purpose, this article will examine the three programmes proposed by the MPA. The first mechanism of the plan is a regional responsibility sharing programme focused on the resettlement of refugees and internally displaced persons (IDPs), known as the 'Solidarity Resettlement' Programme. The second pillar is the integration of refugees and IDPs in safe communities (the 'Solidarity Cities' programme). The third is the 'Borders of Solidarity' programme, which focuses on the development of the border regions of neighbouring countries to benefit displaced Colombians and their hosts, namely Ecuador, Panamá and Venezuela. Finally, the development and effectiveness of these solidarity programmes are considered.

This article is structured in six parts. Following the introduction, the second and third sections provide an overview of important concepts for the understanding of the current development of the Latin American System – regionalism, harmonisation and responsibility sharing. The fourth part presents the evolving system of Latin American asylum law and policy, while the fifth section considers the 2004 MPA and its solidarity programmes. Finally, the conclusions summarise the main aspects of the analysis and research and provide views on the future protection of refugees in Latin America.

## 2. Regionalism and harmonisation

There is a growing trend towards the regionalisation and harmonisation of norms and procedures in a number of instruments concerning the protection of refugees and asylum seekers, such as the regional cooperation system developed by the European Union through its efforts to establish a Common European Asylum System.[11] Considering the fact that Latin America as a region has also been involved in this trend, it is necessary to analyse the notions of regionalisation and harmonisation.

Meeting the protection needs of the asylum seekers, while at the same time promoting cooperation across the world, appears to be one of the central current challenges for the international refugee protection system.[12] Under the existing international regime, the accidents of geography and a country's ability to safeguard its borders determine the distribution of state responsibility for refugees. Consequently, the world's poorer and least capable countries are carrying a disproportionately large share of refugees. Under these circumstances, in order to ensure durable solutions for asylum seekers and refugees, the use of regional responses has been promoted.[13]

The UNHCR takes the position that the adoption of regional approaches is essential for strengthening the international refugee system. The UNHCR has been at the forefront of the design and development of regional approaches that respond to specific regional concerns, in order to guarantee fair burden sharing and international solidarity and ensure that there is conformity with universal standards of refugee protection.[14]

Kneebone and Rawlings-Sanae suggest that 'regional responses shore up the international protection regime by cutting across and perhaps weakening the power of the nation State'.[15] Regional responses developed first because of the restrictive mechanisms aimed towards refugees and asylum seekers over the last 20 years, including, amongst other restrictions, the reduced ability to enter a potential asylum state. Second, regional interventions provide practical solutions to a global problem.[16]

The policies that have been advanced in various regions are intended to overcome weaknesses in the 1951 Convention, and help international refugee law to apply to the various regional refugee issues. According to Fischel de Andrade, 'regional initiatives need to be carried out in a cautious manner given their potential impact and "ripple effects" in other regions' and at no point should the regional approach reduce the standards that have been accepted and set up at the international level.[17]

A regionalist viewpoint takes the position that while bearing in mind global needs, initiatives should be embraced by the entire region, as the parties are united by the common spirit and purpose of the interventions they have developed. Regional responsibility sharing is more achievable than an elaborate and universalised system of human responsibility sharing due to the fact that:

(1) It is difficult for states within a region to insulate themselves from intra-regional refugee flows; (2) there is likely to be a greater sense of political or other responsibility towards the refugees; (3) responsibility sharing would build on existing patterns of regional relationships; (4) there is usually a prevailing sense of regionalism interrelationship.[18]

Currently, there is no universalised system of responsibility sharing for hosting refugees. This is due to the spontaneity of the refugee flows and the responses of the different host states, as well as states' interest in maintaining regional security. Furthermore, refugees are more likely to be welcomed in nearby countries where their social and political cultures are similar.[19]

According to Schuck, a regionally structured system retains numerous significant benefits when compared with the global system, encouraging a 'tradition of regional responsibility for localized refugee flows and solutions, the greater cohesion of interests and values that regions tend to share, and the more intense patterns of interaction that they exhibit'.[20]

A regionalised system of sharing responsibility allows states in the region 'that receive a threat of unmanaged refugee migration to join together in regional grouping to attenuate the impact of such migration'.[21] This ensures that the countries in the region share the responsibility for hosting refugees among themselves.

According to Kneebone, regional *and* national approaches are required.[22] In the first place, global refugee movement trends ought to be acknowledged, along with the influence of regionalism upon such flows.[23] Kneebone suggests that in the global context, a dialogue between the North and the South is necessary. Second, regionalism must develop strategies that promote durable solutions, through joint development-focused projects or joint comprehensive plans.[24] Regional initiatives 'are promoted in the form of harmonisation and burden-sharing by States within the region'.[25]

## 3. Responsibility sharing

The idea of international burden sharing is of vital relevance if the international protection system for victims of persecution, war or natural disaster 'is not to break down under the sheer weight of numbers for lack of proper appreciation of the demands of human solidarity and international legal obligation'.[26]

The notion of burden sharing was first documented in Paragraph 4 of the Preamble of the 1951 Convention, which expressly acknowledges that:

> the grant of asylum may place unduly heavy burdens on certain countries, and that a satisfactory solution of a problem of which the United Nations has recognized the international scope and nature cannot therefore be achieved without international cooperation.[27]

Hathaway and Neve assert that under the Refugee Convention, each state party assumes particular obligations, and nothing in the current legal regime prevents governments from cooperating and offering assets to meet those obligations.[28] In their opinion, burden sharing 'not only makes practical sense as a means to combat the withdrawal of States from the duty to protect refugees, but is consistent with general norms of international law'.[29]

The logic behind burden sharing is motivated by the idea that an equitable distribution of costs and responsibilities in protection will lead to both maximum fairness among states and the greatest openness towards protection seekers. Fairness involves the avoidance of 'peak costs' and better distribution of available resources.[30] However, because not all states can be involved in refugee protection in the same way, Hathaway and Neve argue that 'interest-convergence groups therefore ought to define obligations on the basis of a theory of "common but differentiated responsibility" toward refugees'.[31]

In Latin America, the current developments in the protection of refugees in the region have been influenced by the concepts of responsibility sharing (or responsible sharing of the refugee 'burden') and the 'idea of solidarity', which were reinforced by the MPA. The term responsibility sharing is accordingly used as an alternative to 'burden sharing', which is mostly used to indicate the disparities in the distribution of costs accumulated when handling displaced persons and refugees. Thielemann et al. have highlighted that publications emanating from the mid-1990s favour the reference to responsibility sharing rather than burden sharing, due to the fact that the latter term advances a negative connotation that the refugees are themselves a 'burden'.[32]

The use of the term 'responsibility' instead of 'burden' embodies much more than just a simple altering of terminology, rather it is a complete change in the way refugees and refugee protection are viewed. Instead of the idea of sharing refugees as a burden, it focuses on the individual and collective state responsibility for protecting them from violations of human rights. This idea of responsibility sharing seems to be associated with the concept of 'everyone's responsibility for the privation or needs of any individual or social group'.[33]

Due to the complexity of sharing responsibilities in asylum matters, before selecting the most suitable responsibility-sharing mechanism it is essential for any realistic responsibility-sharing approach to be founded on 'reliable, robust and uncontroversial information' about the states that are under pressure to receive asylum seekers.[34]

This mechanism will have two beneficiaries: host states and protection seekers. First, states will enter such mechanisms to cut total asylum costs. Second, protection seekers will find better protection and in higher numbers. In the absence of an international regime for state cooperation, there is a risk that the disparate sharing of responsibilities for the protection of refugees could undermine the whole international refugee law system.[35]

In 2001, the UNHCR stated in a discussion paper that burden sharing 'is a key to the protection of refugees and the resolution of the refugee problem'.[36] Hathaway and Neve defend the collectivised protection approach 'that allows a balance to be struck between meeting the responsibility to grant asylum and shouldering the burden of financing protection'.[37] This balance is what they term 'common but differentiated responsibility'.[38]

Lastly, sharing the responsibility of receiving refugees may take many forms. Noll's categorisation of the three main approaches to promote cooperation to solve the unequal distribution of asylum seekers are as follows: harmonising refugee and asylum legislation (sharing norms); distributing protection seekers (sharing people); and reallocating funds (sharing money).[39] Each will be further analysed below.

According to Noll, 'sharing norms' is considered a form of sharing responsibilities, in so far as it aims at ensuring a common set of rules to overcome distribution inequalities. The UNHCR strongly recommends that weaknesses in the current instruments should be addressed, including by way of amendment, in order to promote effective standards of substantive or procedural protection.[40]

Sharing norms or norm harmonisation is the practice of adopting law and policy which is complementary and consistent between different states. Potentially, this will have the effect of overcoming unequal asylum distribution because by agreeing on common norms, states reduce the pull factors that make them a desired asylum destination. It is known that policy differences are just one of the factors that influence asylum seekers' choice of host country.

The concept of distributing protection seekers, or 'sharing people', comes from the physical transfer of protection seekers from one host territory to another, and is perhaps the most obvious method to address disparities in refugee burdens.[41] Resettlement is a method of responsibility sharing. Resettlement is the transfer of refugees from a state in which they have acquired asylum to a third state that has earlier agreed to receive them as refugees and grant them legal status, with the possibility of acquiring future citizenship.

In addition to core asylum obligations under the 1951 Refugee Convention, resettlement has been adopted by a community of states that is able to provide protection to a limited number of refugees each year depending on the number of places made available by states. Nevertheless, resettlement is one of the durable solutions offered to refugees, whose need for protection has already been established, and is an important protection instrument and a gesture of international responsibility sharing.

Regarding the policies of sharing people, on the one hand some academics have emphasised the dangers facing both the refugee and the host country, which might not have the necessary social support structure required for the protection of refugees, which would definitely result in a more expensive programme for the group of host countries. On the other hand, advocates of these policies highlight this as the method that efficiently balances the costs incurred by the host territories, both in terms of the cost of receiving and determining who is a refugee, as well as the less measurable costs associated with the integration of protection seekers.[42]

The reallocation of funds (sharing money) is reparative in nature, as it looks to even out existing inequalities through different forms of financial transactions. However as Noll argues, 'a major difficulty in fiscal burden-sharing is the establishment of a distributive key'.[43] This involves decisions about what shall be regarded as a loss under the scheme and how such a loss should be rated.

## 4. The development of the asylum system in Latin America

In this era of global restrictions and mixed migratory fluxes, developments in the region sometimes seem to be the only way forward. If conceived as a way of developing international standards, this Latin American regionalism seems to have a positive effect.[44]

Latin America has a 'generous, long-standing tradition of asylum and protection of refugees' (often referred to as the '*generosa tradición*') and has helped substantively in advancing and developing regional policy approaches, and, consequently, international refugee law towards the protection of victims of forced displacement.[45] This comes as a result of the region's long-established collective efforts. The region has long been considered a leader in such matters by the international community.

Since the endorsement of the two main international refugee law instruments by the treaties discussed below, refugee protection has been mostly improved through regional developments. Latin America, a region that has been regarded as part of this trend, has demonstrated its commitment to strengthening and extending the refugee protection created by the universal system in both the theoretical and practical contexts.[46]

A structure of solidarity and responsibility sharing in refugee protection has been endorsed in the past by Latin American countries, as demonstrated by the Cartagena and San Jose Declarations. Nonetheless, the MPA goes even further by creating a solid plan that would put into motion the idea of regional solidarity. The principle of regional solidarity in Latin American refugee protection denotes a significant conceptual change in the understanding of asylum seekers and the responsibility of states to protect refugees. The engagement with regional solidarity and the generosity that can be found in the Latin American tradition of asylum and refugee protection still play an important role in structuring regional policies, which is in contrast to other regions in the international arena. This approach has been strengthened with 'South–South' cooperation to protect refugees, coupled with the recognition of the role of reciprocal protection.[47]

### 4.1. *1951 Convention and Latin American states*

While discussing the refugee phenomenon in Latin America, it is important to highlight the establishment of the UNHCR and note that almost all Latin American countries have ratified the 1951 Convention Relating to the Status of Refugees and its 1967 Protocol.[48] The 1951 Convention has proved to be a solid instrument that provides international protection to millions of refugees throughout the world. It continues to have direct relevance to many, if not most, contemporary refugee situations. However, regional policy approaches to refugee protection complement and guide actions to resolve, or at least alleviate, the refugee problem.[49]

Regional systems should always be examined parallel to the universal, as they are not meant to replace the universal system, but to complement and supplement it when needed.[50] In this sense, as it will be shown below, the Cartagena Declaration not only ensured the minimum standards of the 1951 Convention, but allowed Latin American states to expand their national systems with a more humane and humanitarian attitude towards refugee protection.[51]

### 4.2. *Cartagena Declaration*

As mentioned above, the earlier definitions of protection seekers in Latin America recognised persecution for political reasons and not for reasons of religious or ethnic affiliation.

However, the region was forced to transform its asylum system after experiencing a massive influx of refugees. In the 1970s and 1980s, Central America experienced social conflicts due to the lack of land for peasants, unequal distribution of wealth, and restricted enjoyment of political rights. This situation mirrored the divisions of the Cold War, as the United States and the Soviet Union supported opposite sides in Nicaragua, El Salvador and Guatemala. The armed conflicts of this period created over two million refugees and internally displaced people, of which only 150,000 were considered refugees under the 1951 Convention.[52]

Latin America's aim was to elaborate a practical and regional solution required to solve this refugee crisis by developing 'an original and pragmatic concept to renew the international protection regime in Latin America, keeping with the peculiarities of the region'.[53] As a result of this, in 1984 the Cartagena Declaration was adopted. It is an agreement that extends the concept of 'refugee'. Cartagena was directly inspired by the first broadened concept of 'refugee' that was developed on a regional scale by the Organisation of African Unity (OAU).[54] Nevertheless, there were differences between the 1969 OAU Convention and the 1984 Cartagena Declaration, as the Cartagena Declaration was aspirational in character and was not intended to be a legally binding instrument.[55] According to Kneebone and Rawlings-Sanae, it 'did not emerge from within a regional organisation but out of an ad-hoc group of experts and ten Latin American governments'.[56]

In extending the concept of a refugee to include those displaced by war, massive violations of human rights or the severe disturbance of public order, the Cartagena Declaration filled a human rights gap, while simultaneously bridged the protection gap.[57] Several states region adopted the declaration as the basis for the refugee policy in the region and incorporated the extended concept of refugee into their national standards, even though it was not formally binding.[58]

Cartagena intended to adjust the focus from the global asylum system to the regional situation, but recommended that the regional refugee concept should complement the 1951 Convention.[59] Therefore, it 'should be viewed as a process that builds upon, and not apart from, the universal body of norms constituted by the 1951 Convention'.[60]

According to the UNHCR, the Cartagena Declaration establishes the model of a harmonised approach, offering guidance for state practice and helping to tackle problems of forced displacement in Latin America.[61] It is part of a trend towards harmonisation and increasing protection and humanitarian assistance for victims of armed conflict and human rights abuses.[62]

### 4.3.  *San Jose Declaration*

In 1994, on the tenth anniversary of the Cartagena Declaration, the San Jose Declaration reiterated the importance of the Cartagena Declaration, and broadened its scope in order to extend protection, in particular, to the internally displaced.

In its fifth conclusion, the 1994 San Jose Declaration:

> [Urges] governments to encourage, with the collaboration of UNHCR, a process of progressive harmonization of rules, criteria and procedures concerning refugees, based on the 1951 Convention and the 1967 Protocol relating to the status of refugees, the American Convention on Human Rights, and the Cartagena Declaration.[63]

The declaration proposed to evaluate the Cartagena Declaration and to reanimate and strengthen the commitment of the countries in the American continent in the search for solutions.

The San Jose Declaration on Refugees and Displaced Persons mentions the necessity of confronting the problem of internally displaced people in the region. It states that the violation of human rights is one of the causes of dislocation and that, therefore, the protection of such rights and the strengthening of the democratic system are the best measures in the search for durable solutions.[64]

### 4.4. *Mexico Declaration and Plan (MPA)*

In 2004, on its 20th anniversary, the Cartagena Declaration provided the principled basis for the adoption of the 'Mexico Declaration and Plan of Action to Strengthen the International Protection of Refugees in Latin America' (MPA).[65] The MPA is a regional framework developed in order to deal with the complex humanitarian crisis resulting from forced displacement in Latin America. Consequently, within a 'South–South' approach, this 'solidarity' emphasises the importance of the responsibility sharing of global southern countries, as well as cooperation with refugees and displaced people.[66]

According to Lavanchy, the MPA 'aimed at better equipping the States to address current challenges in a spirit of solidarity and cooperation'.[67] It defines actions with regard to protection and proposes an agreement of durable measures for the refugee issue, especially in relation to two situations that urgently needed an answer: the increasing flow of refugees centred on the urban cores of Latin America and the phenomenon of crowded borders.

For this purpose, the objectives of the plan are aligned with the principles of Cartagena through two components: (1) protection and (2) an innovative component on durable solutions and regional solidarity.

The protection component of the MPA focuses on four specific areas: strengthening the legal and operational framework for the protection of refugees and IDPs in the region to be on a par with international instruments; promoting legal research and doctrinal development, including training for refugee workers; strengthening the national commissions for refugee status determination; strengthening the national and regional protection networks; and asking the media to publicise the values of solidarity, respect, tolerance and multiculturalism in their networks and publications.

The durable solution component of the MPA has highlighted the significance of the spread of 'best practices' in the area in a bid to enhance the region's South–South cooperation. Three solidarity programmes have been developed in relation to durable solutions[68] to improve the quality of asylum. As such, one of the main strands of the proposal is the adoption of the three 'solidarity' programmes to facilitate durable solutions for refugees (predominantly from Colombia) in countries in the region. One of the mechanisms of the plan is a regional responsibility-sharing programme focused on the resettlement of refugees and IDPs, called the 'Solidarity Resettlement Programme'. The second, the 'Solidarity Cities Programme', was developed in order to promote local integration and self-reliance of people in need of protection in urban areas. Finally, the 'Borders of Solidarity Programme' focused on the development of the border regions of neighbouring countries to benefit displaced Colombians and their hosts. The solidarity programmes will be studied in-depth in the second part of this article.

The MPA has emphasised the importance of the dissemination of 'best practices' in the region for South–South cooperation, including the need to focus on and address precise scenarios with the help of the international community in the durable solution component.[69] Among the most pertinent commitments of this component is the inclusion of the 'idea of solidarity in all of its actions'.[70]

As applied in Latin America, regional solidarity has emphasised the need for sharing the responsibility for assisting victims of human rights violations, thereby defining a more positive strategy in the context of refugees' reception. By assuming the idea of solidarity, the MPA introduces a more humane and relatively fresh dialogue in international refugee law, as it uses the term 'responsibility sharing' instead of 'burden sharing'. Moreover, it should be stressed that the MPA embodies not only a change in semantics, but also a reformation of the manner in which refugees are understood, 'not as a problem and a situation of sharing refugees but as a responsibility for protection with victims of violations of human rights'.[71]

### 4.5. *Brasilia Declaration*

In 2010, the Brasilia Declaration on the Protection of Refugees and Stateless Persons in the Americas[72] was adopted. The declaration has three main features that merit particular attention. The first element is that countries have agreed to respect the principle of non-refoulement without restrictions. The principle of non-refoulement expands upon the basic definition found in the 1951 Refugee Convention by including within its scope 'non-rejection at the border and indirect non-refoulement' and 'non-penalization of illegal entry and non-discrimination'.[73] Second, the declaration supports the incorporation of gender, age and diversity considerations into national laws on refugees and IDPs. Accordingly, paragraph eight of the declaration states that member states agree 'to promote the values of solidarity, respect, tolerance and multiculturalism'. The third feature encourages states to embrace mechanisms to address 'new situations not foreseen by the international instruments for the protection of refugees'.[74]

### 5. The Mexico Plan of Action and its solidarity programmes

With the adoption of the MPA, Latin American countries improved their refugee protection instruments for people seeking asylum from persecution. At the regional level, they have followed new commitments to share the responsibilities to strengthen refugee protection.[75]

The MPA represents a step forward in strengthening the protection of human rights and the affirmation of the universality of human dignity. The MPA expresses Latin American solidarity with countries that currently have the highest number of refugees and are experiencing a larger burden on their protection systems due to the disproportionally large influxes of Colombian refugees into their territories.

The MPA highlights the regional willingness enforcing the 'spirit of Cartagena',[76] ensuring advancement in both international refugee law and protection, and revising earlier commitments by making them stronger and more efficacious to face the 'new challenges of forced migration and refugee crises'.[77] The spirit of Cartagena is reflected through the features in the MPA, which require Latin American countries to find humane solutions when replying to the challenges of the humanitarian crises.[78]

The proposal contained in the MPA for the responsibility for solidarity is 'built on (1) the regional tradition of refugee protection in Latin America, (2) the "re-birth" of resettlement, and (3) the principle of solidarity'.[79]

The consolidation of the objectives and programmes of the MPA carries with it a dual responsibility. The first responsibility, which is of regional character, refers to the need for states to act together to solve their common problems, reflecting a notion of 'regional solidarity' and shared responsibility. The second responsibility is of an international character. The success of the regional programme of resettlement in Latin America could encourage similar initiatives in other parts of the world, revealing the importance of cooperation at regional and intercontinental levels.

The 'idea of solidarity' has vast importance in international refugee law, since it encompasses one of the main concepts that establish the responsibility of the international community towards refugees. 'Regional solidarity' and the global acceptance of Southern countries working together in order to share the responsibilities of protecting refugees are the two fundamental concepts of establishing such cooperation.[80]

### 5.1. *Borders of Solidarity*

'Borders of Solidarity' was created to support the border regions of neighbouring countries such as Ecuador, Panamá and Venezuela to shelter displaced Colombians. The programme's main objective is to identify and respond to the humanitarian and protection needs of refugees. Local integration is promoted through comprehensive strategies that benefit people in need of international protection as well as the local host population. To ensure impact and sustainability, this programme is closely connected to regional development and national plans to combat poverty.

This proposal focuses attention on new forms of thinking about border zones, border lives and how different actors might form a dialogue to improve the reception, assistance and protection of displaced groups in a region marked by deep social inequalities and political violence.[81] It focuses on the population of refugees, establishing protection for asylum seekers near the borders and requires that 'border officials have to be trained in a way to ensure access to adequate refugee status determination procedures and respect for human rights'. This approach is clearly a departure from the dominant view around the world, which regards refugees as a security issue and is traditionally linked to tighter controls.[82]

Concerning this programme, opinions on the function of borders as spaces of life differ based on the varying assumptions of each group and the ways that they participate in the political discussion. Some groups dealt with the management of movement, whereas others enriched the conditions of life for marginal groups. A few groups were also able to interrupt the political procedures responsible for making the marginalisation feasible in the first place.[83]

### 5.2. *Solidarity Resettlement*

'Solidarity Resettlement' is a regional responsibility sharing programme focused on the resettlement of refugees and IDPs, based on principles of international solidarity and responsibility sharing. It benefits a limited number of refugees who face protection risks in their countries of asylum. Its objective was an explicit call to transform Latin America in general, and South America in particular, into the biggest and most promising emerging resettlement area in the world.

While further consolidation is needed, the experiences of countries such as Brazil, Argentina and Chile can be seen as pioneering initiatives, from which important lessons can be drawn. Brazil and Chile were the first countries to receive the solidarity resettlement programme. 'Both countries already had Memoranda of Understanding (MOUs) on resettlement with UNHCR and had experience with resettlement in the past.'[84]

One of the most innovative as well as symbolic programmes of the MPA is solidarity resettlement. From its implementation, over 900 refugees with particular protection requirements have been resettled – mainly from Costa Rica and Ecuador – in Argentina, Brazil, Chile and Uruguay. Many countries in the Southern Cone have been making major policy and operational commitments to safeguard the sustainable management of the reset-tlement programme.[85]

On the one hand, it shows that a more effective approach to public policies should be introduced, so that the integration prospects of a higher number of resettled refugees may be improved. Funding is also a challenging and pressing issue.[86]

On the other hand, however, resettlement in solidarity can lead to a more humane approach to resettlement. This is due to two main factors. First, it can establish a new model of dialogue among states and actors involved in refugee protection based on the concept of solidarity. As a result, the paradigm of 'burden sharing' may lose its former prevalence in this field. Second, by focusing on both the needs of individuals and the con-cerns of states, resettlement in solidarity can actually become a viable tool in refugee pro-tection. In light of the above, it is important to promote this initiative and its implementation, with the aim of strengthening the refugee protection regime with due respect for human dignity.[87]

Solidarity resettlement is a concept that promotes a different approach to protecting refugees whilst they are in real crises. It adds a new paradigm in the dialogue between states and actors who are involved in refugee protection. In this scenario, the countries of first asylum, which are overwhelmed by massive arrivals, find new hope through durable solutions. Consequently, solidarity resettlement is not only a suitable alternative, but a remarkable advancement in the international protection regime as it broadens the narrow global humanitarian paradigm. In Latin America, this discussion appears to have reverberated more strongly since – while strengthening the states' commitment to refugee protection by building solidarity resettlement – it brings about a shift from the concept of burden sharing to that of responsibility sharing.[88]

Although resettlement countries have reiterated their commitment to the regional pro-gramme and have assumed greater operational responsibilities, the programme continues to require external support from the international community. Therefore, the consolidation and sustainability of the programme depends largely on a stronger commitment by states on financial matters and the involvement of partners who have accompanied this process.

### 5.3. *Solidarity Cities*

'Solidarity Cities' was adopted in order to encourage the local integration of persons in need of protection in urban areas. It is intended to avoid, as far as possible, so-called irregular or secondary movements and seeks overall to offer more effective protection that encompasses the refugee's economic and cultural rights and social duties.

This programme is one of the most novel components of the MPA. The achievement of self-sufficiency through the local integration of refugees has continued to be one of the major challenges for refugee care programmes in Latin America. Refugees face complex socio-economic situations, but they are also forced to compete with other disadvantaged sectors of their host communities.

On the other hand, it promotes a different attitude towards the urban context. The city is presented as an open space and a place for opportunities to be explored and experienced.[89] It is therefore essential, in the first instance, to encourage public officials to recognise the particular situation of refugees and the differences that exist with other migratory groups and, in the long term, for them to incorporate these perspectives into a local public agenda. Effective local integration is achieved through the execution of public policies that take into account the social, economic and cultural rights and obligations of refugees.[90]

The Cities of Solidarity programme represents a novel strategy offering refugees better options and opportunities for local integration. This programme is solely dependent upon the improvement of the local integration of refugees in urban settings. This initiative has a number of positive approaches such as the establishment of new partnerships with local governments and civil society, and the identification of institutions that are interested in helping refugees.[91] However, the cities involved must go far beyond declarations of the principles understood in the agreements. Plans of Action made by municipalities are considered a departure point from the complicated process, the accomplishment of which is a long-term challenge that needs to be observed and assessed as it develops.

## 6. Conclusion

Since the adoption of the MPA, Latin American countries have increased their efforts to strengthen their refugee protection systems. Furthermore, new commitments are being made to ensure cooperation and to share the responsibility to protect refugees at the regional level.

Consequently, Latin America as a region has developed particular regional policy approaches towards better protection for refugees and also political asylum seekers through various normative and institutional developments. Hence, when speaking of the harmonisation of refugee definitions in Latin America, one should preferably rely first on the 1951 Convention's (global) concepts of a refugee, and second on the 1984 Cartagena Declaration (regional), without forgetting the regional definition of 'asylee', which is often of practical importance.

Latin American countries have perceived that the regional nature of numerous refugee issues calls for 'South–South' collaboration in providing protection. This collaboration is based on the standard of 'regional solidarity', the development of the concept of responsibility sharing in the region, and the acknowledgement that nations in the South need to cooperate in sharing the responsibility for refugee protection.

The 1984 Cartagena Declaration on Refugees is a compilation of best practices based on the 1951 Convention relating to the Status of Refugees and its 1967 Protocol, together with the *generosa tradición* of asylum in Latin America. The MPA, created during the 20-year celebration of the Cartagena Declaration, defines the framework for regional action with regard to protection and proposes an agreement of durable measures for the refugee issue. It focused especially on two situations that urgently needed a response: the increasing flow of refugees centred on the urban cores of Latin America, and the phenomenon of crowded borders. The MPA's proposals included the adoption of three programmes: 'Solidarity Cities', 'Borders of Solidarity' and 'Solidarity Resettlement'. In proposing these programmes, Latin American governments recognised that the MPA needed to be both aspirational and practical in its approach and profess the establishment of strategies that are more humane than international refugee law. Latin America continues to increase its dedication to refugee protection and laws, and to develop solutions motivated by the 'human rights approach and by the value of solidarity'.[92]

The central challenge is still to reinforce the institutional presence of states in the border areas to promote respect for human rights and a sustainable development process, to benefit local populations and people in need of international protection. The MPA represents a step forward in strengthening the protection of human rights and the affirmation of the universality of human dignity. It does this by focusing on the current regional challenges in a spirit of solidarity and cooperation with countries that currently have the highest number of refugees in Latin America, especially those fleeing from the violence in Colombia. It has addressed many of these regional challenges, through innovative programmes that have allowed progress in the promotion of durable solutions. The leading role of the governments has been noteworthy in establishing public policies to facilitate the refugees' incorporation into social and economic programmes, and the increasing role of local authorities, civil society and the private sector in the integration processes. However, the refugee population continues to face serious difficulties that impede their full enjoyment of rights, and their social and productive inclusion. Further to the principal role of states, it is crucial to persist in promoting international cooperation and the presence of civil society to preserve the humanitarian space and to reinforce refugee protection.

The consolidation of the objectives and programmes of the MPA also carries with it a dual responsibility. The first is of a regional character, referring to the need for regional solidarity and the willingness of states to act together to solve common problems in order to share the responsibility for protecting refugees. Second is of an international character, as the success of the regional programme of resettlement in Latin America could encourage similar initiatives in other parts of the world, revealing the importance of cooperation at the regional level. The MPA reflects the importance of the notion of international solidarity and responsibility sharing in international refugee law, as it supports concepts that establish the responsibility undertaken by the international community regarding refugees.

## Acknowledgements

I would like to thank Professor Susan Kneebone for generously sharing her time and expertise. I am enormously thankful for this support and opportunity. I also would like to thank Janelle Kenny for her rigorous academic editing.

## Funding

This work was supported by the CAPES Foundation, Ministry of Education of Brazil, under Grant [number BEX 0796/14-0].

## Notes

1. The expression Latin America will be used as defined by the United Nations Statistical Division, that is: Argentina, Belize, Bolivia, Brazil, Chile, Colombia, Costa Rica, Ecuador, El Salvador, Guatemala, Guyana, Honduras, Mexico, Nicaragua, Panamá, Paraguay, Peru, Suriname, Uruguay and Venezuela. See: Liliana Lyra Jubilut, 'Fora and Programmes for Refugees in Latin America', in *Regional Approaches to the Protection of Asylum Seekers: an International Legal Perspective*, ed. Ademola Abass and Francesca Ippolito (Surrey: Ashgate, 2014), 245.
2. Although the complex concept of political asylum in Latin America is not the main object of this article, it seems important to briefly accentuate the differences between political asylum and refugee status as per the 1951 Refugee Convention. Political asylum is primarily a political measure in order to provide protection to individuals who are persecuted for political crimes, or common crimes committed for political reasons. On the other hand, 'refuge' is arguably a humanitarian measure for those who have 'a well-founded fear of being persecuted for reasons of race, religion, nationality, political opinion, or membership of a particular social group'. The regional development of political asylum in the American continent occurred

due to the internal political conflicts and to the instability of governments in the region. This distinction between concepts and systems occurs only in Latin America, while for the rest of the world the terms 'asylum' and 'asylum seeker' are used to identify the status of a refugee, not a 'political asylee'. See Liliana Lyra Jubilut, *O Direito Internacional dos Refugiados e sua Aplicação no Ordenamento Jurídico Brasileiro* (São Paulo: Método, 2007), 37; Flavia Piovesan, 'O direito de asilo e a proteção internacional dos refugiados', in *O direito internacional dos refugiados: uma perspectiva brasileira*, ed. Nádia Araújo and Guilherme Assis de Almeida (Rio de Janeiro; São Paulo: Renovar, 2001), 27; and Stefania Eugenia Barichello, 'A evolução dos instrumentos de proteção do Direito Internacional dos Refugiados na América Latina', *Universitas: Relações Internacionais 10*, Brasília, no. 1 (2012), 33. See also the following English-language sources: José H. Fischel de Andrade, 'Regional Policy Approaches and Harmonisation: A Latin American Perspective', *International Journal of Refugee Law* 10, no. 3 (1998): 389, at 398–99; and Liliana Lyra Jubilut, 'Fora and Programmes for Refugees in Latin America', in *Regional Approaches to the Protection of Asylum Seekers: an International Legal Perspective*, ed. Ademola Abass and Francesca Ippolito (Surrey: Ashgate, 2014).

3. Regional Refugee Instruments & Related, *Cartagena Declaration on Refugees, Colloquium on the International Protection of Refugees in Central America, Mexico and Panama*, 22 November 1984, http://www.refworld.org/docid/3ae6b36ec.html.

4. Article 1 of the convention as amended by the 1967 Protocol provides the definition of a refugee as: 'A person who owing to a well-founded fear of being persecuted for reasons of race, religion, nationality, membership of a particular social group or political opinion, is outside the country of his nationality and is unable or, owing to such fear, is unwilling to avail himself of the protection of that country; or who, not having a nationality and being outside the country of his former habitual residence as a result of such events, is unable or, owing to such fear, is unwilling to return to it.' See: UN General Assembly, *Convention Relating to the Status of Refugees* (1951) 189 UNTS 137. Opened for Signature 28 July 1951. Entered into Force 22 April 1954.

5. Regional Refugee Instruments & Related, *Mexico Declaration and Plan of Action to Strengthen International Protection of Refugees in Latin America*, 16 November 2004, http://www.refworld.org/docid/424bf6914.html.

6. This is a concept that I will return to throughout this article. The armed socio-political conflict that Colombia has been going through for more than 40 years has become a permanent worry for human rights organisations, mainly because of widespread violence and mass violations of human rights perpetrated by networks of both guerrilla and parliamentary groups. Colombia is a typical example of the 'crowded borders phenomenon', because of the flow of asylum seekers and also internally displaced persons fleeing from violence crossing Colombia's borders in search of international protection in Venezuela, Panamá, Ecuador, and other States of the region. See: UNHCR, *Hacia una visión compartida de las víctimas del conflicto colombiano en los países vecinos* (Caracas: ACNUR, 2003); A. Rangel, 'Colômbia: um país de contrastes' *Revista Diplomacia, Estratégia e Política* 8 (2007).

7. Liliana Lyra Jubilut, 'Fora and Programmes for Refugees in Latin America', in *Regional Approaches to the Protection of Asylum Seekers: An International Legal Perspective*, ed. Ademola Abass and Francesca Ippolito (Surrey: Ashgate, 2014), 260.

8. *Mexico Declaration and Plan of Action to Strengthen International Protection of Refugees in Latin America*, Chapter Three.

9. See Philippe Lavanchy, 'The Mexico Declaration and Plan of Action: Reaffirming Latin America's Generous Tradition of Asylum and Innovative Solutions', *International Journal of Refugee Law* 3, no. 2 (2006): 450; William Spindler, 'The Mexico Plan of Action: Protecting Refugees Through International Solidarity', *Forced Migration* Review 24 (2005): 64; Tristan Harley, 'Regional Cooperation and Refugee Protection in Latin America: A "South-South" Approach', *International Journal of Refugee Law* 26, no. 1 (2014): 22.

10. See Liliana Lyra Jubilut and Wellington Carneiro, 'Resettlement in Solidarity. A New Regional Approach towards a More Humane Durable Solution', *Refugee Survey Quarterly* 30, no. 1 (2011): 63; Fabio Varoli, 'Cities of Solidarity: Local Integration in Latin America', *Forced Migration Review* 34 (2010): 44; Carolina Moulin, 'Borders of Solidarity: Life in Displacement in the Amazon Tri-Border Region', *Refuge* 26, no. 2 (2009): 41; Ana Guglielmelli White, 'A Pillar of Protection: Solidarity Resettlement for Refugees in Latin America', *UNHCR New Issues in Refugee Research* 239 (2012): 1.

11. See Eiko Thielemann, Richard Williams, and Christina Boswell, *What System of Burden-sharing between Member States for the Reception of Asylum Seekers?* (Brussels: European Parliament – Policy Department Citizens' Rights and Constitutional Affairs, 2010); Eiko Thielemann, 'Editorial Introduction', *Journal of Refugee Studies* 16, no. 1 (2003): 225; and Gregor Noll *Negotiating Asylum. The EU Aquis, Extraterritorial Protection and the Common Market of Deflection* (The Hague: Martinus Nijhoff Publishers, 2000).

12. Susan Kneebone and Felicity Rawlings-Sanae, 'Introduction', in *New regionalism and Asylum Seekers: Challenges Ahead*, ed. Susan Kneebone and Felicity Rawlings-Sanae (Oxford: Berghahn Books, 2007), 1.

13. Asha Hans and Astri Suhrke, 'Responsibility Sharing', in *Reconceiving International Refugee Law*, ed. James C. Hathaway (The Hague, The Netherlands: Martinus Nijhoff Publishers, 1997), 83.

14. Kneebone and Rawlings-Sanae, 'Introduction', 1.

15. Ibid.

16. Ibid.

17. José H. Fischel de Andrade, 'Regional Policy Approaches and Harmonisation: A Latin American Perspective', *International Journal of Refugee Law* 10, no. 3 (1998): 389, at 391.

18. Hans and Suhrke, 'Responsibility Sharing', 108.

19. Bill Frelick. 'Afterword: Assessing the Prospects for Reform of International Refugee Law', in *Reconceiving International Refugee Law*, ed. James C. Hathaway (The Hague, The Netherlands: Martinus Nijhoff Publishers, 1997), 147.

20. Peter H. Schuck, 'Refugee Burden-Sharing: A Modest Proposal', *Yale Journal of International Law* 22 (1997): 243, at 249.

21. Frelick, 'Afterword: Assessing the Prospects', 152.

22. Susan Kneebone, 'Conclusions; Challenges Ahead', in *New Regionalism and Asylum Seekers: Challenges Ahead*, ed. Susan Kneebone and Felicity Rawlings-Sanae (Oxford: Berghahn Books, 2007), 221, at 229.

23. Ibid.

24. Ibid.

25. Kneebone and Rawlings-Sanae, 'Introduction', 1.

26. Jean-Pierre L. Fonteyne, 'Burden-Sharing: An Analysis of the Nature and Function of International Solidarity in Cases of Mass Influx of Refugees', *Australian Year Book of International Law* 8 (1978–80): 162, at 166–7.

27. *Convention Relating to the Status of Refugees.*

28. James C. Hathaway and R. Alexander Neve, 'Making International Refugee Law Relevant Again: A Proposal for Collectivized and Solution-Oriented Protection', *Harvard Human Rights Journal* 10 (1997): 115, at 169.

29. Ibid.

30. Thielemann, 'Editorial Introduction', 225.

31. Hathaway and Neve, 'Making International Refugee Law Relevant Again', 144.

32. See Thielemann et al., 'What System of Burden-sharing'.

33. Jubilut and Carneiro, 'Resettlement in Solidarity', 70.

34. Thielemann et al., 'What System of Burden-sharing', 111.

35. Tristan Harley 'Regional Cooperation and Refugee Protection in Latin America: A "South-South" Approach', *International Journal of Refugee Law* 26, no. 1 (2014): 22.

36. UNHCR, 'Burden Sharing: Discussion Paper Submitted by UNHCR', in Fifth Annual Plenary Meeting of the Intergovernmental Asia-Pacific Consultations on Refugees, Displaced Persons and Migrants (APC), 2001, http://www.apcprocess.net/Inter-active/past%20apc%20papers/burden_sharingUNHCR.htm.

37. Hathaway and Neve, 'Making International Refugee Law Relevant Again', 145.

38. Ibid.

39. Noll, *Negotiating Asylum*, 270.

40. UNHCR, 'Burden Sharing'.

41. Thielemann, 'Editorial Introduction', 225.

42. Ibid.

43. Noll, *Negotiating Asylum*, 272.

44. Jubilut, 'Fora and Programmes for Refugees in Latin America', 245.

45. Lavanchy, 'The Mexico Declaration', 450.

46. Flavia Piovesan and Liliana Lyra Jubilut, 'Regional Developments: Americas', in *The 1951 Convention Relating to the Status of Refugee and its Protocol. A Commentary*, ed. Andreas Zimmermann (Oxford: Oxford University Press, 2011), 205; and Jubilut, 'Fora and Programmes for Refugees in Latin America', 261.

47. See: Lavanchy, 'The Mexico Declaration', 450; Harley, 'Regional Cooperation', 22.

48. The exceptions are Cuba and Guyana, which are not party to either treaty. See: Jubilut, 'Fora and Programmes for Refugees in Latin America', 245.

49. Fischel de Andrade, 'Regional Policy Approaches', 389.

50. Jubilut, 'Fora and Programmes for Refugees in Latin America', 255, 263.

51. Piovesan and Jubilut, 'Regional Developments: Americas', 205.

52. *Cartagena Declaration on Refugees, Colloquium on the International Protection of Refugees in Central America, Mexico and Panama* (1984), http://www.refworld.org/docid/3ae6b36ec.html.

53. Jubilut and Carneiro, 'Resettlement in Solidarity', 66–7.

54. Kneebone and Rawlings-Sanae, 'Introduction', 8.

55. Jubilut, 'Fora and Programmes for Refugees in Latin America', 253.

56. Kneebone and Rawlings-Sanae, 'Introduction', 8.

57. Ibid., 9; and Jubilut, 'Fora and Programmes for Refugees in Latin America', 255.

58. Ibid.

59. Jubilut, 'Fora and Programmes for Refugees in Latin America', 263.

60. Fischel de Andrade, 'Regional Policy Approaches', 401.

61. UNHCR. *The Mexico Plan of Action to Strengthen International Protection of Refugees in Latin America. Main Achievements and Challenges During the Period 2005–2010* (2010), http://www.pamacnur2010.com/MPAprogressEnglish.pdf.

62. Ibid.

63. *San Jose Declaration on Refugees and Displaced Persons* (1994), http://www.refworld.org/docid/4a54bc3fd.html.

64. Ibid., Preamble.

65. *Mexico Declaration and Plan of Action to Strengthen International Protection of Refugees in Latin America*, 16 November 2004, http://www.refworld.org/docid/424bf6914.html.

66. Guglielmelli White, 'A Pillar of Protection', 3.

67. Lavanchy, 'The Mexico Declaration', 451.

68. The chapter on Durable Solutions recognised voluntary repatriation as the best solution for refugees, however it did not anticipate the need to create a specific regional programme.

69. Jubilut, 'Fora and Programmes for Refugees in Latin America', 260–1.

70. Ibid., 260.

71. Jubilut and Carneiro, 'Resettlement in Solidarity', 70; Jubilut, 'Fora and Programmes for Refugees in Latin America', 261; and Harley, 'Regional Cooperation', 22.

72. *Brasilia Declaration on the Protection of Refugees and Stateless Persons in the Americas*, 11 November 2010, http://www.refworld.org/docid/4cdd44582.html.

73. Ibid.

74. Ibid.

75. Harley, 'Regional Cooperation', 22.

76. Jubilut, 'Fora and Programmes for Refugees in Latin America', 256.

77. Jubilut and Carneiro, 'Resettlement in Solidarity', 68.

78. Ibid.

79. Ibid., 71.

80. Harley, 'Regional Cooperation', 22.

81. Moulin, 'Borders of Solidarity', 41.

82. Jubilut and Carneiro, 'Resettlement in Solidarity', 74.

83. According to Moulin, 'understandings of solidarity … speak to each of these perspectives – managerial, faith-based, and autonomous – stressing the problems and also the positive aspects that might be learned from approaching borders through the lenses of solidarity'. See: Moulin, 'Borders of Solidarity', 41.

84. Guglielmelli White, 'A Pillar of Protection', 5.

85. UNHCR, *The Mexico Plan of Action to Strengthen International Protection of Refugees in Latin America*.

86. Marcia A. Vera Espinoza 'Mapping Refugee Resettlement in Latin America: Actors and Processes in Chile and Brazil', in *SLAS 2014. 50th Anniversary Conference* (London, 2014).

87.  Ibid.
88.  Jubilut and Carneiro, 'Resettlement in Solidarity', 71.
89.  Varoli, 'Cities of Solidarity', 44.
90.  Ibid.
91.  Jubilut and Carneiro, 'Resettlement in Solidarity', 63.
92.  Piovesan and Jubilut, 'Regional Developments: Americas', 224.

# Human security and external burden-sharing: the European approach to refugee protection between past and present

Paolo Biondi

*School of Advanced Study, University of London, UK*

The discourse surrounding the link between human security and the European Union's policy on external burden-sharing is connected to the concept of securitisation developed in the 1990s, when the language of human security was first used to promote solutions in the regions-of-origin of refugees through external burden-sharing. External forms of burden-sharing, nevertheless, can be traced back to the UNHCR's use of its 'good offices' in the 1960s to promote 'regional solutions in Asia, and reflect a slow evolution since the adoption of the 1951 Convention. In order to understand this evolution this article adopts an analysis informed by policy mapping of targeted representative cases combined with a comparative approach towards those cases. It proposes for the subject to be addressed from the perspectives of the states; protection seekers; and the balance of refugees' rights and state security. This article argues that the concept of external burden-sharing is compatible with effective refugee protection and their more rational distribution, but only when it offers long-term solutions based on genuine protection and not as a surrogate to the granting of asylum in the European Union. According to the analysis provided, this article concludes that the current European Union policy on refugee protection is implicitly guided by a restrictive rationalisation of movements as a result of a slow evolution of a distorted and not effectively implemented version of external burden-sharing. First through promoting local solutions and then the human security concept. Yet, this policy cannot represent an acceptable long-term alternative to territorial asylum or an admissible form of external burden-sharing, because protection seekers' movements are guided by the safety and effectiveness of protection and the current European Union external approach does not offer such protection.

## 1. Introduction

The Office of the United Nations High Commissioner for Refugees (UNHCR) has stressed for many years that the great majority of refugees find/seek protection in developing countries, and that the developed countries offer asylum to a small residual number.[1] This uneven distribution is linked to the fact that many of the causes provoking refugee flows have their foundation in developing countries and refugees have the tendency to seek asylum in the closest safe place in order to favour a return when possible.

Yet, it seems that other factors may have influenced the concentration of refugees in certain areas rather than others. This could be the result of developed countries' efforts to promote solutions for asylum seekers in their own country or region of origin on the basis of protecting their own interests, rather than the interests of those seeking protection.

I argue in this article that some concepts, such as the external burden-sharing and the concept of human security as applied to the protection of asylum seekers and refugees, seem to be used for this purpose. Yet both in a certain way revised in scope and distant from the original concepts' aims. For the purposes of this article, by 'external burden-sharing' I refer to the way developed European Union (EU) states focus efforts of protection in countries of origin or third countries, rather than accepting asylum seekers into the EU.[2]

This article first examines if this manipulation of concepts is a real and concrete phenomenon, and asks if it is something new, or has evolved from past practices. Second, it investigates and suggests how the principles of external burden-sharing and human security are interpreted in this context and if there is a way to re-establish a balance that the statistics confirm to be uneven.

In order to test the above hypotheses, this article adopts a framework of analysis based on policy mapping combined with a comparative approach over time, with targeted representative cases serving as thematic comparison. This method is used to draw parallels between the past and the current EU response to refugee crises, and to show how the original concept of human security has been translated into the EU's current practice of external burden-sharing.

This article is divided into five sections. The first is a historical background on the evolution of external burden-sharing and state-centric conceptions of security in Europe. The second section draws parallels between the concept of human security and the practice of external burden-sharing. The third section describes the inclusion and interpretation of human security in the EU external dimension of refugee protection. The fourth section elaborates on the different perspectives in the interpretation of the human security and external burden-sharing concepts. Lastly, the fifth section puts the analysis into the context of the EU's response to the Syrian refugee crisis.

## 2. The evolution of burden-sharing and state-centric security in Europe

The 1951 Convention Relating to the Status of Refugees[3] represented a turning point in terms of refugee definition, but it excluded several groups from protection. This safeguarded, in a certain way, states' sovereignty and promoted discretion for the large category of humanitarian refugees falling outside of the scope of the convention.

Thus the refugee regime created a binary distinction between refugees falling under the convention, and those falling under the definition of 'humanitarian' refugees.[4] Arguably, this distinction can be explained by the context in which the convention was drafted, with its focus on Europe and reflection of anti-communist Western political ideals.[5]

Despite these apparent limitations, the interpretation and progressively more extensive mandate of the UNHCR have been used to overcome large crises all around the globe. However, the responses of states to these crises have been very different, varying from those which are very successful and based on the classic granting of asylum, to those with a mix of asylum and external humanitarian assistance. Finally, those where the response has been much more restrictive, both in terms of asylum and humanitarian assistance. The grade of divergence has depended on the interests at stake.

Some crises have been relatively successfully addressed, such as the 1956 Hungarian refugee crisis for instance, where prima facie[6] status was granted. This was later used as a precedent in other refugee crises in the developing world.[7] In addition to legal practice[8] and the impact of a number of favourable strategic and political interests of states,[9] the *prima facie* status solution was possible due to the temporary protection offered by Austria being backed by resettlement opportunities in 37 countries, in particular the United States. Similarly, in 1973, Chileans, alongside other Latin American refugees, were settled in Europe and elsewhere, assisted in their claims by the fact that Chile was going through a promising process of democratisation and stabilisation.[10]

Other crises have seen a mixture of success and compromise, as beyond Europe the protection of refugees was constrained by the geographic and temporal limitation of the convention. After the Protocol of 1967 lifted some of these limitations, protection was limited by the non-eligibility criteria contained therein,[11] but also by constraints of a political nature that made de facto refugees not entitled to protection. Despite these limitations, in both the Hong Kong (1957–1963) and the Indo-Chinese (1975–1979) crises, the problem of non-eligibility was solved using either the UNHCR's 'good offices',[12] or the humanitarian assistance towards 'people's external displacement'[13], but also through resettlement[14] or substantial financial contributions to the first countries of asylum.[15] Subsequent to these crises however, the method of return became the principal solution to dealing with refugees,[16] arguably motivated by states' economic or strategic interests.[17]

Between 1987 and 1994, the International Conference on Central American Refugees (CIREFCA), the European Community (EC) and its single states contributed substantially to regional refugee stabilisation through financial resources. This was possible because the EC states were again interested in the political stability of the region, but also because they wanted to promote and strengthen economic relations and because no physical resettlement to Europe was involved.[18]

By way of contrast, the European response to the refugee emergency created by the war in the former Yugoslavia (1991–2001), was far more restrictive. Political and socio-cultural conditions no longer favoured refugees' reception in Western Europe, and the United States (US) no longer accepted big groups of refugees from Europe. Since the crisis was on the EU's doorstep, solutions in the region of origin in the name of people's human security and the 'right to remain' were immediately preferred. This was implemented through the creation of safe zones during 1992–1995 in Bosnia, with the UNHCR providing solution-oriented support to internally displaced persons (IDPs) through its good offices.[19]

The responses to this crisis can be seen to be linked with the notion of human security that started developing at that time. Solutions in the region of origin in the name of people's human security and the 'right to remain' were immediately promoted through the use of the good offices[20] or local temporary protection,[21] but in this case as a choice and not as an alternative to the non-eligibility issue as in the past.

Refugee crises have been addressed with varying degrees of success and commitment according to states' wider interests. UNHCR humanitarian assistance has been used in certain cases to promote in-country or in-region solutions as a means to fill the normative gaps or to create space for manoeuvre in an inactive political system. Additionally, humanitarian assistance provided by the UNHCR has also operated as an alternative to territorial asylum, a concept that has not been favoured due to the lack of institutionalised burden-sharing.

Over time, European states' preference for humanitarian law and external forms of burden-sharing, rather than refugee law and asylum, has become a consolidated practice. To the European states' adopting this approach, humanitarian assistance has represented a less demanding alternative to providing asylum. In the absence of other possible solutions, this can be seen as a 'rationalist approach', as only when relevant linkages exist between realpolitik and the capacity of European states to absorb refugees, has resettlement to Europe been offered.

Nevertheless, subsequently the 'local doctrine' has been used to prevent the amplification of crises, and local assistance has been employed in the name of people's human security and right to remain; this time as a priority and not as a last resort. This has promoted a slow tendency towards containment caused by the low risk to states of offering humanitarian assistance, an increased focus on preventive actions and containment, as well as a larger number of refugee flows and subsequent increased costs.[22]

But states' interests and security are not the only concern, as the human security of all refugees must also be taken into account. This means that the concept of refugees' human security must be evaluated correctly and translated into practice effectively. Preventive activities at or near the refugees' source by working on local solutions and containing the displacement represent a limited responsibility sharing mechanism[23] and cannot be always prioritised.

## 3.  Human security and burden-sharing

As evidenced by some of the above cases, wider political or economic concerns with a state-centric security approach based on containment in other regions is premised on the need to maintain an ordered and integrated environment within the territorial boundaries of a nation state.[24] It is the state's role to define its community of citizens and then to protect its economic, social and cultural welfare with a state-centric conception of security based on an inclusion/exclusion dichotomy where identity is premised on the sharing of common values.[25]

Most recently, there has been an endeavour to mitigate this state-centric approach through the use of the concept of human security. This paradigm officially made its appearance in the 1994 United Nations Development Programme (UNDP) Human Development Report, coinciding with the Balkan crisis, but the idea had been around since the 1980's when the Brandt Commission stressed that 'security must be reconceived with people foremost in mind'.[26]

Human security is no longer just about protecting states and the people within their boundaries from external threats or aggressions. It also embraces transnational[27] protection, from governments and non-state actors, with the single individual at its centre, protected 'from sudden and hurtful disruptions in the daily pattern of life'.[28]

As will be discussed below, human security is people-centred and preventive in nature, based on international and transnational cooperation and multilateralism. It seeks protection and empowerment with long-term solutions. Arguably, human security also takes into account various natural, economic, social, ecological and humanitarian threats, such as the original humanitarian purpose of refugee protection that aims at effective solutions.[29] It does not have a precise definition but guarantees protection against any kind of security threats, including threats to civil, political, economic and social rights. The concept of human security exists and operates outside the standard conventional norms and rules of human rights and does not have a legal framework. Nevertheless human rights and human security are interrelated, interdependent and mutually reinforcing.[30]

Human security tries to improve upon the protection offered by the current minimum human rights and refugee law standards through more favourable interpretation and good practices going beyond national interests, political strategy and conventional norms.[31] This means that the enforcing rules of human security are not well defined but are strongly connected to the concept of the responsibility to protect (R2P) and humanitarian intervention in cases involving IDPs and those who have been forcibly displaced. In the context of asylum seekers and refugees, it has been proposed that it should include states' responsibility to grant open borders and asylum for those fleeing crimes of genocide, ethnic cleansing, crimes against humanity, and war crimes,[32] but also generalised violence.

Yet, the concept of human security's vague characteristics, lack of legal framework and enforceability makes it an easy target for alternative interpretation. While human security tries to overcome the gaps and limitations in the legal protection framework of refugee law represented by the lack of open borders and obligation to grant asylum, it is constricted by states that try to mitigate their obligations by interpreting its content and doctrine in a state-centric and responsibility-limiting fashion.

This is the exact effect of the securitisation discourse just described, which tries to make use of the extra-EU burden-sharing policy through the argument of better protecting refugees' rights in the region of origin, by using a restricted version of the concepts of humanitarian assistance and human security. A reason for the existence of this discourse could be ascribed to the way refugees are perceived as a menace to the host country's sovereignty and security by increasing demands on resources.[33]

This argument leads to an exaggerated policy of containment and absence of physical burden-sharing veiled by the language of security[34] that leads paradoxically to closed borders, limited asylum and solutions in the regions of origin, but more as a palliative than an effective remedy.

The challenge, therefore, is to apply the original human security concept in a way that yields constructive and protective outcomes for refugees.[35] This means facilitating refugee protection in their countries and regions when this is possible, but, when required, providing open-border territorial asylum. The aim is also to be realistic and take into account the host countries' legitimate interests and concerns for their own community's security. Accordingly, states should be allowed to choose how to rationalise their fair share of responsibility, either by granting asylum or providing external quality support, taking into account that in certain cases protection can be in the region of origin.

For some time, however, the approach of most states' within the EU seems to have been to prioritise entirely external solutions, in order to limit their immediate territorial responsibility regardless of the quality of protection offered and the consequences for refugees.

## 4.   The EU refugee agenda and the interpretation of the human security doctrine

In 1993 the High Commissioner for Refugees, Sadako Osaka, introduced the concept of 'preventive protection' of refugees. This concept emphasised the 'right to remain' in one's home over the right to leave,[36] a clear recognition of the right of people to remain in safety in their countries and the right not to be forced into exile.

In Osaka's words 'preventive activities can help to contain human catastrophe by creating time and space for political process'. This statement reflected a vision very much akin to the human security concept. A vision which was focussed on individuals rather than states, and aimed at implementing preventive solutions in order to avoid people having to leave their regions in situations where complete safety of those people could be assured.

However, in practice Osaka's doctrine has been translated by the EU into the creation of the safe zones in Bosnia, and promotion of local solutions in the case of Kosovo. The concept of human security and preventive protection was used as a legitimation of the burden management and external burden-sharing policy in the region of origin, but resulted, in fact, in a policy of containment rather than effective assistance through quality protection.

In 1994 the EC continued on the restrictive agenda, adopting a 'Communication on Immigration and Asylum Policies', which outlined elements such as action on migration pressure and control of migration flows and integration.[37] The new strategy would see efforts towards the restoration and perpetuation of peace and respect of human rights aligned with humanitarian assistance to enable asylum-seeking persons to stay in the nearest safe area to their home.

Since then, the use of EU soft law as a tool to control irregular migration to Europe has become an agreed-upon official position. In 1998 a step forward was made, and a strategy paper[38] made clear that the Refugee Convention had become less applicable to the modern-day areas of concern and that solutions required not only asylum and resettlement but also transnational cooperation and creative comprehensive approaches.[39] This strategy paper represented a continuation of the reform of protection, and a transition from protection concepts based on asylum law, to mostly politically guided and oriented concepts[40] of assistance in the regions of origin using preventive capacity building, practical cooperation and *ex-post facto* humanitarian assistance.

This development led to the creation of the High-Level Working Group on Migration and Asylum,[41] mandated with the task to prepare comprehensive action plans for the countries of origin and transit of migrants in order to assist them in dealing with migration through capacity building in order to limit access to the EU.[42]

In 1999, the Tampere Conclusions provided space for a professed vision of readmissions, and the fight against irregular migration began to be perceived as the top priority. In 2003, the United Kingdom made a proposal to process asylum seekers' applications outside Europe in specific offshore transit processing centres.[43] The British approach emerged after the introduction of the UNHCR's Convention Plus,[44] an operative framework that among several aspects stressed the need to have greater protection and a more comprehensive arrangement of solutions in the region of origin.[45]

A few member states affected by the inevitable increased pressure stemming from the ineffectiveness of EU policy as well as the enlarged refugee crisis developed a series of measures designed to limit or prevent applicants from reaching their borders.[46] This resulted in the dog-chases-tail situation of even more focus being placed on developing external solutions.

Convention Plus, along with the other EU policy measures, therefore, endorsed an approach focussed on a European vision of durable solutions in the regions of origin with little account paid to effectiveness or alternatives.

This mapping of policymaking inevitably leads to evidence that the European approach to extra-regional burden-sharing has changed very little since the local solutions policy of the good offices of the 1960's. Rather, it has just adapted to the contemporary realities and challenges, while making use of new mechanisms for the same scope: limit the granting of territorial asylum. This can be seen in practice first in Yugoslavia and subsequently with more refined measures in other countries in its neighbourhood, such as Morocco, Libya, Tunisia and Mauritania.

It is also evident that the contemporary EU approach is gradual, in the sense that its external dimension focuses on the country of origin, the region of origin, countries of transit, and as a last resort, on protection in the EU. Despite this, priority is always given to solutions closer to the source of flows, regardless of their effectiveness, on the basis that in this way the spontaneous arrival of asylum seekers can be contained. But this policy has exactly the opposite effect. The more the EU contains refugees with ineffective preventive or *ex-post facto* activities through external burden-sharing or human security, the more desperate refugees are to leave the area.

The point now is to take account of this reality and restore a balance relatively quickly.

## 5. Human security and burden-sharing: a question of perspectives

Today, the complex relationship between EU external burden-sharing and human security must be addressed from three different perspectives in order to provide the full picture: the state, the people in transit, and the balance of refugees' rights and states' interests.

### 5.1 *The state perspective*

This involves the movement of people from a state or region to a new national or regional territory. The risk of a change in the territory's ethnic composition can be perceived as a threat to the host community, disrupting the assumed harmony within the host state,[47] and resulting in political destabilisation. Refugees and asylum seekers can provoke feelings of insecurity, particularly when presented by politicians and the media as a threat.[48] Thus the state and its policymakers' struggle to unite diverse groups of people might be threatened by the perceived added burden of accepting and integrating foreign nationals.[49]

The same matter can also be considered in a strictly economic light. In this case there can be a tendency to raise the drawbridge to inflows of people during an economic recession,[50] either solely because of the related costs attendant with the influx of asylum seekers, or because of the risks to the unemployment rate. In this case refugees are accepted on the basis of a strategic benefit or for profit, with states' attitudes towards refugees fluctuating from openness, during times of prosperity, to concerns about absorption capacity in times of austerity and recession.[51]

States' solidarity towards refugees, therefore, oscillates according to their economic condition but it is also measured in terms of internal security, integration prospects, public opinion and realpolitik.

This is the reason why states, and the EU in our specific case, increasingly prefer to provide assistance and protection through external forms of burden-sharing, justified through the use of human security's arguments, far from their borders, to rationalise the perceived burden of hosting protection seekers or to simply regulate their movement. Protection through asylum and resettlement is reduced to a limited number of individuals in order to control intakes and ethnic composition.

The practical result of this is that when the EU perceives the risk of spontaneous arrivals it tries to deflect protection seekers through a 'gradual concentric circles approach',[52] with the EU at its centre.

### 5.2 *People in transit*

From the perspective of the people on the move, the concepts of human security and external burden-sharing are framed within the notion of 'freedom from fear', as enshrined in President Roosevelt's doctrine and included in the Preamble of the Universal Declaration of Human Rights.[53] This is the right not to feel fear because of conflicts or war and to remain in one's own home. It includes the possibility to remain in the country of origin, sustained by the international community with humanitarian assistance provided by other states, as a form of 'remote burden-sharing'. But this is not always either possible nor does not offer effective protection.

The risk in these cases is that there might be an abuse of such solutions, even against the interests of the subject protected and even when such solutions are not recommendable. Therefore, rather than a right it might become an obligation to remain.

For this reason, invoking the concept of human security must also be framed in the same terms as the 'well-founded fear of being persecuted' of the 1951 Refugee Convention,[54] constituting a fundamental requirement for seeking asylum. In this case, human security connected to the concept of external burden-sharing is expressed by the right to leave one's own country and to seek quality protection elsewhere, when the local government or the international community cannot offer effective protection and safety to IDPs, and to seek quality protection elsewhere. This exercise of human security rights occurs especially in the case of refugees fleeing extended and protracted conflicts that are forced to seek temporary protection or asylum somewhere else.

Therefore, this also brings into play the responsibility of neighbouring countries or those farther away to share such a burden and offer protection. The burden imposed on any of these countries can and must be compensated for by the support of other countries in the form of cooperation and external burden-sharing when the fair share of responsibility of the country goes beyond its capacity. This again can be in the classic form of humanitarian assistance, but it must not be over-relied upon.

That is why support can also be through physical relocation outside of the region when this is necessary and when other forms of external burden-sharing are ineffective or unsafe, both for refugees and the local hosting countries. Protection seekers' movements are always guided by the dual motivators of safety and quality of protection and will keep moving until they are provided, no matter what the cost.

The problem escalates when it comes to making the choice about how to promote the human security of the people of concern through external burden-sharing, making the best decision from the options available and limiting the discretion linked to varying states' interests. The protection seekers have, according to the doctrine of R2P, the right to remain in their home country or region in safety, but IDPs and refugees do not yet meet the threshold of the R2P prevention or intervention in their own right.[55]

The protection of IDPs and refugees' is peripheral to the R2P doctrine, and may be excluded from activities under the prevention pillar.[56] The major reason for engaging in preventive activities and securitisation of conflicts or their amplification is in relation to the containment of population displacement in order to avoid refugee outflows, but only because the movement of these outflows is recognised as a potential burden.[57] Therefore the focus in most cases is more on containment and neighbouring states' protection rather than people's safety, in contrast to what the concept of human security proposes. It is a focus on IDPs and refugees' securitisation at any cost within the perimeter of a given area.

Therefore, making the best decision from the options available, and limiting the discretion linked to states' interests, means that when the security of the right to remain, either in the country of origin or in any other country cannot be effectively granted, onward movement must always be favoured. This movement could be towards the closest country able to offer protection through a corridor passage supported and maintained by the international community. Where the right to remain in one's state is unavailable, as an alternative, IDPs should not be refused entry to another state even if they might constitute a potential burden. In this case a responsibility would fall on the host state to grant either asylum or temporary protection.

The logic behind this is, in accordance with the rules governing the R2P preventive pillar, justified by the need to maintain a high threshold for human rights protection.[58] Letting IDPs and refugees exit from a state may assist in preventing crimes of genocide, ethnic cleansing, crimes against humanity and war crimes.[59] It can also prevent the amplification of conflicts when motivated by ethnic hate or persecution, which in general fall more strictly under the R2P preventive pillar.

Yet, even if the enforcement of the right to leave is in certain cases preferable, as we have seen, it is not in most cases a consolidated practice.

### 5.3   The balance of refugees' rights and states' security

States and refugees have conflicting aspirations when it comes to their security protection, interests and rights. The safeguards of national sovereignty and of the human security of protection seekers clash in terms of interests.

States have the discretionary right to grant protection to humanitarian refugees[60] and an obligation for refugees under the convention. However, states in the first instance are interested in protecting their community. The state's option to offer temporary or prolonged protection under well-established rules may thus conflict with states' claim to security. This is especially true in cases of mass influx, which might threaten the security (even the very survival) of the nation state.[61] Thus invoking security concerns and refusing entrance or movement has the aim of preserving protection and relieving pressure on national capacity, but also of rationalising movement and allocation.

Protection seekers instead aspire to find a temporary or more permanent place to seek protection, and their movements are guided by the natural desire to reach a place where their rights will be respected. When they find opposition on their way to these aspirations and rights, they keep moving until they find what they consider a reasonable treatment in line with what can be defined humane and effective protection – even if sometimes this means protection seekers pay a high price, both in economic and human terms.

Thus states tend to favour their interests over those of protection seekers, interpreting the rules in their favour. Protection seekers do the same, but considering their relatively weak impact on the rules, they play across them, sometimes with no choice other than to try to get around them or battle against them.

Countries are obliged to keep their borders open, even if this is not always a legal obligation but more of a moral one.[62] It is an obligation 'to do something', but in practice highly discretionary and usually results in at least temporary protection.[63] States can choose to open their borders or not, but in most cases this choice is dependent on the choices of other states – often far from the region – that by offering effective assistance or resettlement through physical burden-sharing can re-establish the balance in the security discourse towards protection seekers.

Often, however, the EU deflects arrivals of protection seekers, and increasingly adopts extra-regional burden-sharing as a priority, preferring to secure its community and push for local solutions. The problem is that this choice is in most cases based on very discretionary and self-oriented interests, which tend to simplify a complex problem by providing palliative solutions in line with short-term securitisation agendas and with little regard to effectiveness.[64]

It seems indeed that states, both in and out of the region of the flow of protection seekers, have legitimate arguments for restrictiveness but those farther away have no corresponding effective and realistic international obligations to offer cooperation or solutions. On the other side, the countries in the region have hypothetical obligations to do something, but provided with little support, assistance from the West in most cases is more likely to arrive if certain political interests are at stake.

The lack of constructive dialogue results in most cases with both the convention and humanitarian refugees remaining contained and forced to resort to alternative exit ways and extra-regional movements, which in many cases involve human smuggler routes.

## 6. Five EU responses to the Syrian refugee crisis

The EU response to the Syrian refugee crisis is a perfect example of the union's gradual concentric circles approach. The approach followed four gradual measures that, to a great extent, reflect the EU's approach to the external burden-sharing described above.[65]

The EU promoted political transition, provided assistance with financial and practical aid in the country and to the neighbouring hosting states, granted asylum to a limited number of refugees and safeguarded and increased border security.

The EU worked on promoting political transition in the country while contributing to various meetings in Geneva under the auspices of the UN. It has supported several initiatives, including various UN statements and resolutions, which condemn the regime's actions, calling for a cessation of violence and for the support of the UN Syrian Observer Missions. It supported attendance at the Friends of Syria Group's meetings and called for documentation and investigation of the human rights abuses committed by the Syrian regime.[66]

At the regional level, the EU is coordinating actions with the League of Arab States (LAS) in its political responses to the Syrian crisis by supporting the LAS observer mission commenced in December 2011, commending imposition of LAS sanctions, supporting the Arab Plan of Action and applauding LAS demands to Assad to end the violence and step aside.[67]

Since 2012, the EU has given around €230 million in humanitarian aid to the Syrian refugee crisis, both inside and outside the country, making the EU the leading international donor.[68] According to the EC, this amounts to more than 53% of the international response, placing Europe's total monetary contribution at well over a quarter of a billion euro.[69] The EU offered further financial support of 58 million euro to Lebanon in 2013,[70] and total support to the region amounted to 1.1 billion euro to January 2014.[71]

The EU's Civil Protection Mechanism has coordinated the allocation of pooled EU funds to respond to the Syrian crisis. The EU Civil Protection Mechanism operated in April 2012 to help Turkey cope with the influx of refugees, and in September 2012 to assist Jordan.[72]

The EU has also discussed establishing a Regional Protection Programme (RPP) in cooperation with the UNHCR. Such a programme would focus on increasing reception capacity and improving protection in host countries, the provision of humanitarian assistance, return of displaced persons, and integration and resettlement.[73]

The EU offered 12,340 resettlement places, roughly the number of refugees registered in Lebanon during the final five days of November 2013.[74] Later, the EU, Switzerland and Norway pledged 14,600 resettlement or humanitarian admission places.[75] Some countries, such as Sweden, Germany and the United Kingdom, offered other resettlement places, even if very limited in terms of numbers and oriented towards only the most vulnerable. Sweden called for more solidarity, recalling that the EU, following the Swedish, path could settle no less than 100,000 refugees.[76]

Italy deployed a maritime surveillance mission in 2013, called Mare Nostrum, aimed at giving support to migrant' boats in distress but also to work against the people smugglers operating in the area. To date, the mission has saved almost 150,000 migrants in distress. The member states and the EU as a whole have been implementing several forms of border control and cooperation with third countries based on their individual national security needs as a result of Syrian flows.

Even if the EU approach covers a wide spectrum of actions, it is de facto focussed on the containment of the crisis in the region or to the external boundaries of the EU. The promotion of political transition in the region had little or no effect. As internal protection was therefore not a realistic option, neighbouring countries have granted protection seekers several forms of temporary protection. The EU insisted on the allocation of resources to hosting countries, yet the geopolitical interests linked to the economic interests in the region are not that relevant. Consequently, the financial support to the hosting countries has been, even if generous, inadequate to offer protection seekers durable solutions that are different from previous cases, such as the CIREFCA.

Unlike the Hungarian case and in some part the Indo-Chinese and Chilean cases, the political and strategic interests of the West to resettle refugees are not so relevant. There is apparently less absorption capacity, since this crisis also coincides with other crises closer to the EU's borders, in particular the Libyan crisis; therefore only relatively small relocation schemes have been set in place.

The spontaneous arrivals, mostly provoked by the containment approach and the lack of effective local solutions, are being controlled by the EU in third countries and at the EU's borders, sometimes with tragic consequences.

In sum, the overall poor and ineffective solutions promoted by the EU in its external dimension at all stages cannot be considered effective and legitimate forms of external burden-sharing to constitute an alternative to the classic granting of open borders and asylum. This has resulted, as a consequence, in more and more extra-regional and secondary movements and the tragedy of the Syrian refugees is already beyond the Yugoslav worst-case scenario.


## 7. Conclusion

Following the slow evolution from the UNHCR's humanitarian assistance to the concept of preventive protection and the right to remain, the historical overview and analysis in this article has evidenced a focus by European states on implementing local solutions. This was in part provoked by the limited extension of the refugee definition, and in part because of political constraints, but mostly due to the desire to contain displacement and rationalise movements.

Focussing on IDPs or on local protection measures can promote early solutions as IDPs are likely to be the refugees of tomorrow and not all people have the means to seek protection far away. Yet, this focus on IDPs and local solutions must not be stretched too far. This article has argued, in line with other authors, that since 1951 there has been a binary interpretation between conventional and humanitarian refugees, but it stresses that both types have been penalised by the discretionary exercise of protection and over-stretched use of external burden-sharing and human security, that does not distinguish between the two categories.

According to their original purpose, the doctrines of human security and external burden-sharing were to be implemented gradually, by promoting, through concentric circles, protection from the country or region of origin until its centre, represented by the West or more developed countries – but only in so far as protection can be effective and in the interest of those to be protected. They thus invoke free movement when effective protection is at risk.

In line with this approach, the Western and the EU approach to protection seekers in the past – as today – has been gradual. But in its progression these states sometimes exercise too much discretion and force for solutions that limit their immediate territorial responsibility. Therefore, solutions are preferred as much as possible far from their backyards, forcing local human security of IDPs first and then refugees, even if this might not effectively safeguard their rights.

This article has argued that this practice is not in the best interests of either the categories of protection seekers to be protected or the Western and EU countries. I have argued that the best approach is to provide consistent support that reduces the likelihood of external flows – but only when preventive and *ex-post facto* activities will result in effective humanitarian assistance or durable solutions, which as such can serve as a foundation for lawful forms of external burden-sharing. Local or regional solutions can be considered permissible only if they result in a protection equivalent or comparable to that which could be sought and offered through the classic granting of asylum.

This leads to the conclusion that external forms of burden-sharing can work as a rationalisation of burden and movements only when they offer effective protection. When the support is not substantial, in good faith, or possible given the circumstances, the result will always be ineffective and have as a consequence external flows, which are better promoted at the earliest stage possible, without people's lives.

Therefore, the external burden-sharing cannot always be considered *a priori* a legitimate or lawful form of assistance or rationalisation of movements, and external movement shall be granted for all kinds of protection seekers irrespective of their status to maintain a high threshold for protection against human rights violations.

## Disclosure statement

No potential conflict of interest was reported by the author.

## Notes

1. Eighty-six percent of the world refugees are hosted in developing countries. UNHCR *Global Trends Report* (2013), 2, http://unhcr.org/trends2013/.
2. The term 'burden sharing' in this article is used to describe the financial assistance, humanitarian provisions, and resettlement contributions supplied by developed states for refugee protection and durable solutions to the country of origin, host states of first asylum or countries of secondary movement in other regions.
3. (1951) 189 UNTS 137. Opened for Signature 28 July 1951. Entered into Force 22 April 1954.
4. Susan Kneebone, 'The Refugee Definition and Humanitarian Protection', in *Research Handbook on International Human Rights Law*, ed. Sarah Joseph and Adam McBeth (Cheltenham, UK: Edward Elgar Publishing, 2010), 216.
5. National Security Council, 'Psychological Value of Escapees from the Soviet Orbit', Security Memorandum, 26 March 1953. See also James C. Hathaway, *The Law of Refugee Status* (London: Butterworths, 1991), 25.
6. Prima facie refugee determination is performed on the basis of the objective circumstances leading to the mass displacement and the evident refugee character of the individuals concerned. See UNHCR, *Handbook for Emergencies*, 2nd ed. (UNHCR, 2000), 13; UNHCR, 'Note on International Protection' (31 August 1993) UN Doc. A/AC.96/815 [27]. UNHCR Global Consultations, 'Protection of Refugees in Mass Influx Situations: Overall Protection Framework' (EC/GC/01/4) (19 February 2001), 18.
7. Leon Gordenker, *Refugees in International Politics* (New York: Columbia University Press, 1987), 39.

8. Ibid., 39. See also UNHCR, *Handbook for Emergencies*, 13; UNHCR, 'Note on International Protection'; UNHCR Global Consultations, 'Protection of Refugees in Mass Influx Situations'.
9. Andreas Gémes, 'Deconstruction of a Myth? Austria and the Hungarian Refugees of 1956–57', in *Time, Memory, and Cultural Change*, ed. Sean Dempsey and David Nichols (Vienna: IWM Junior Visiting Fellows' Conferences, Vol. 25, 2009).
10. Tony Kushner and Katharine Knox, *Refugees in an Age of Genocide. Global, National and Local Perspectives during the Twentieth Century* (London: Frank Cass, 1999), 280–90.
11. The Refugee Convention contains a number of restrictions relating to the eligibility of an individual to be considered a refugee. Beyond the temporal and geographic limitation of Article 1 (B), Article 1(D) excludes individuals who were (at the time of the 1951 Convention) already receiving protection or assistance from another United Nations (UN) agency. This provision continues to apply to Palestinian refugees receiving assistance from the United Nations Relief and Works Agency for Palestine Refugees in the Near East (UNRWA). The 1967 Protocol removed these restrictions; however it also gave state parties the option to continue to apply them.
12. Guy S. Goodwin-Gill and Jane McAdam, *The Refugee in International Law* (Oxford: Oxford University Press, 2007), 27.
13. Ibid.
14. Aristide R. Zolberg, *Escape from Violence: Conflict and the Refugee Crisis in the Developing World* (Oxford: Oxford University Press, 1989), 157–160. Astri Suhrke, 'Burden-Sharing During Refugee Emergencies: The Logic of Collective Action Versus National Action', *Journal of Refugee Studies* 11, no. 4 (1998): 406.
15. The Japanese pledged 60 million dollars, equivalent to almost half of the cost of the UNHCR budget, for the Indochinese refugees in 1979.
16. Suhrke, 'Burden-Sharing During Refugee Emergencies', 406; and Richard Towle, 'Processes and Critiques of the Indo-Chinese Comprehensive Plan of Action: An Instrument of International Burden-Sharing?', *International Journal of Refugee Studies* 18, no. 3–4 (2006): 537.
17. Zolberg, *Escape from Violence*, 173.
18. Alexander Betts, 'Comprehensive Plans of Action: Insights from CIREFCA and the Indochinese CPA' (UNHCR New Issues In Refugee Research Working Paper No. 120, January 2006), 62.
19. Guy S. Goodwin-Gill, 'International Protection and Assistance for Refugees and the Displaced: Institutional Challenges and UN Reform' (paper presented at the Refugee Studies Workshop, 24 April 2006).
20. Ibid.
21. Elena Jileva, 'Larger Than the European Union: The Emerging EU Migration Regime and Enlargement', *Migration and the Externalities of European Integration*, ed. in Sandra Lavenex and Emek M. Ucarer (Lanham, MD: Lexington Books, 2002).
22. Gil Loescher, 'The UNHCR and World Politics: States Interests vs. International Anatomy', *International Migration Review* 35, no. 1 (2002): 44, at 45.
23. The term 'responsibility sharing' is used to define how the normative responsibility for refugee protection should be shared between states and what this means in legal terms when there is a lack of international cooperation or solidarity for the scope of burden-sharing.
24. Mehreen Afzal, 'Rethinking Asylum: The Feasibility of Human Security as New Ratione Personae Protection', *Journal of International Law & Policy* 3 (2005): 2, 29–30.
25. Ibid.
26. James Bernard Quilligan, 'The Brandt Equation: 21st Century Blueprint for the New Global Economy' (2002), 13, http://www.brandt21forum.info/BrandtEquation-19Sept04.pdf.
27. Transnational security is referred as a 'paradigm for understanding the ways in which governments and non-State actors, functioning within and across borders, interact and affect the defence of States and their citizens'. See Richards H. Shultz, Roy Godson, and George Quester, eds, *Security Studies for the 21st Century* (Washington, D.C., and London: Brassey's Inc, 1997).
28. United Nations Development Programme (UNDP), *Human Development Report* 22 (1994), 23.
29. Kneebone, 'The Refugee Definition and Humanitarian Protection', 230–1; and Michael Barnett and Thomas G. Weiss, eds, *Humanitarianism in Question: Politics, Power, Ethics* (Ithaca and London: Cornell University Press, 2008), 5.

30. Wolfgang Benedek, 'Human Security and Human Rights Interaction', in *Rethinking Human Security*, ed. Moufida Goucha and John Crowley (Oxford: Wiley-Blackwell, 2008), 98.

31. Ministerial Meeting of States Parties to the 1951 Convention and/or its 1967 Protocol Relating to the Status of Refugees, Geneva, Switzerland, 12–13 September 2001, Declaration of States Parties to the 1951 Convention and/or its 1967 Protocol Relating to the Status of Refugees, 2, 6, UN Doc. HCR/MMSP/2001/09 (16 January 2002).

32. Brian Barbour and Brian Gorlick, 'Embracing the "Responsibility to Protect": A Repertoire of Measures Including Asylum for Potential Victims', *International Journal of Refugee Law* 20 (2008): 533–61.

33. Bhupinder S. Chimni, 'Globalization, Humanitarianism and the Erosion of Refugee Protection', *Journal of Refugee Studies* 13 (2000): 243, 244.

34. Ibid.

35. Eve Lester, 'Socio-Economic Rights, Human Security, and Survival Migrants: Whose Rights? Whose Security?', in *Human Security and Non-Citizens: Law, Policy and International Affairs*, ed. Alice Edwards and Carla Ferstman (Cambridge: Cambridge University Press, 2010).

36. UN General Assembly, *Universal Declaration of Human Rights*, 10 December 1948, Article 13.

37. Commission of the European Communities, Communication to the Council and the European Parliament on Immigration and Asylum Policies, COM (94) 23 final, 23 February 1994.

38. Council of the European Union, Note from the Presidency to K4 Committee: Strategy Paper on Immigration and Asylum Policy, CK4 27, ASIM 170, 9809/98 (OR.d) 1 July 1998, http://www.proasyl.de/texte/europe/eu-a-o.htm.

39. Ibid., 27 and 37.

40. Ibid., 41.

41. See 'High Level Working Group on Asylum and Migration. Report to the European Council in Nice', Council Document 13993/00JAI 152 AG 76, of 29 November 2000, 51. See also, Maria-Teresa Gil-Bazo, 'HLWG Action Plans: Assessment of the Human Rights Dimension', in ECRE, 'The ECRE Tampere Dossier. A Compilation of Non and Inter-Governmental Observations on the Special Meeting of the European Council on the Establishment of an Area of Freedom, Security and Justice', 15–16 October 1999, Tampere, Finland; and a selection of presentations made at the 'ECRE EU Tampere Summit Parallel Meeting', June 2000, 59–60.

42. Maria-Teresa Gil-Bazo, 'The Practice of Mediterranean States in the Context of the European Union's Justice and Home Affairs External Dimension. The Safe Third Country Concept Revisited', *International Journal of Refugee Law* 18, no. 3–4 (2006): 589.

43. See Madeline Garlick, 'The EU Discussions on Extraterritorial Processing: Solution or Conundrum', *International Journal of Refugee Law* 18, no. 3–4 (2006): 601.

44. See UNHCR High Commissioner's Forum, *Convention Plus Targeting of Development Assistance for Durable Solutions to Forced Displacement*. FORUM/2005/8, 10 February 2006, http://www.unhcr.org/437d9f152.html.

45. Ibid.

46. Katy Long, *No Entry: A Review of UNHCR's Response to Border Closure in Situations of Mass Refugee Influx* (UNHCR PDES, 2010).

47. Afzal, 'Rethinking Asylum', 29–30.

48. Ibid.

49. Ibid., 31.

50. Andrew Geddes, 'Migration as a Foreign Policy? The External Dimension of EU Action on Migration and Asylum' (report presented at the seminar 'Migration as Foreign Policy', Stockholm, 21 April 2009), 10, http://www.sieps.se/sites/default/files/528-2009-2rapport.pdf.

51. See Dallal Stevens, *UK Asylum and Law Policy-Historical and Contemporary Perspectives* (London: Sweet & Maxwell, 2004), 14.

52. For an overview of the EU's external 'concentric circles' cooperation see Alexander Betts, 'Towards a Mediterranean Solution? Implications for the Region of Origin', *International Journal of Refugee Law* 18, no. 3–4 (2006): 666, 671.

53. UN General Assembly, *Universal Declaration of Human Rights*, 10 December 1948, Preamble.

54. Refugee Convention, Article 1.

55. Chimni, 'Globalization, Humanitarianism and the Erosion of Refugee Protection', 252.

56. UNHCR, *Refugees, Internally Displaced Persons and the 'Responsibility to Protect'* (PDES, 2010), 8.

57. Chimni, 'Globalization, Humanitarianism and the Erosion of Refugee Protection', 252.

58. Long, 'No Entry', 15.
59. Barbour and Gorlick, 'Embracing the "Responsibility to Protect"', 561.
60. Kay Hailbronner, 'Non-Refoulement and Humanitarian Refugees', *Virginia Journal of International Law* 26, no. 4 (1986): 857, 869.
61. Long, 'No Entry', 1–2.
62. The preamble to the 1951 Convention states that: 'The grant of asylum may place unduly heavy burdens on certain countries, and that a satisfactory solution of a problem of which the United Nations has recognized the international scope and nature cannot therefore be achieved without international co-operation.' The ExCom Conclusion on International Cooperation and Burden and Responsibility Sharing in Mass Influx Situations, agreed in 2004, focuses specifically on the question of how to balance refugees' rights against the security and capacity questions surrounding mass influx. It reiterates the normative principle that 'persons who arrive as part of a mass influx seeking international refugee protection should always receive it at least on a temporary basis'. However, in addressing practical responses to burden-sharing the conclusion underlines the continued reluctance of states to share the physical realities, rather than simply the financial costs, of refugee crises. Hathaway stresses that there is a legal basis for restricting non-refoulement if a state's basic national survival is threatened by a mass influx. Katy Long stresses instead that there is a presumption that in this case, in order to balance the rights of the refugees against the state's security, the burden will be shared between states (James Hathaway, *The Rights of Refugees under International Law* (Cambridge: Cambridge University Press, 2005), 367). This dilemma is better expressed by the fact that 'just as a refugee has a right to seek asylum, but no State has the obligation to grant it, a host State has at least in theory the obligation to protect all members of a mass influx from *refoulement* while the international community has no legal obligation to burden-share'. For more on this topic see Long, 'No Entry', 12, 13.
63. Hathaway, *The Law of Refugee Status*, 26.
64. See Betts, 'Towards a Mediterranean Solution?', 666–71.
65. Migration Policy Centre, 'The EU Response to the Syrian Refugee Crisis. What Next?' (MPC research report 2012/14), http://www.migrationpolicycentre.eu/docs/MPC%202012%2014.pdf.
66. Ibid.
67. Ibid.
68. Ibid.
69. European Commission, Press Release (24 October 2012), 'Justice and Home Affairs Council: 25–26 October 2012', http://europa.eu/rapid/press-release_MEMO-12-807 en.htm.
70. European Commission, Press Release (10 September 2013), 'Lebanon, Further Support of 58 Million Euro to Deal with Syrian Crisis', http://europa.eu/rapid/press-release_IP-13-826_en.htm.
71. European Union, Press Release (14 January 2014), 'Syrian Crisis: EU Pledges Additional Funding for Humanitarian Aid as Needs Continue to Rise', http://europa.eu/rapid/press-release_IP-14-17_en.htm.
72. Migration Policy Centre, 'The EU Response to the Syrian Refugee Crisis'.
73. Euroactic and Reuters, 'EU Considers Syrian Refugee Protection' (24 July 2012), http://www.euractiv.com/global-europe/eu-considers-syrian-refugee-prot-news-514079.
74. Amnesty International, 'Briefing: An International Failure: The Syrian Refugee Crisis' (13 December 2013), http://www.amnesty.org/ar/library/asset/ACT34/001/2013/ar/8a376b76-d031-48a6-9588-ed9aee651d52/act340012013en.pdf.
75. ECRE, 'Sweden Calls for Solidarity with Syria's Refugees – EU Could Resettle 100,000 People if all States Resettle Proportionally as Many Refugees as Sweden' (4 April 2014), http://ecre.org/component/content/article/70-weekly-bulletin-articles/665-sweden-calls-for-solidarity-with-syrias-refugees-eu-could-resettle-100000-people-if-all-states-resettle-proportionally-as-many-refugees-as-sweden.html.
76. Ibid.

# Networks and norm entrepreneurship amongst local civil society actors: advancing refugee protection in the Asia Pacific region

Alice M. Nah

*Centre for Applied Human Rights, University of York, UK*

Research on transnational advocacy networks has tended to focus on how non-state actors from developed countries interact with those from developing countries to pressure states, often by drawing in liberal Western states. This article adds a different perspective, focusing on how local civil society actors in different locales interact with each other to persuade their own governments 'from below'. It examines how these actors facilitate norm emergence amongst Asian states on issues with little domestic traction and for which there are well-developed international norms, standards and procedures. In studying the way local civil society actors conduct norm entrepreneurship, it is important to recognise the political, material and ideational conditions that constrain their work; their positionality and fragility in their own societies; and the way they relate to other actors working on the same issues. Focusing on the case of the Asia Pacific Refugee Rights Network, it is argued that working through a formalised network has changed the ways and the conditions under which local civil society actors engage in norm entrepreneurship on refugee protection. It has changed the attributes of actors, helping them develop visibility, capacity and connectedness through the formation of a 'community of practice'; it has changed power relations between them and other actors – in particular, the United Nations High Commissioner for Refugees; it has facilitated the development of 'regional imagination' and the practice of 'scale shifting', helping local actors move beyond domestic contexts to engage with state and non-state actors through regional and international fora. It has also introduced shifts in the dynamics of norm entrepreneurship by introducing a new actor – the network itself, which exercises agency through a Secretariat – and intra-network sensitivities, which need careful attention to prevent member disengagement.

## Introduction

In November 2008, over 110 participants from around 70 civil society groups and organisations based in 13 countries in the Asia Pacific region met in Kuala Lumpur to discuss the protection of refugees. It was an unprecedented gathering. Service providers, advocacy groups, lawyers and refugee community-based organisations in countries of asylum – such as Malaysia, Thailand, India, Nepal, Japan, South Korea and Australia – met human rights groups and activists in refugee-producing countries such as Myanmar, Indonesia, Sri Lanka and Pakistan. Organisations located in different countries serving refugees from the same country of origin were able to share their experiences, compare notes and discuss the challenges they faced. Previously isolated in their work, championing issues with little domestic traction in their own countries, they experienced unexpected camaraderie.

The issues of their concern were – and indeed continue to be – pressing. In spite of the presence of millions of refugees and the existence of some of the largest and most protracted encampment situations in the world, only a minority of states in the Asia Pacific region are party to the 1951 Convention Relating to the Status of Refugees and its 1967 Protocol.[1] There are no regional conventions that explicitly recognise the rights of refugees.[2] Further, most states neither have domestic legislation recognising refugees nor functioning national asylum systems. Without formal legal recognition, many refugees have been treated as irregular migrants and have been subject to arrest, detention, punishment for immigration offences and deportation. Many refugees have been forced to eke out a living in the shadow economy, suffering violations of their labour and human rights. Some have languished indefinitely in immigration detention centres and prisons without access to protection. Some have fallen prey to traffickers in search of safety. In India, Bangladesh, Nepal and Thailand, hundreds of thousands of refugees have been kept indefinitely in overcrowded refugee camps.

At the conference, participants expressed joy and surprise at meeting like-minded people, having felt alone and alienated in their work. They also shared common frustrations and concerns – with their governments, with the United Nations High Commissioner for Refugees (UNHCR), and with fellow citizens unsympathetic to the protection of refugees. The participants discussed a range of issues – from the challenges involved in gaining government recognition of the status and rights of refugees, to the abuses refugees face in detention, to the specific risks that women and children experience, and the inability of refugees to gain access to health care.[3] A unanimous observation at the conference was that it was crucial for states in the region to protect refugees. To achieve this aim, the participants resolved to stay connected and to work together – the Asia Pacific Refugee Rights Network (APRRN) was born.

How do local civil society actors work together to facilitate the adoption of new norms amongst states? What are the challenges they face in facilitating 'norm emergence' on issues with little domestic traction and for which there are well-developed international norms? How does the formation and formalisation of a transnational advocacy network influence the ways and the conditions under which they engage in norm entrepreneurship?

In this article, I analyse the role that local civil society actors play in advocating for refugee protection in the Asia Pacific region. This case study is particularly interesting because of the persistence of most states in the region in 'rejecting' norms on refugee protection in spite of the institutionalisation and implementation of these norms in most parts of the world. Scholars refer to this as the 'Asian exceptionalism' to refugee protection[4] or the 'Asian rejection' of refugee law.[5] This is a case where norm diffusion has not been successful in spite of the significant effort of both state and non-state actors in promoting these norms over decades – it is a case of the 'dog who didn't bark'.[6]

The domestic conditions for norm entrepreneurship on refugee protection have been unfavourable. Local civil society actors have had to contend with the dominant nationalist ideas that the rights and welfare of citizens take precedence over those of non-citizens, and that non-citizens with irregular status are 'criminals'. State officials in Asia also tend to see refugee protection as a 'UNHCR problem' or an 'international problem', rather than a domestic or regional one requiring long-term, local solutions. The treaty-based international refugee rights regime has become very technically sophisticated and exclusive, involving negotiations between actors and in spaces that exclude many Asian local civil society actors. Compared to other actors in the field of refugee protection – in particular,

UNHCR and international non-governmental organisations (INGOs) – local civil society actors also tend to be smaller, less resourced, less financially stable, and more vulnerable to political attack.

This article focuses on the very early stage of the norm 'life cycle', the phase of 'norm emergence' as identified by Martha Finnemore and Kathryn Sikkink.[7] It focuses on the ways and the conditions under which local civil society actors conduct norm entrepreneurship on unpopular issues where there are well-developed international norms, standards and procedures. Scholarship on transnational advocacy networks tends to focus on the interactions between transnational actors and local actors, and on the involvement of liberal Western states in socialising norm violators.[8] This article seeks to add a different perspective, by focusing on how local civil society actors interact with each other through a formalised network in order to persuade governments 'from below'.

In studying norm entrepreneurship amongst local civil society actors, it is important to recognise the political, material and ideational conditions that constrain their work; their positionality and fragility in their own societies; and the ways they relate to other actors working on the same issues. Focusing on the case of APRRN, I argue that working through a formalised civil society network has changed the ways and the conditions under which local actors in Asia engage in norm entrepreneurship in four main ways. First, it has changed the attributes of actors, helping them develop visibility, capacity and connectedness. It does this through the formation of a 'community of practice',[9] a 'safe space' through which civil society actors with common goals interact with each other to strengthen their own knowledge, expertise, practices and connections. Second, it has changed power relations between them and other actors – in particular, UNHCR. UNHCR is often the most dominant influence in socialising local civil society actors with respect to refugee protection norms. It is also often a gatekeeper – not just of issues but also of tactics and strategies for advocacy. By networking with each other, local civil society actors are able to gain alternative perspectives on issues and to engage with UNHCR in multiple ways.

Third, working through a network has helped local civil society actors to move beyond their local contexts and to develop a 'regional imagination' about their struggle. It has facilitated 'scale shifting', coordinating claims-making at different levels than where the claims first began,[10] thus opening up more diverse fora for engagement with states. When its members construct governmental audiences for advocacy, their primary strategy is not to draw in Western liberal states to pressure their own states 'from above'. Instead, using a range of tactics and strategies, they appeal to their own governments and to governments in the region as concerned citizens and residents to adhere to norms on the basis that it constitutes 'appropriate behaviour'.

Last but not least, the Network has introduced shifts in the dynamics of norm entrepreneurship in two ways. It has introduced a new actor – the Network itself, which exercises its own agency through a secretariat – which sometimes (inadvertently) competes with local civil society actors in norm entrepreneurship. It has also introduced intra-network sensitivities that need careful attention – in particular, the need to ensure that power, leadership and participation are balanced between members with different identities. If unattended to, these can lead to member disengagement.

### Norm emergence, norm entrepreneurs

In their landmark paper, Martha Finnemore and Kathryn Sikkink define a norm as a 'standard of appropriate behaviour for actors with a given identity'.[11] They identify three phases in a norm 'life-cycle' in international politics – norm emergence, norm acceptance and norm internalisation. Drawing upon the work of Cass Sunstein,[12] they observe that norm entrepreneurs – agents who build support for the adoption of new norms – play a key role in the first phase. Norm entrepreneurs persuade a critical number of states to adopt new norms, often through an organisational platform. A key task in this endeavour is to create and frame issues so that they resonate with local audiences.[13]

The states that adopt these norms then act as norm leaders, socialising other states to do the same. After a tipping point is reached, a norm cascade occurs, in which states rapidly take on these new norms.[14] These norms are then internalised and institutionalised to the point that they are taken for granted. Finnemore and Sikkink note that: 'Up to the tipping point, little normative change occurs without significant domestic movements supporting such change.'[15] What is the 'work' that goes into building such support at the domestic level? What are the preconditions for 'persuasion'? How do norm entrepreneurs with similar goals relate to each other?

Reflecting on the process of norm diffusion in Southeast Asia, Amitav Acharya contrasts a moral cosmopolitan perspective – in which transnational agents 'teach' cosmopolitan norms through 'moral proselytism' and regard local resistance to such norms as 'illegitimate' or 'immoral' – with a perspective that emphasises the importance of examining the domestic conditions that influence the receipt of new norms and the role that local actors play as norm-makers and norm brokers.[16] Acharya observes that contestation between transnational norms and local beliefs and practices reduces the likelihood of norm diffusion. Local agents need to engage in 'constitutive localisation', reconstructing norms so that they become congruent with local beliefs and practices. 'The success of norm diffusion strategies and processes', Acharya argues, 'depends on the extent to which they provide opportunities for localization'.[17] He further states,

> The prospect for localization also depends on its positive impact on the legitimacy and authority of key norm-takers [states], the strength of prior local norms, the credibility and prestige of local agents, indigenous cultural traits and traditions, and the scope for grafting and pruning presented by foreign norms.[18]

Acharya's analysis suggests why it is difficult for local civil society actors to persuade Asian states to commit to refugee protection. In addition to the existence of unfavourable local beliefs, the scope for 'grafting' (associating a new norm with a pre-existing norm) and 'pruning' (adjusting foreign ideas to fit more easily with local beliefs and practices) is limited. Local civil society actors seek the commitment and compliance of Asian states to the rules, principles, standards and procedures of the international refugee rights regime, a regime rooted in the 1951 Convention and its 1967 Protocol and supervised by UNHCR, who in turn is advised by an inter-state body, the Executive Committee.[19] As such, while local civil society actors engage in reframing, applying and strategically deploying international norms to local settings, their desire for state commitment to an existing international regime delimits the extent to which they (are willing to) adapt such norms.

Scholars have assessed how different types of actors have engaged in norm entrepreneurship on different issues – from influential individuals[20] to federal agencies,[21] regional organisations[22] and states.[23] There is also a large and growing body of work that examines how local civil society actors act individually and transnationally to (re)interpret, (re)represent and (re)constitute 'global' ideas, principles and norms for domestic contexts.[24]

## Local actors, transnational networks

Muthiah Alagappa provides a useful definition of 'civil society actors', referring to them as 'self-organised, self-governing, nonstate, non-profit, nonprivate institutions that employ nonviolent means to achieve a public interest or good through collective action'.[25] *Local* civil society actors typically comprise citizens and non-citizens who engage in activities at the domestic level to achieve outcomes with governments.[26] As such, they are distinct from regional and international NGOs in terms of how they operate and how they are structured, governed and resourced.

Local civil society actors are uniquely located socio-politically vis-à-vis their own governments. As 'insiders' they are able to shape public opinion in the local vernacular, and to engage with the judiciary, legislature and executive with local legitimacy. They can raise critical reflections on 'appropriate behaviour' without facing some of the legitimacy challenges that INGOs face.[27] They cannot be immediately dismissed as 'outsiders' who 'interfere' in the domestic affairs of a state. Their advocacy challenges the preconception that refugee protection is a 'Western idea', particularly salient in postcolonial, nationalistic societies.

However, states shape the level of influence that local civil society actors have on national policy debates. As Robert Pekkanen observes in the case of Japan, the government's imposition of structural and ideational constraints on domestic civil society organisations has made it difficult for them to establish their authority and legitimacy based on expertise, which, in turn, limits their influence on policy-making. Political opportunities for the advancement of rights also often occur when states are particularly concerned about their reputation, or domestic political elites perceive themselves to be vulnerable to condemnation.[28] Unfortunately, it is also in these moments of heightened perceived vulnerability when state and non-state actors react by threatening activists.

Sally Engle Merry also points out that local civil society actors can be vulnerable as they 'vernacularise' human rights ideas.[29] As intermediaries between global and local contexts, they can be distrusted and misconstrued as being 'disloyal'. Indeed, in his report to the UN General Assembly in October 2015, the UN Special Rapporteur on the Situation of Human Rights Defenders identified defenders seeking to protect the rights of minorities and refugees as one of the 'most at-risk' groups of defenders.[30]

There has been a growing body of work on how civil society actors work through transnational advocacy networks to facilitate change in state behaviour. Margaret Keck and Kathryn Sikkink provide the classic definition of such networks, referring to them as 'networks of activists, distinguishable largely by the centrality of principled ideas or values in motivating their formation'.[31] They observe that transnational advocacy networks help local actors gain momentum on issues with their own governments through building international pressure from 'outside' – what they call the 'boomerang' effect.

Scholarship on such networks has tended to focus on how transnational actors – often based in the Global North – collaborate with local actors to change state behaviour, often by involving liberal, Western states. There has been less scholarship on how local civil society actors in the Global South work together to build state commitment to people-centred norms without involving Western states. As César Rodríguez-Garavito observes, shifts in the relative power of states means that human rights work is now conducted in a 'multipolar world order', in which:

> states and NGOs in the Global North no longer have sole control over the creation and implementation of human rights standards, as new actors (from transnational social movements to transnational corporations to Global South states and NGOs) emerge as influential voices.[32]

Drawing on his experiences in Latin America, he describes how local civil society actors collaborated to put simultaneous pressure on their own states and another powerful state in the region to achieve their goals, bypassing a traditional ally, the United States – what he refers to as a 'multiple boomerang' strategy.[33]

Although the primary aim of local civil society actors is to convince their own states of the need to adopt norms, such engagements can be located at multiple levels – at local, national, regional and international fora. Social movement theorists observe that agents who operate at one level sometimes shift the scale of their action, either moving 'upwards', from local action outwards, or 'downwards', applying practices at a broader level to a local context.[34] They define a 'scale shift' as 'a change in the number and level of coordinated contentious actions to a different focal point, involving a new range of actors, different objects, and broadened claims'.[35] As Sidney Tarrow elaborates, scale shifting involves five mechanisms: coordination (planning collaboration across space) brokerage (facilitating such linkages), theorisation (generalising an idea from a particular reality so that it can be applied to other realities), target shifting (focusing on a new target), and claim shifting (changing the nature of the claim).[36] Formal networks can facilitate such scale shifting by identifying opportunities and fora for collaborative action and maximising the participation of members in these.

## Refugee protection in the Asia Pacific region: an overview

UNHCR noted the presence of 3.5 million refugees and 1.4 million stateless persons in the Asia Pacific region in 2015, with the majority of refugees originating from Afghanistan and Myanmar.[37] Most refugees in this region seek asylum in neighbouring countries. A smaller proportion of refugees travel across multiple borders to reach their preferred destination, sometimes after various periods of settlement in different countries. Refugees from Myanmar, for example, often travel through Thailand to reach Malaysia, and refugees from Sri Lanka, Afghanistan and Myanmar often travel through Indonesia and Malaysia in an attempt to reach Australia. Refugees from outside the region are relatively small in number, coming primarily from the Middle East and Africa. Well-developed smuggling and trafficking networks cut across Asian states, often involving chains of smugglers and traffickers. On the whole, the movements of refugees in this region are 'mixed' with the movement of migrant workers, students and tourists, and constitute only a very small proportion of people on the move. Over two-thirds of refugees live outside of camps, typically in urban areas with insecurity.[38]

In countries with relatively large refugee populations, the UNHCR takes on operational responsibilities belonging to states, such as refugee status determination (RSD), protection intervention, community services and resettlement, acting as a 'surrogate state'.[39] Without the resources to fully substitute for the role of a state, UNHCR's capacity to protect refugees is limited. In Thailand and Malaysia, for example, asylum seekers wait years for UNHCR to register and determine their status, a situation that UNHCR itself recognises as a significant protection problem. The lack of prospects for repatriation and local integration has led UNHCR to rely upon resettlement as a means of 'unlocking' protracted refugee situations. In 2013, Nepal, Thailand and Malaysia were the top three countries in the world from which UNHCR-assisted resettlement occurred.[40] However, resettlement only benefits a fraction of the refugee population – most refugees live in limbo, waiting with fear and uncertainty for a durable solution.

Nationalist pride and anti-colonial sentiments can colour the way governments interpret the efforts of UNHCR. In the Asia Pacific region, refugees are often seen as politically sensitive populations, as threats to national security, and as unwanted 'irregular migrants'.[41] The advice of UNHCR thus touches on how a state manages foreign relations and national security, which are fundamental expressions of state sovereignty.[42] Governments sometimes dismiss UNHCR's interventions as a 'Western imposition'. The Eurocentric origins of the 1951 Convention and the 1967 Protocol, and the perceived exclusion of the perspectives of Asian governments in their drafting, do not help in this matter.[43]

In South and Southeast Asia, only one of the eight members of the South Asian Association for Regional Cooperation (SAARC)[44] – Afghanistan – and only two of the 10 members of the Association of Southeast Asian Nations (ASEAN) – Cambodia and the Philippines – are parties to the 1951 Convention and its 1967 Protocol.[45] The lack of legal infrastructure poses a significant challenge for their protection. The existing practice in South and Southeast Asia is that states accommodate refugees on the basis of 'hospitality' or humanitarian concern rather than obligation. States have preferred to negotiate over the protection of specific groups of refugees rather than grant asylum to all refugees in a systematic and impartial manner. These negotiations have tended to be temporal, contingent and politicised, informed by foreign policy considerations and the political affiliations of government leaders.

While UNHCR, scholars and practitioners alike have praised Asian states for protecting refugees on humanitarian grounds, this non-binding, non-legal approach has resulted in uncertain protection.[46] As Martin Jones notes critically, this 'protection space' approach also

> privileges international interests, fora, and UNHCR as the negotiator; devalues the normative strength of obligations towards refugees; and, allows the underlying responsibility for the provision of refugee protection to drift from the state to UNHCR.[47]

The operational environment for refugees in Australia, New Zealand and the Pacific is somewhat different. While many states are party to the 1951 Convention and the 1967 Protocol, there is significant variation in the way they protect refugees. Australia, in particular, has interpreted its international obligations in controversial ways – engaging in 'third-country processing' (sending asylum seekers arriving by boat to Nauru and Manus Island in Papua New Guinea for the determination of their protection claims); practicing the mandatory detention of non-citizens unlawfully present in its territory, resulting in the non-reviewable and indefinite detention of asylum seekers[48]; and in 2014, negotiating a multi-million dollar transfer arrangement with Cambodia, in which refugees recognised in Nauru would be 'resettled' to Cambodia.[49]

China,[50] Japan and the Republic of Korea are all party to the 1951 Convention and 1967 Protocol. The latter two countries have introduced domestic law on refugees and conduct RSD. However, asylum seekers do not have full access to fair and timely RSD procedures. These countries detain asylum seekers, and tend to provide protection only as a matter of discretion and humanitarian action rather than as a matter of responsibility or obligation.[51] Asylum seekers and refugees are largely marginalised and excluded from society, resulting in serious discrimination, destitution, homelessness and abuse.[52]

## Local civil society actors and challenges to norm entrepreneurship on refugee protection

In many countries in the Asia Pacific region, local civil society actors are the main service providers to refugees. They engage in a wide range of activities, from education, legal aid in domestic courts, legal representation for RSD (conducted by states and UNHCR), and medical assistance, to shelters, livelihood projects, welfare support and resettlement referrals.[53] They also advocate for reforms in laws, policies and administrative practices using a range of tactics and strategies, so that refugees are formally recognised and their rights protected.

For example, amongst APRRN members, in South Korea, the Korean Public Interest Lawyers' Group (Gonggam), Dongcheon Public Interest Foundation, Refuge Pnan, Nancen, and Advocates for Public Interest Law played a key role in drafting and advocating for a domestic Refugee Act that was passed in 2012 and took effect in 2013.[54] Members of the Migration Working Group in Malaysia use human rights mechanisms such as the Universal Periodic Review Process to advocate for refugee protection.[55] In India, the Organisation for Eeelam Refugees Rehabilitation, which runs and supports most of the services in camps for Sri Lankan refugees, is the primary interlocutor and advocate for refugee issues with the Indian government, NGOs and donors. In addition to providing legal and social assistance to refugees, the Japan Association for Refugees conducts policy advocacy, pressuring Japan to adhere to its international obligations concerning refugees.[56]

Nevertheless, building momentum and support for refugee protection continues to be an uphill task. When arguments for refugee protection are made, a common opposing refrain – from government officials, the public, and some civil society actors – is that governments should first focus on improving the conditions of (disenfranchised) citizens before focusing on non-citizens.[57] Local civil society actors also contend with strong beliefs and practices that erode refugee protection, such as the perception of migrants with irregular status as 'criminals'. As described earlier, most refugees in the Asia Pacific region are part of 'mixed migration flows' – that is, they often travel using the same routes as other migrants and rely on the same smuggling networks to cross borders. Refugees sometimes have mixed motives, fleeing from their country of origin not just out of fear of persecution but also to seek a better life. As such, in public imagination, they are easily dismissed as irregular migrants. In states where there is strong securitisation of migration and no national asylum systems, refugees are legally and socially indistinct from irregular migrants. Antipathy towards irregular migrants makes it challenging to build public support for refugees.

As stated earlier, government officials in Asia tend to see refugees as an 'international' or 'UNHCR' problem, rather than a domestic problem. In Southeast Asia, this is part of the legacy of the Comprehensive Plan of Action for Indochinese Refugees (from 1988–1996), in which states agreed to host refugee populations temporarily while UNHCR conducted RSD and arranged for their resettlement or repatriation. This 'arrangement' still forms the basis of government officials' expectations today. In Malaysia, government officials expect UNHCR to conduct RSD and blame them for not resettling refugees quickly enough. In Thailand, government officials still call the decades-old refugee camps along the Thai-Burma border 'temporary shelters'. As a result of this line of thinking, government officials do not focus on local integration as a durable solution, thinking instead that the 'right' treatment of refugees is their return or resettlement.

The international refugee regime has also grown in complexity over time. In order to participate in global debates concerning refugees, local civil society actors concerned about the rights and welfare of refugees have had to learn unfamiliar terminology, procedures, standards, and systems – such as those related to RSD, the care of vulnerable groups (such as unaccompanied minors and survivors of sexual and gender-based violence), and resettlement. International negotiation and strategy development concerning refugee protection tends to privilege some types of actors while excluding others. For example, every year, states, UNHCR and NGOs discuss global resettlement through the Annual Tripartite Consultations on Resettlement in Geneva. While these discussions are a key part of global strategising on protection,[58] and while Thailand, Nepal and Malaysia have historically been amongst the top five countries from which UNHCR-assisted refugees have been resettled, local civil society actors in these countries have rarely participated in these dialogues, because they are not directly involved in resettlement. In summary, the professionalisation of refugee protection has alienated local civil society actors and refugees.

Local civil society actors are also different operationally and structurally from UNHCR and INGOs. Often formed and run by very committed, independent-minded, strong-willed leaders, they tend to be smaller and have fewer resources than their international and regional counterparts. They often struggle to meet overwhelming needs and to keep programmes viable in the face of scarce financial resources. In most countries in Asia, governments do not fund domestic refugee programmes. Some institutional donors do not support civil society groups in middle- and high-income countries; some require grantees to have formal registration as a non-profit organisation, which is difficult for groups restricted by domestic laws. Local civil society actors are also subject to scrutiny, surveillance and regulation by state authorities; they can be targeted easily by their own governments for their activities.[59]

## Networking for refugee protection: forming a transnational 'community of practice'

The APRRN was set up specifically to foster collaboration between members and to equip them to influence state behaviour on refugee protection. It does this through joint advocacy, capacity strengthening, and knowledge/resource sharing and outreach.[60] In an effort to create a 'safe space' for civil society, membership in the Network is restricted to civil society actors alone – those who work for the government, intergovernmental bodies and the media are not permitted to join this network. At point of writing, in 2015, APRRN has 136 organisational and 114 individual members.[61] Most of APRRN's organisational members comprise local civil society groups and organisations based in the Asia Pacific region, such as legal aid providers, service providers, human rights advocacy organisations, universities and refugee community-based organisations.[62] Its individual members primarily comprise academic scholars, researchers, students and lawyers.

When APRRN was formed in 2008, its members created working groups so that they could interact with each other in a number of ways. There are four geographic working groups: South Asia, Southeast Asia, East Asia, and Australia, New Zealand and the Pacific, and five thematic working groups: Legal Aid and Advocacy, Immigration Detention, Women and Girls at Risk, The Right to Health, and Statelessness. This crosscutting structure enables APRRN members to work on multiple issues at the same time and to avoid 'gate-keeping' in issue adoption,[63] which is important, given the complexities of the issues that refugees face in the region.

A steering committee comprising elected and appointed members provides strategic leadership to the Network; a secretariat based in Bangkok operationalises its plans.[64] The steering committee is responsible for governance, and is accountable to APRRN's members who meet at its biannual conference, the Asia Pacific Consultation on Refugee Rights (APCRR).[65] Over time, APRRN has become more formalised, transitioning from a member-driven network to a secretariat-based one.

### *Strengthening visibility, capacity and connectedness*

APRRN helps to make visible local civil society support for refugees, thus positioning refugee protection as an issue of domestic interest. The work of APRRN members is featured in APRRN's newsletters, wiki pages, blog, Facebook pages and tweets. APRRN organises panels and sessions at regional and international conferences, creating opportunities for APRRN members to build support for refugee protection with civil society groups working on other issues. It provides its members and external stakeholders with a network of contacts that they can use to identify and access those with knowledge, skills and expertise on refugees in different countries. Before APRRN was formed, it was difficult to work out who was doing what and where with refugees across the region.[66]

APRRN's activities have fostered the building of a 'community of practice' amongst its members. APRRN members consult each other on thorny problems, express solidarity, discuss ideas and share resources through APRRN events and communication channels. In addition to its biannual conference, APRRN runs specialist courses and workshops aimed at strengthening the technical expertise of members on the international refugee rights regime as well as on specialist topics such as refugee mental health, legal aid provision, and ending and limiting immigration detention. APRRN also releases joint statements to draw attention to human rights violations and state practices that erode refugee protection. These public statements not only reiterate the principles, standards and values which APRRN members promote, the process of writing them is an important way in which members debate advocacy positions and develop consensus.[67]

APRRN's added value is most evident when it facilitates collaboration between civil society actors in different locales who work on the same issue. In 2015, for example, in response to the maritime crisis in which Rohingya refugees and Bangladeshi migrants were left stranded at sea by smugglers and traffickers, the APRRN Secretariat facilitated a number of teleconferences through which local civil society actors pieced together their understanding of the movements and government responses, and coordinated advocacy initiatives. Similarly, when UNHCR announced that year that it was fundamentally rethinking its approach to RSD, recognising its structural inability to process overwhelming caseloads according to procedural and other standards, APRRN's Legal Aid and Advocacy Working Group met in teleconferences to discuss their engagement with UNHCR.

The interactions and relationships between members at APRRN activities have led to a number of bilateral and multilateral collaborations initiated by members themselves. In Indonesia for example, dialogues facilitated by APRRN members and UNHCR led to the formation of the Indonesian Civil Society Network for Refugee Protection (SUAKA) in 2012, which provides legal assistance to asylum seekers, conducts advocacy, and engages with refugee communities on protection issues.[68] Similarly, in Pakistan, APRRN members formed a national Refugee Rights Network (RRN-Pakistan) in 2015 to strengthen their advocacy with the government of Pakistan.[69]

### *Reconfiguring power relations with UNHCR*

A key way in which APRRN has changed the way in which local civil society actors engage in refugee protection is the way it has reconfigured power relations between them and UNHCR. The relationship between UNHCR and local civil society actors is multi-layered, ambivalent and complex. In many countries in the Asia Pacific region, UNHCR takes the lead role in advocating for refugee protection. Many civil society actors are dependent on UNHCR for resources, expertise and the preservation of 'protection space'.

Partnerships with UNHCR are particularly important in contexts where refugees are vilified as irregular migrants, as these partnerships legitimise the work of local civil society actors. As such, local civil society actors often work under the protection of UNHCR – but also under its shadow. Their understanding of refugee protection, prioritisation of issues, and imagination of possibilities tends to be shaped in large part by what they are told by UNHCR officers based in country offices.[70] While UNHCR desires the support, services and cooperation of local service providers, it is usually less welcoming of their criticism. The attitudes of individual UNHCR officers range from respect for the work of local civil society actors to disdain.

APRRN events and communication structures provide members with ways of obtaining alternative perspectives on issues, thus reducing UNHCR's dominance in defining and framing domestic protection agendas. For example, one of the more contentious issues between local civil society actors and UNHCR has been the way that UNHCR conducts registration and RSD in countries such as Malaysia, Indonesia and Thailand. Most UNHCR country offices do not welcome the involvement of civil society actors in these procedures. However, APRRN members who provide RSD legal aid have been able to come together to raise concerns as a collective with UNHCR about the way RSD is conducted, when they would otherwise have been silenced.

APRRN members have helped each other to develop productive working relationships with UNHCR based on positive experiences elsewhere. For example, when Ara Legal Initiative, a provider of RSD legal aid in India, launched its organisation and programmes, the APRRN Secretariat put it in contact with Brian Barbour, the Chair of the Legal Aid and Advocacy Working Group, who had already developed standard operating procedures with UNHCR in Hong Kong. As a result, Ara Legal Initiative was able to finalise its own letter of understanding (LOU) with UNHCR, secure access to RSD interviews, and reach agreement with UNHCR to provide all asylum seekers with detailed reasons for rejection when this occurs, whether or not they are legally represented.[71] Other legal aid providers in India can also sign this LOU with UNHCR, which is available as a template.

APRRN facilitates member engagement with UNHCR at different levels, for example, through organising meetings with UNHCR's regional office in Bangkok and with its Asia Bureau in Geneva. These meetings are particularly helpful when dialogue with UNHCR country offices has deteriorated. Before APRRN existed, UNHCR relations with civil society largely occurred at the country level with a handful of local actors, often their implementing partners. APRRN provides UNHCR with an interlocutor with whom it can discuss regional priorities, policy positions and good practice with a much broader constituency of civil society actors. This engagement helps UNHCR to understand the nature, interests and potential of civil society in the region, which strengthens the way it engages with them.[72]

### *Scale-shifting: regional imagination, alternative political opportunities*

Not only does APRRN help its members to develop a 'regional imagination' on refugee protection, but it helps them situate their own experiences within the context of the broader refugee movement. APRRN conferences, workshops and meetings provide members with an audience of peers. These interactions serve as a mirror of sorts through which local civil society actors can reflect on their own domestic and regional roles. As Hotaeg Lee, of Refuge Pnan in South Korea observes, deliberations at APRRN's East Asia Working Group meetings prompted a sense of responsibility amongst Korean NGOs for leading efforts for refugee protection at the domestic and sub-regional level.[73] This multi-level perspective helps local civil society actors recognise opportunities for collaboration and advocacy at sub-regional, regional and international levels.

The target audience of APRRN's members are states in the Asia Pacific region. They call on these states to commit to higher standards of behaviour in a number of ways. Rather than shaming these states before liberal states in Europe and North America, their dominant strategy is to appeal to these states as concerned (and outraged) citizens and residents who witness the suffering of refugees and believe that this should not happen in their own countries. They appeal for their own states to demonstrate behaviour that is morally upright – not because such behaviour is good for 'international image', but because it is the right thing to do.

When APRRN members do appeal to other governments, these are primarily other governments from within the region. There are two main types of such appeals. The first are appeals to regional blocs, such as SAARC and ASEAN, whose collective behaviour influences the individual behaviour of states. Second, APRRN, together with organisations such as the International Detention Coalition, have organised multilateral roundtables that bring together civil society actors and government officials from a number of adjacent states.[74] The purpose of these dialogues is to focus on constructive problem solving, collaboration and the development of 'pilot projects' as a method of trust building. These roundtables are unique because they are non-adversarial in tone, focused on practical solutions, and subtly appeal to governments to show leadership in the region.

There is untapped potential for engagement in sub-regional and regional processes. For example, over the past decade, there has been unprecedented development in the regional infrastructure for human rights in Southeast Asia. In 2009, ASEAN established the ASEAN Intergovernmental Commission on Human Rights (AICHR) whose 2010–2015 Work Plan[75] includes thematic studies on issues such as migration; trafficking in persons, particularly women and children; child soldiers; and women and children in conflicts and disasters – all of which are related to refugee protection. In 2012, ASEAN adopted the ASEAN Human Rights Declaration, which states at Article 16: 'Every person has the right to seek and receive asylum in another State in accordance with the laws of such State and applicable international agreements.' In November 2015, ASEAN members signed its first legally binding regional treaty, the ASEAN Convention Against Trafficking in Persons, Especially Women and Children, which bears on the protection of refugees.

At a broader geographical level, in 2009 states reaffirmed their commitment to the multilateral Bali Process on People Smuggling, Trafficking in Persons and Related Transnational Crime, co-chaired by Australia and Indonesia. At that time, there was an increase of asylum seekers arriving by boat to Australia, the Rohingya were being forcibly expelled from Myanmar, and there was a humanitarian crisis in north-east Sri Lanka.[76] In 2011, members of the Bali Process endorsed a Regional Cooperation Framework to reduce irregular migration in the Asia Pacific region. Although UNHCR's attempts to feature refugee protection strongly in this framework have not been successful,[77] the Regional Support Office that operationalises the framework is open to dialogue with civil society actors on irregular migration and refugee protection.

APRRN's value lies in facilitating norm entrepreneurship and collaborative relationships amongst local civil society actors in different locations across the region, and in identifying (and indeed creating) political opportunities for advocacy at sub-regional, regional and international levels. APRRN members are often too engrossed in their own work at the domestic level, and too overwhelmed by the daily needs of refugees to engage effectively at these broader levels. The APRRN Secretariat can help members participate in these by monitoring developments in these processes, building alliances with relevant stakeholders, briefing APRRN members on the technicalities and politics of these processes, developing advocacy strategies and facilitating the participation of members in key meetings at crucial moments. At the time of writing, there is consensus amongst states, civil society and UNHCR that regional cooperation and regional solutions are required for refugee-related crises in South and Southeast Asia, such as the maritime movement of Rohingya. The APRRN Secretariat is well placed to facilitate the engagement of members in the development of such regional cooperation arrangements.

### Managing intra-network sensitivities

The formation and formalisation of APRRN has changed the ways in which local civil society actors relate to each other. These reconfigurations of ties also bring about new challenges, however. The first is how APRRN creates and maintains space for local civil society actors (both members and non-members) to advocate for refugee protection without 'taking over' scarce resources and political space. As it is a unique network, it has become the 'go-to' civil society actor on refugee protection in Asia. When UNHCR, states or civil society groups want Asian civil society voices in workshops or events, they often turn to the APRRN Secretariat. APRRN Secretariat staff can either decide to attend these events themselves, or recommend the participation of the most relevant member – in most cases, the member closest to the ground and/or the one with the greatest expertise or knowledge of issues.

Apparently simple decisions like these are not easy to make. On one hand, strengthening the work of members is the raison d'être of the Network. Participation in events and meetings can be valuable opportunities for APRRN members to build their own visibility, conduct advocacy and engage in networking. On the other hand, to continue to exist, the Secretariat needs to ensure that it remains relevant to movement building.[78] That is, its own visibility – as a group of experts, coordinators and facilitators – is important. Should they extend invitations to members, or attend events themselves? When allocating such resources, transparency, fairness and collective accountability in decision-making is important. Otherwise, it is easy for decisions to be made on (what are perceived to be) arbitrary criteria and for members to feel resentful.

The power relations between members also need careful navigation. Sub-regional identities and related sensitivities matter. At a broad level, it is important for there to be 'balance' in participation across the four sub-regions in the Network – South Asia; Southeast Asia; East Asia; and Australia, New Zealand and the Pacific – so that one sub-region does not dominate in terms of leadership and decision-making. It is also particularly important for 'Northern' members in the Network to respect the agency and views of 'Southern' members, and to refrain from 'telling them what to do'. Such behaviour is frowned upon (often implicitly, in the 'Asian way'), and would work against the ethos of APRRN, which values mutual respect and solidarity. Similarly, it is important for the Network to consider gender, class and other identity-based dynamics in the life of the Network, and to ensure that all members enjoy inclusion and substantive equality.

A lack of attentiveness to intra-network sensitivities can result in member disengagement. Emphasising the importance of recognising the voluntary nature of civil society networks and thus the capacity for members to exit the network (or to remain dormant), Kathryn Sikkink observes,

> For networks-as-actors, network nodes choose whether to participate in networks. This gives networks their informal nature and means that you can't 'lock-in' either members or commitments. Thus networks must create benefits for network members, what many authors refer to as network externalities, in order for networks to continue to exist. These benefits may be of a very diverse sort – but because networks are voluntary, nodes will exit if they do not perceive benefits, and seek out other kinds of arrangements.[79]

## Conclusion

Local civil society actors play a key role in persuading states to adopt new norms. Crucially, they do so as 'insiders' appealing to their states to adhere to standards of 'appropriate behaviour'. However, they often face significant challenges in doing so. Without an understanding of the political, ideational and material constraints on their work, it is easy for outsiders to dismiss their efforts as being 'weak'. This can delegitimise and disempower them, especially if such thinking leads to their exclusion from processes and fora relevant to their work.

Working through a formalised network can change the ways and the conditions under which local civil society actors engage in norm entrepreneurship. As the case of APRRN demonstrates, participation in a formalised network can strengthened the visibility, capacity and connectedness of local civil society actors. It can reconfigure power relations between them and other powerful actors. It can facilitate the development of 'regional imagination' and help them engage in 'scale shifting' in order to maximise opportunities for advocacy at multiple levels.

A formalised network also becomes an actor in itself even as it functions as an organisational platform for members. If the aim of the network is to foster norm entrepreneurship amongst members, it is important for it to avoid taking over the role of members, absorbing valuable resources and opportunities for advocacy. Working in a diverse network introduces sensitivities between members. In order to prevent member disengagement, it is important for these sensitivities to be understood and managed so that an enabling environment can be created for norm entrepreneurship to flourish amongst members until the desired norm cascade occurs.

## Acknowledgements

This article is based on the author's observations as one of the founding members of APRRN as well as an analysis of data produced by APRRN. As a volunteer for FORUM Asia, the author was the main organiser of the inaugural conference in 2008 described in this article. She served as APRRN's first chair (2008–2010) and subsequently as a steering committee member (2010–2014; 2015–present). The views expressed in this article are the author's own, and do not represent the official view of APRRN. This article was presented at a workshop organised by Susan Kneebone on 'Comparative Regional Protection Frameworks for Refugees: Norms and Norm Entrepreneurs' on 15 November 2013 at the Institute of Advanced Legal Studies, London. The author is indebted to Alexander Betts, Brian Barbour, Helen Brunt, Vivienne Chew, Tamara Domicelj, Petrice Flowers, Martin Jones, Susan Kneebone, Julia Mayerhoffer, Mauricio Angel Morales, Aeden Pillai, Alejandro Peña and James Thomson for their constructive comments on earlier drafts of this article. Any mistakes remain the author's own.

## Disclosure statement

No potential conflict of interest was reported by the author.

## Notes

1. UN General Assembly, *Convention Relating to the Status of Refugees* (1951) 189 UNTS 137. Opened for signature 28 July 1951. Entered into force 22 April 1954; UN General Assembly, *Protocol Relating to the Status of Refugees* (1967) 606 UNTS 267. Opened for signature 31 January 1967. Entered into force 4 October 1967.
2. Although note that there are non-binding instruments. See for example the *Bangkok Principles on the Status and Treatment of Refugees*, 31 December 1966, http://www.refworld.org/docid/3de5f2d52.html (accessed 16 December 2015).
3. Resources from this conference, called the Asia Pacific Consultation on Refugee Rights, can be found at https://sites.google.com/site/apcrr2008/Home (accessed 14 December 2015).
4. See for example B.S. Chimni, Miyoshi Masahiro, and Li-ann Thio, *Asian Yearbook of International Law: Volume 14 (2008)* (London: Routledge, 2010).
5. Sara E. Davies, 'The Asian Rejection?: International Refugee Law in Asia', *Australian Journal of Politics & History* 52, no. 4 (2006): 562–75.
6. Jeffrey T. Checkel, 'Norms, Institutions, and National Identity in Contemporary Europe', *International Studies Quarterly* 43, no. 1 (1999): 86.
7. Martha Finnemore and Kathryn Sikkink, 'International Norm Dynamics and Political Change', *International Organization* 52, no. 4 (1998): 887–917.
8. Thomas Risse and Kathryn Sikkink, 'The Socialization of International Human Rights Norms into Domestic Practices: Introduction', in *The Power of Human Rights*, ed. Thomas Risse, Stephen C. Ropp, and Kathryn Sikkink (Cambridge: Cambridge University Press, 1999), 1–38.
9. Jean Lave and Etienne Wenger, *Situated Learning: Legitimate Peripheral Participation* (Cambridge: Cambridge University Press, 1991); Etienne Wenger, Richard Arnold McDermott, and William Snyder, *Cultivating Communities of Practice: A Guide to Managing Knowledge* (Cambridge, MA: Harvard Business Press, 2002); Etienne Wenger, *Communities of Practice: Learning, Meaning, and Identity* (Cambridge: Cambridge University Press, 1999).
10. Sidney Tarrow, *The New Transnational Activism* (Cambridge: Cambridge University Press, 2005).
11. Finnemore and Sikkink, 'International Norm Dynamics and Political Change', 891.
12. Cass R. Sunstein, 'Social Norms and Social Roles', *Columbia Law Review* 96, no. 4 (1996): 903–68; Cass R. Sunstein, *Free Markets and Social Justice [Electronic Resource]* (New York: Oxford University Press, 1997).
13. Robert D. Benford and David A. Snow, 'Framing Processes and Social Movements: An Overview and Assessment', *Annual Review of Sociology* 26 (1 January 2000): 611–39; Rodger A. Payne, 'Persuasion, Frames and Norm Construction', *European Journal of International Relations* 7, no. 1 (2001): 37–61.
14. Finnemore and Sikkink, 'International Norm Dynamics and Political Change'. The authors suggest that this 'tipping point' is often reached when about one-third of states make formal commitments to a new norm.
15. Ibid., 902.
16. Amitav Acharya, 'How Ideas Spread: Whose Norms Matter? Norm Localization and Institutional Change in Asian Regionalism', *International Organization* 58, no. 2 (2004): 239–75.
17. Ibid., 241.
18. Ibid., 247–8.
19. Alexander Betts, 'Institutional Proliferation and the Global Refugee Regime', *Perspectives on Politics* 7, no. 1 (2009): 53–8.
20. Daisuke Madokoro, 'How the United Nations Secretary-General Promotes International Norms', *Global Responsibility to Protect* 7, no. 1 (2015): 31–55.
21. Steven Hetcher, 'The FTC as Internet Privacy Norm Entrepreneur', *Vanderbilt Law Review* 53, no. 6 (2000): 2041–61.
22. Michelle Pace, 'Norm Shifting from EMP to ENP: The EU as a Norm Entrepreneur in the South?', *Cambridge Review of International Affairs* 20, no. 4 (2007): 659–75; Issaka K. Souaré, 'The African Union as a Norm Entrepreneur on Military Coups D'état in Africa (1952–2012): An Empirical Assessment', *The Journal of Modern African Studies* 52, no. 1 (2014): 69–94; David Lewis, 'Who's Socialising Whom? Regional Organisations and Contested Norms in Central Asia', *Europe-Asia Studies* 64, no. 7 (2012): 1219–37.
23. Christine Ingebritsen, 'Norm Entrepreneurs Scandinavia's Role in World Politics', *Cooperation and Conflict* 37, no. 1 (2002): 11–23.

24.  Margaret E. Keck and Kathryn Sikkink, *Activists Beyond Borders: Advocacy Networks in International Politics* (Ithaca, NY: Cornell University Press, 1998); Sanjeev Khagram, James V. Riker, and Kathryn Sikkink, *Restructuring World Politics: Transnational Social Movements, Networks, and Norms* (Minneapolis: University of Minnesota Press, 2002); Sally Engle Merry, 'Transnational Human Rights and Local Activism: Mapping the Middle', *American Anthropologist* 108, no. 1 (2006): 38–51; Richard Price, 'Transnational Civil Society and Advocacy in World Politics', *World Politics* 55, no. 4 (2003): 579–606; Thomas Risse, Stephen C. Ropp, and Kathryn Sikkink, eds, *The Power of Human Rights* (Cambridge: Cambridge University Press, 1999).
25.  Muthiah Alagappa, 'Civil Society and Political Change: An Analytical Framework', in *Civil Society and Political Change in Asia: Expanding and Contracting Democratic Space*, ed. Muthiah Alagappa (Stanford, CA: Stanford University Press, 2004), 34.
26.  See also Amitav Acharya, 'Local and Transnational Civil Society as Agents of Norm Diffusion' (paper presented at the Global Governance Workshop, Department of International Development, Queen Elizabeth House, University of Oxford, June 1–3, 2012). http://amitavacharya.com/sites/default/files/Local%20and%20Transnational%20Civil%20Society%20as%20Agents%20of%20Norm%20Diffusion.pdf
27.  Vivien Collingwood and Louis Logister, 'State of the Art: Addressing the INGO "Legitimacy Deficit"', *Political Studies Review* 3, no. 2 (2005): 175–92; Alan Hudson, 'NGOs' Transnational Advocacy Networks: From "Legitimacy" to "Political Responsibility"?', *Global Networks* 1, no. 4 (2001): 331–52; Sarah Lister, 'NGO Legitimacy: Technical Issue or Social Construct?', *Critique of Anthropology* 23, no. 2 (2003): 175–92; Michael Edwards, *Legitimacy and Values in NGOs and Voluntary Organizations: Some Sceptical Thoughts* (London: Earthscan, 1999).
28.  Susan Burgerman, *Moral Victories: How Activists Provoke Multilateral Action* (Ithaca, NY: Cornell University Press, 2001).
29.  Merry, 'Transnational Human Rights and Local Activism'.
30.  UN General Assembly, 'Situation of Human Rights Defenders', A/70/217, 30 July 2015, http://www.un.org/ga/search/view_doc.asp?symbol=A/70/217.
31.  Keck and Sikkink, *Activists Beyond Borders*, 1.
32.  César Rodríguez-Garavito, 'The Future of Human Rights: From Gatekeeping to Symbiosis', *Sur - International Journal on Human Rights* 20 (2014): 499.
33.  César Rodríguez-Garavito, 'Multiple Boomerangs: New Models of Global Human Rights Advocacy', *openDemocracy*, 21 January 2015, https://www.opendemocracy.net/openglobalrights/c%C3%A9sar-rodr%C3%ADguezgaravito/multiple-boomerangs-new-models-of-global-human-rights-advoc (accessed 24 December 2015).
34.  Tarrow, *The New Transnational Activism*.
35.  Doug McAdam, Sidney Tarrow, and Charles Tilly, *Dynamics of Contention* (Cambridge: Cambridge University Press, 2001), 331.
36.  Tarrow, *The New Transnational Activism*, 122.
37.  UNHCR, '2015 UNHCR Regional Operations Profile – Asia and the Pacific', 2015, http://www.unhcr.org/pages/4a02d8ec6.html (accessed 24 December 2015).
38.  Ibid.
39.  Michael Kagan, '"We Live in a Country of UNHCR": The UN Surrogate State and Refugee Policy in the Middle East', Policy Development and Evaluation Service, Research Paper No. 201 (Geneva: United Nations High Commissioner for Refugees, February 2011); Amy Slaughter and Jeff Crisp, 'A Surrogate State? The Role of UNHCR in Protracted Refugee Situations', Policy Development and Evaluation Service, Research Paper No. 168 (Geneva: United Nations High Commissioner for Refugees, January 2009), http://www.unhcr.org/4981cb432.html (accessed 24 December 2015).
40.  UN High Commissioner for Refugees, 'UNHCR Global Resettlement Statistical Report 2013' (UNHCR, 2014), http://www.unhcr.org/52693bd09.html (accessed 24 December 2015).
41.  See also Susan Kneebone, 'ASEAN and the Conceptualization of Refugee Protection in Southeastern Asian States', in *Regional Approaches to the Protection of Asylum Seekers: An International Legal Perspective*, ed. Professor Ademola Abass and Professor Francesca Ippolito (Aldershot: Ashgate Publishing, 2014), 295–323.
42.  B.S. Chimni, 'Status of Refugees in India: Strategic Ambiguity', in *Refugees and the State: Practices of Asylum and Care in India, 1947–2000*, ed. Ranabir Samaddar (New Delhi:

SAGE Publications India, 2003), 443–71. As Chimni opines, countries such as India are concerned that accession to the convention would allow greater intrusion by the UNHCR of its national refugee regime.

43. B.S. Chimni, 'The Birth of a "Discipline": From Refugee to Forced Migration Studies', *Journal of Refugee Studies* 22, no. 1 (2008): 11–29; Davies, 'The Asian Rejection?'

44. Bangladesh, Bhutan, India, Maldives, Nepal, Pakistan and Sri Lanka are not state parties.

45. Brunei Darussalam, Indonesia, the Lao People's Democratic Republic, Malaysia, Myanmar, Singapore, Thailand and Vietnam are not state parties. Timor Leste, not yet an ASEAN member, is a state party.

46. Alice M. Nah, 'Struggling with (Il)legality: The Indeterminate Functioning of Malaysia's Borders for Asylum Seekers, Refugees and Stateless Persons', in *Borderscapes: Hidden Geographies and Politics at Territory's Edge*, ed. Prem Kumar Rajaram and Carl Grundy-Warr (Minneapolis: University of Minnesota Press, 2007), 35–64; Pia Anjolie Oberoi, *Exile and Belonging: Refugees and State Policy in South Asia* (Oxford: Oxford University Press, 2006); Ranabir Samaddar, ed., *Refugees and the State: Practices of Asylum and Care in India, 1947–2000* (New Delhi: SAGE Publications India, 2003).

47. Martin Jones, 'Moving beyond Protection Space: Developing a Law of Asylum in South East Asia', in *Refugee Protection and the Role of Law: Conflicting Identities*, ed. Susan Kneebone, Dallal Stevens, and Loretta Baldassar (London: Routledge, 2014), 257.

48. Robyn Sampson, 'Mandatory, Non-Reviewable, Indefinite: Immigration Detention in Australia', in *Immigration Detention: The Migration of a Policy and Its Human Impact*, ed. Amy Nethery and Stephanie J. Silverman (London and New York: Routledge, 2015), 104–13.

49. See ABC News, 'Cambodia to Take Refugees in $40 Million Deal with Australia', ABC (Online ed., 26 September 2014), http://www.abc.net.au/news/2014-09-26/cambodia-to-take-refugees-in-40-million-deal-with/5773282 (accessed 16 December 2015).

50. The obligations of the 1951 Convention do not extend to Hong Kong through the historic application of Article 40, first during British colonial rule and more recently by China.

51. Brian Barbour, 'Protection in Practice: The Situation of Refugees in East Asia', 2 *Nanmin Kenkyu Journal* [Refugee Studies Journal] 81 (2012) (published in Japanese; English original available at: http://www.refugeestudies.jp/)

52. Ibid.

53. Howard Adelman, ed., *Protracted Displacement in Asia: No Place to Call Home* (London: Ashgate, 2013); Sriprapha Petcharamesree, 'International Protection and Public Accountability: The Roles of Civil Society', in *The UNHCR and the Supervision of International Refugee Law*, ed. James C. Simeon (Cambridge: Cambridge University Press, 2013), 275–85.

54. Hans Schattle and Jennifer McCann, 'The Pursuit of State Status and the Shift toward International Norms: South Korea's Evolution as a Host Country for Refugees', *Journal of Refugee Studies* 27, no. 3 (2014): 317–37.

55. See: http://wao.org.my/file/file/Migration%20Working%20Group%20Joint%20UPR%202013%20Submission.pdf (accessed 14 December 2015).

56. Petrice Flowers, *Refugees, Women, and Weapons: International Norm Adoption and Compliance in Japan* (Stanford, CA: Stanford University Press, 2009).

57. See also Chimni, 'Status of Refugees in India: Strategic Ambiguity'.

58. UNHCR, 'UNHCR Position Paper on the Strategic Use of Resettlement' (Annual Tripartite Consultations on Resettlement, Geneva, 2010), http://www.refworld.org/pdfid/4c0d10ac2.pdf (accessed 24 December 2015).

59. Asia Pacific Refugee Rights Network, 'Human Rights Lawyer and APRRN Member Threatened in Sri Lanka', *Asia Pacific Refugee Rights Network*, 1 March 2013, http://www.aprrn.info/1/index.php/news/178-human-rights-lawyer-and-aprrn-member-threatened-in-sri-lanka (accessed 14 December 2015). In June 2013, for example, Sri Lankan human rights lawyer Lakshan Dias, one of the founding members of APRRN, was subject to surveillance and questioning. Human rights groups were concerned that he would be abducted, tortured and forcibly disappeared.

60. Constitution of the Asia Pacific Refugee Rights Network, http://www.aprrn.info/1/images/APRRN-Constitution-2014-final.pdf (accessed 14 December 2015).

61. Personal communication with Julia Mayerhoffer, APRRN Interim Executive Director, 7 October 2015.

62. A public list of the APRRN's members can be found on its website, http://www.aprrn.info/1/index.php/about-us/membership (accessed 14 December 2015).

63. R. Charli Carpenter, 'Governing the Global Agenda: "Gatekeepers" and "Issue Adoption" in Transnational Advocacy Networks', in *Who Governs the Globe?*, ed. Deborah D. Avant, Martha Finnemore, and Susan K. Sell, Cambridge Studies in International Relations (Cambridge: Cambridge University Press, 2010), 202–37.

64. Constitution of the Asia Pacific Refugee Rights Network, http://www.aprrn.info/1/images/APRRN-Constitution-2014-final.pdf (accessed 14 December 2015).

65. Since the first Asia Pacific Consultation on Refugee Rights (APCRR1) in 2008, APRRN members have met again in Bangkok in 2009 and 2010, Seoul in 2012, and Bangkok in 2014. The reports from these conferences are available on the APRRN's website.

66. I am indebted to James Thomson for sharing this observation (personal communication, 6 November 2015).

67. Nevertheless, the APRRN's joint statements now include a standard disclaimer: 'While APRRN statements are prepared in consultation with APRRN members, they do not necessarily reflect the views of all APRRN members.' See for example, APRRN Statement, 'Japan's Review of their Refugee Status Determination System Raises New Concerns', http://www.aprrn.info/1/images/PDF/APRRN_Japan_Statement_29052015.pdf (accessed 14 December 2014).

68. APRRN Newsletter, September 2013. More information on SUAKA can be found on its website, http://suaka.or.id/ (accessed 14 December 2015).

69. See SSRN, 'Launching Ceremony: Refugee Rights Network (RRN) Pakistan', 2015, http://rrnpk.org/launching-ceremony-of-rrn-pakistan/ (accessed 14 December 2015).

70. Chimni, 'The Birth of a "Discipline"'. In his seminal paper, Chimni notes that the UNHCR plays a significant role in the production and dissemination of knowledge about refugees. I argue that this observation applies to the way that local civil society actors understand the realities, limits and possibilities of refugee protection.

71. Personal communication with Brian Barbour, 13 October 2015.

72. I am indebted to James Thomson for sharing these observations (personal communication, 6 November 2015).

73. Peter Hayes and Kiho Yi, *Complexity, Security and Civil Society in East Asia: Foreign Policies and the Korean Peninsula* (Cambridge: Open Book Publishers, 2015).

74. For example, the Regional Experts Roundtable on Alternatives to Detention for Children, 19–20 November 2015, Bangkok, Thailand.

75. http://www.dpiap.org/resources/pdf/AICHR_5_YEAR_work_plan2010-2015_12_07_04.pdf (accessed 14 December 2015).

76. Susan Kneebone, 'The Bali Process and Global Refugee Policy in the Asia–Pacific Region', *Journal of Refugee Studies*, 29 June 2014.

77. Ibid.

78. It is often difficult to justify the 'added value' of coordination and facilitation to donors through traditional rubrics of 'impact' and 'effectiveness'. Most discernible outcomes are by definition the product of partnerships and often have long gestation periods.

79. Kathryn Sikkink, 'The Power of Networks in International Politics', in *Networked Politics: Agency, Power, and Governance*, ed. Miles Kahler, Cornell Studies in Political Economy (Ithaca, NY: Cornell University Press, 2009), 230.

# The ethics of resettlement: Australia and the Asia-Pacific Region

Maria O'Sullivan

*Faculty of Law, Monash University, Melbourne, Australia*

One of the key problems at the heart of refugee protection today is that there are large numbers of refugees attempting to seek asylum and insufficient political will in many asylum-host states to receive refugees in their territories. A proportion of these attempt to come to Australia to seek refuge – either by requesting a resettlement place through the auspices of the United Nations High Commissioner for Refugees, or by arriving directly in Australian territory (by boat or plane). Asylum-seekers who arrive by boat are disadvantaged and penalised under Australian law in that they are excluded from Australian territory and processed offshore in third countries. Successive Australian governments justify these measures by emphasising that resettlement is the 'proper' mode for claiming asylum which ensures protection is given to those refugees who are most in need. This raises fundamental ethical questions: are those chosen by resettlement countries such as Australia necessarily the refugees who are most in need? Is resettlement as a concept ethical? And should resettlement be utilised to prevent and penalise spontaneous arrivals attempting to seek asylum in a country?

## I.  Introduction

Contemporary refugee policy is facing a number of fundamental questions about how to fairly and equitably share the 'burden' of refugee flows. The numbers of refugees worldwide seeking protection far exceeds the number of protection places available, making asylum a 'scarce resource'. There are currently 19.5 million refugees worldwide[1] and it is widely recognised that developing countries and those neighbouring refugee-producing states bear an unfair share of hosting refugees.[2] Indeed, it is estimated that 86% of refugees are now hosted by developing countries.[3] Given those figures, it may be asked whether receiving states in the industrialised world, such as Australia, Canada, the United States (US) and Europe, are engaged in sufficient 'burden-sharing' and what constitutes an adequate legal and ethical response to this crisis.

Resettlement is the process by which persons assessed by the Office of the United Nations High Commissioner for Refugees (UNHCR) as refugees are selected to travel to and resettle permanently in another country.[4] It is perceived as an important aspect of refugee protection: it has long been one of UNHCR's three durable solutions[5] and UNHCR constantly urges developed states to resettle more refugees.[6] However, resettlement places offered in the industrialised world are very low in comparison to demand.[7]

This is starkly illustrated by the response to the Syrian crisis: it is estimated that the neighbouring Middle-Eastern countries of Lebanon, Jordan, Turkey, Iraq and Egypt now host more than four million registered refugees from Syria.[8] In contrast, major industrialised countries have made available only 96,688 places to Syrian refugees via resettlement since 2013 (plus an open-ended pledge by the US).[9] These 'burden-sharing' dynamics in relation to developing countries are also reflected in the Asia Pacific region, where a significant proportion of the 3.5 million refugees are hosted in countries such as Pakistan (1.6 million refugees)[10] and Malaysia (98,000 refugees).[11]

The ability of countries to meet the levels of current resettlement needs, both worldwide and in the Asia Pacific region, is therefore very limited. In the context of Australia, the number of persons seeking protection via the resettlement programme is very high, ranging from 40,000 to 50,000 in past years.[12] In response, Australia offers a quota of 13,750 protection places per year, from which both onshore and resettlement places are allocated.[13]

In addition to a deficit in resettlement places, there are also ethical questions raised as to how resettlement programmes operate. Three states have traditionally been the leaders in resettlement: the US, Canada and Australia.[14] A number of researchers argue that resettlement decisions in these states are politically influenced by factors such as foreign policy and electoral interests.[15] Interestingly, these three states also have restrictive policies for those asylum-seekers who attempt to claim refugee status onshore, particularly if they do so without prior authorisation.[16] Thus, whilst resettlement is used as a humanitarian measure, it is also used by some states as justification for controlling the entry of other asylum-seekers. It can therefore be used as part of a broader policy of deterrence.

An example of this is Australian policy and discourse which positions resettlement as the central focus of a managed migration system. It disadvantages and penalises 'unauthorised maritime arrivals' – those attempting to enter Australian territory by boat to seek asylum – as interfering with that orderly system. In doing so, the government has framed resettlement as providing asylum to those most in 'need' of protection. Political and media discourse in Australia reinforces this discourse by using the language of a 'queue',[17] which boat arrivals are portrayed as evading (thereby taking protection places away from 'genuine' refugees waiting in overseas camps). It has also entered into arrangements with other countries in the Asia Pacific, namely Papua New Guinea and Nauru, to process and resettle those asylum-seekers who attempt to seek asylum in Australia by boat (called 'offshore processing' and 'regional resettlement'). Further, the Australian government promotes an idealised form of resettlement based on a notion of the deserving 'camp refugee' which represents an overly simplistic picture of the broad spectrum of experiences of those awaiting resettlement, including the large numbers of asylum-seekers residing in urban environments.[18]

Against this background, this article seeks to deconstruct the notion of resettlement from various ethical perspectives. It will use Australia's refugee policy as an example. Australia will be the focus because in addition to prioritising resettlement as the primary avenue for refugee protection, it also carries out a concomitant (linked) penalisation of boat arrivals. Further, it will discuss the ethics of resettlement agreements made between states, such as those agreed between Australia and countries in the Asia Pacific region. This article will be structured as follows: Part II will briefly discuss the way in which UNHCR posits resettlement as serving protection needs, before discussing, in Part III, how Australia operates its resettlement programme. Part IV will then analyse the operation of Australia's resettlement regime from an ethical perspective.

## II.  Resettlement and protection needs

Most states in the world are bound by obligations towards refugees set out in international treaties and regional arrangements. The primary treaty on refugee protection is the 1951 Convention on the Status of Refugees ('the Refugee Convention'),[19] to which there are 146 state parties. The preamble to the convention recognises the need for burden-sharing amongst states, stating that:

> ...the grant of asylum may place unduly heavy burdens on certain countries, and that a satisfactory solution of a problem of which the United Nations has recognized the international scope and nature cannot therefore be achieved without international cooperation.

Despite this invocation for international cooperation, the convention does not oblige states to take refugees directly from overseas locations (such as from camps in Africa). In this sense, resettlement is a voluntary, discretionary act by states. Although international cooperation via resettlement is not a binding obligation, UNHCR classifies it as 'a vital instrument of international protection, integral to comprehensive protection and durable solutions strategies'.[20] It has stated that it serves three important purposes:

> *First*, it is a tool to provide international protection and meet the specific needs of individual refugees whose life, liberty, safety, health or other fundamental rights are at risk in the country where they have sought refuge.
>
> *Second*, it is a durable solution for larger numbers or groups of refugees, alongside the other durable solutions of voluntary repatriation and local integration.
>
> *Third*, it can be a tangible expression of international solidarity and a responsibility sharing mechanism, allowing States to help share each other's burdens, and reduce problems impacting the country of first asylum.[21]

The latter emphasis on burden-sharing is of interest to the present discussion as it illustrates the framing of resettlement as a responsibility-sharing mechanism. However, as will be discussed below, resettlement is a tool used by only a small number of industrialised countries and does not currently operate to significantly reduce the impact of refugee flows on countries of first asylum.

The policies of UNHCR are important as it is responsible for referring refugees for resettlement to states. It has set out categories of those in need who will be eligible for recommendation for resettlement:

- those with immediate protection needs stemming from their lack of legal status, including those at risk of *refoulement*, arbitrary detention and persecution;
- particularly vulnerable refugees with needs that cannot be met in the asylum country including survivors of torture and violence, people with serious medical issues, women and girls, and some children and adolescents; and
- those who do not have current or future prospects of integrating into the local community or returning home safely.[22]

In order to refer refugees to resettlement countries like Australia, which have their own national priorities, UNHCR also considers whether the refugee is likely to meet the resettlement country's additional selection criteria, and whether they will fit within the government's priorities and quotas.[23]

It is acknowledged that, historically, resettlement has protected large numbers of refugees, but it has also served the interests of states. On the latter point, UNHCR recognises that in the aftermath of World War II and during the Cold War there was a 'desire of governments to facilitate the movement of certain people for foreign and domestic policy reasons'.[24] For instance, research indicates that there were strong ideological reasons underpinning resettlement of USSR refugees during the Cold War (support of defection from communist states and the need for labour in the post-war economic boom).[25] Due to a number of factors, including the significant increase in refugee numbers and the decreased influence of ideological factors, resettlement numbers worldwide have fallen dramatically in the past 30 or so years.[26] Globally, only one in ten persons in need of resettlement will be granted that outcome annually.[27] Resettlement has been critiqued as 'resource intensive' and a 'luxury solution'.[28] Indeed, there is a global 'resettlement crisis' due to limited resettlement places and an emphasis on return as the favoured solution.[29]

I will now turn to discuss how Australia operates its domestic resettlement programme.

## III. Australia's resettlement policy

### (A) *The development of refugee protection and resettlement in Australia*

Australia is a party to the 1951 Refugee Convention and its 1967 Protocol.[30] It therefore has an international legal obligation to deal with asylum-seekers who arrive in its territory or come under its jurisdiction in accordance with that convention. This means, amongst other things, that Australia must not return a refugee to a country where his life or freedom would be threatened on account of his race, religion, nationality, membership of a particular social group or political opinion (the *non-refoulement* principle).[31] As a party to the Refugee Convention, Australia is also obliged to grant refugees certain political and socio-economic rights.[32]

During the post-World War II period, Australia received substantial numbers of refugees and displaced persons under its general immigration intake.[33] Research has indicated that the decision to accept these persons were largely influenced by Cold War foreign policy considerations and the need for labour.[34] The immigration intake was also highly influenced by the so-called 'White Australia policy' which permitted authorities to discriminate on racial grounds.[35] Immigration and refugee policy in Australia changed quite dramatically in the 1970s when the White Australia policy was dismantled and Australia took in substantial numbers of refugees during the Indo-Chinese wars. During this period, Australia also formulated its first comprehensive Australian policy on refugees. This reinforced Australia's responsibility to admit refugees for resettlement and recognised that although Australia was a signatory to the 1951 Refugee Convention, the decision to accept refugees was the prerogative of the Australian government.[36]

Interestingly, Australia's response to refugee flows from Indo-China in the 1970s has informed its current emphasis on the need for orderly migration systems. Australia was involved in the Comprehensive Plan of Action (CPA) agreed to as a response to the Indo-Chinese boat arrivals. One of the objectives of this was to discourage the organisation of clandestine departures and to replace them with a reinvigorated and more effective system for regular departure and orderly migration.[37] As Susan Kneebone has noted:

> The CPA, designed to stem the flow of these people, had an important role in the development of Australian policy to spontaneous refugee arrivals. It reinforced the trend to selective resettlement, and the distinction between onshore asylum seekers and offshore refugees which persists in Australian refugee policy today.[38]

The selective nature of Australia's resettlement programme has continued from the 1980s to the present. Although the constitution of the intake has been influenced heavily by the geographical origin of conflict regions (e.g. the former Yugoslavia in the 1990s), there is also evidence that political interests have been a significant factor, with a heavy emphasis on resettlement from Africa in the late 1990s and early 2000s.[39] For instance, in the financial year 2003–2004, over 70% of refugee resettlement grants were allocated to Africa whilst only 24% were allocated to the Middle East and South-West Asia.[40] This was so despite the large numbers of asylum-seekers fleeing conflict areas in Afghanistan and Iraq during that time. This is also indicative of the prioritisation given to camp refugees in Australia's resettlement system.

Australian refugee policy underwent a major shift in 2001 due to a number of factors: the heightened border security which occurred after 9/11 and the political debates surrounding the refusal by Australian authorities to allow entry of a boat carrying asylum-seekers during the *MV Tampa* incident of August 2001.[41] The government discourse painted the asylum-seekers as 'queue jumpers' and the incident led to a number of legal changes, including the creation of the offshore processing system (the so-called 'Pacific Solution') later that same year.[42] A common link between these acts has been the emphasis on border security and deterrence of spontaneous asylum-seeker arrivals, specifically, those arriving by boat. These restrictive policies have, for the most part, been continued by successive governments.

I now turn to examine two particular features of the current operation of Australia's resettlement programme: First, the demarcation between the 'offshore' resettlement programme (operated via UNHCR referrals from source regions) and spontaneous boat arrivals who are deemed 'unauthorised' and treated accordingly. Second, the link between resettlement programme and spontaneous arrivals which mean that any protection visas[43] granted to boat arrivals are subtracted from the yearly resettlement quota.

#### (B) *Particular features of the Australian resettlement programme*

##### (i) *Resettlement versus onshore arrivals*

Australian law and policy makes a clear demarcation between 'resettlement' and 'onshore' arrivals. Under the resettlement programme, Australia sets a yearly quota for receiving refugees directly from countries hosting refugees, such as those in Africa and South-East Asia. These are usually persons who have been assessed to be refugees by UNHCR. However, refugees can also 'self-refer' by applying directly to the Australian embassy in the country to which they flee. Under both referral procedures, Australian authorities make a decision as to which refugees will be granted a resettlement visa. This visa decision is based on, amongst other things, applicable national priorities and the ability of the applicant to settle into Australian society.[44]

Australia sets a yearly limit for its refugee and humanitarian intake and has historically set that quota at around 13,750 places.[45] The offshore component of the refugee and humanitarian programme has two categories.

- The Refugee category for people subject to persecution in their home country and in need of resettlement. The majority of applicants who are considered under this category are identified and referred by UNHCR to Australia for resettlement.[46]

- The Special Humanitarian Program category for people who, while not being refugees, are subject to substantial discrimination amounting to a gross violation of their human rights in their home country.[47]

## (ii)   Onshore refugee visas and the 'resettlement queue'

One of the main problems with the way Australia's resettlement system operates is that any protection visas which are granted by Australian immigration authorities to refugees who apply *onshore* are subtracted from the quota set for resettlement visas under the Offshore Special Humanitarian Resettlement programme. That is, Australia links the two programmes numerically – distinguishing between refugees based on the means by which they made their asylum application. Australia is unique in this sense – no other country in the world formally subtracts onshore arrival refugee places from its resettlement quota. The reasoning of government authorities is that such an arrangement ensures that those most in need are given protection, rather than those that utilise people smugglers.[48]

This differentiated regime is reflected in the widespread public perception in Australian society that there is a resettlement 'queue' which boat arrivals are evading. Many commentators have argued that there is no 'resettlement queue'. As the leading international refugee law commentator, Jane McAdam notes:

> UNHCR's resettlement process does not operate like a queue, but more like a triage system in which needs are constantly reassessed. Someone who arrives today with an acute resettlement need, such as extreme vulnerability on account of sexual abuse or disability, may be prioritized ahead of someone who has been waiting for ten years.[49]

A number of non-governmental organisations (NGOs) in Australia have criticised the unwarranted linkage between the onshore and offshore visa system established in Australia. The Refugee Council of Australia points out that the two programmes are designed to meet quite different international responsibilities: the onshore protection programme aims to meet Australia's obligation as a party to the Refugee Convention whilst the offshore resettlement programme is a voluntary contribution to the sharing of responsibility for refugees for whom no other durable solution is available.[50] NGOs have also stated that the deterrence-based policies endorsed by both major parties in Australia 'are based on the highly problematic and erroneous premise that applying for resettlement from overseas is the only "right way" to seek protection as a refugee'.[51]

This prioritisation of resettlement is becoming more pronounced under Australian policy: in the financial year 2014–2015, a minimum of 11,000 places have been set aside for the overall offshore resettlement programme within the 13,750 total.[52] This represents a significant increase in the offshore allocation compared to previous years. There are two important changes to note here. First, there has been a significant shift in balance *within* the offshore stream: more places will be allocated to Special Humanitarian component and fewer for the Refugee component. Within this, priority is to be given to *family members* proposed through the Special Humanitarian programme (increased from 500 to 5000).[53] This represents a significant emphasis on family reunion over the protection of refugees. Second, this has implications for onshore refugee applications as only the *balance* of the yearly quota will be set aside for Permanent Protection visas granted onshore (for those who arrive with a visa, that is, by plane). Any onshore protection visa grants arising from Refugee Convention status will therefore be numerically limited. This can be done because legislation now permits the Minister for Immigration to place a yearly 'cap' on numbers of onshore protection visas granted.[54] This will effectively mean even if a person has been found by Australian authorities to be a refugee, they may have to wait an underdetermined period to be given a protection visa. Related legislative provisions also now provide that those boat arrivals who are not subjected to transfer to an offshore centre and are permitted to lodge a protection visa application[55] can only receive a temporary protection visa of three years' duration and will not be given a permanent protection visa.[56]

## (C) *Resettlement and penalisation of boat arrivals*

As part of the prioritisation given to orderly migration flows, the Australian Migration Act establishes a clear demarcation between 'lawful' and 'unlawful' non-citizens, which is dependent on the holding of a visa. This is illustrated by sub-section 4(2) of that legislation, which gives primacy to the visa system as the only source of lawfulness of entry and stay in Australia:

> (2) To advance its object, this Act provides for visas permitting non-citizens to enter or remain in Australia and the Parliament intends that this Act be the only source of the right of non-citizens to so enter or remain.

Sub-section 42(1) of the Migration Act specifically provides that subject to certain exceptions not generally applicable to asylum-seekers, 'a non-citizen must not travel to Australia without a visa that is in effect'. Following on from this, asylum-seekers who arrive by boat (without a visa) are designated as 'unauthorised maritime arrivals'.[57] Those asylum-seekers who arrive in Australia without such authorisation are subject to draconian policies. Boat arrivals are subject to lengthy mandatory detention and exclusion from Australian territory.[58] They are liable to be transferred from Australian territory to the Pacific Island states of Nauru and Papua New Guinea ('offshore countries'), where they are detained and their claims are processed. What is significant about this regime is that any persons recognised as refugees by these offshore countries are no longer resettled in Australia, but will be resettled in the offshore countries or other states in the region, including Nauru and Cambodia.[59] This is controversial for a number of reasons. First, UNHCR and many international and national NGOs, have found that conditions in the offshore locations breach fundamental human rights of asylum-seekers.[60] In particular, the UNHCR has stated that the offshore centres lack fair, efficient and expeditious systems for assessing refugee claims.[61] Second, it is arguable that Australia should be the country which accepts those persons found to be refugees under the extraterritorial processing system, rather than providing funds to countries in the region so that they may 'resettle' those refugees. This is particularly so given that conditions in such countries may not permit safe resettlement. Amnesty International has questioned the ability of Papua New Guinea to successfully and safely resettle large numbers of refugees, noting it is:

> ... an impoverished country with high rates of unemployment, serious problems with violence – particularly against women – and a general intolerance for outsiders ... It has a poor track record of protecting the limited numbers of refugees it has received to date. The prospects of successfully integrating larger numbers of refugees from a greater variety of cultures and faiths are dim.[62]

Likewise, many commentators (including the author) have raised concerns over the use of Cambodia as a country to which refugees processed under the extraterritorial regime can be resettled.[63] This raises a question as to whether a country such as Australia can 'outsource' both its processing and settlement obligations under the Refugee Convention. The above analysis is relevant to resettlement because although there is substantial public concern and political debate as to how to deter asylum-seekers from making what is often a danger-ous journey by boat from Indonesia to Australia,[64] the punitive approach taken to those asylum-seekers who arrive by boat is also influenced significantly by the dichotomy between the 'proper' orderly resettlement route and the 'unlawful' boat arrival cohort.

### (D)  *Regionalising resettlement in the Asia-Pacific region*

The use of offshore processing and resettlement by Australia is part of its attempt to estab-lish a wider regional framework between countries in South-East Asia. Some groundwork for this has been done via creation of the 'Regional Cooperation Framework' agreed at the Bali Process in 2011.[65] As part of a drive towards regionalism in the Asia-Pacific region and a strong political desire to stop unauthorised boat arrivals, Australia has attempted to fina-lise agreements with neighbouring countries to take refugees. For instance, in 2011, the Australian government controversially finalised an 'arrangement' with Malaysia, under which up to 800 asylum-seekers who arrived by sea in Australia were to be transferred to Malaysia for assessment of their claims to be refugees. In return, Australia agreed to receive 4000 recognised refugees from Malaysia (the so-called 'Malaysian Solution').[66] Interestingly, the swap was to be accompanied by an increase in resettlement numbers for Australia, with the Australian prime minister agreeing that in exchange 'Australia will expand its humanitarian program and take on a greater burden-sharing responsibility for resettling refugees currently residing in Malaysia.'[67] Such an increase was made in the year 2012–2013, when the resettlement quota was raised to 20,000 places, but it has since been reduced back to its historical level of 13,750.[68] Ultimately, the transfer pro-visions of the Malaysian Arrangement could not be carried out as the High Court of Aus-tralia held that the ministerial declaration underlying the arrangement failed to comply with the Migration Act.[69] The government did implement the resettlement provisions of the arrangement, although it did so by taking those places from the regular offshore programme instead of providing additional places as it had originally indicated it would.

Following this High Court decision, the Australian government commissioned a three-member 'Expert Panel on Asylum Seekers' to review Australia's refugee policy. This was in part a response to the High Court's decision on the Malaysian Solution, and was also prompted by a number of fatalities of asylum-seekers at sea, and an extended and highly publicised parliamentary debate about the direction of Australia's refugee policy.[70] The report (released in 2012) advocated, amongst other things, a more regional approach to resettlement in order to decrease the demand for people smugglers and therefore to halt unauthorised boat arrivals. Specifically, the report recommended that the Australian huma-nitarian programme should be more focused on asylum-seeker flows moving from source countries into South-East Asia.[71] The panel stated:

> Australia needs a substantially increased and *more regionally focused* Humanitarian Program while still maintaining capacity to respond to other regions of concern to Australia and UNHCR such as Africa. Such an initiative would serve Australian national interests as well as our international engagement. It would enhance the scope of our cooperation with regional partners.[72]

Despite this, the current government has moved away from this regional focus in the area of resettlement. Under a policy introduced in late 2014, persons recognised as refugees by UNHCR in Indonesia will no longer be accepted for resettlement in Australia.[73] This raises questions about Australia's labelling of resettlement as the only means by which asylum-seekers should obtain protection and the 'queue' rationale underlying refugee policy in Australia. It also appears to contradict the rationale of preventing deaths at sea, as arguably granting resettlement to recognised refugees in Indonesia is one way in which to reduce the numbers of asylum-seekers attempting to reach Australia by boat.

### (E) *Resettlement and unauthorised arrivals in Canada and the US*

Before turning to analyse Australia's resettlement regime from an ethical perspective, it is worth noting that Australia is not the only resettlement country which penalises or deters 'unauthorised' asylum-seeker arrivals. I note that similar prioritisation of resettlement is reflected in policy in the US and in Canada which offer significant numbers of resettlement places and also deter spontaneous arrivals. For instance, as is the case with Australia, Canada has traditionally been a country which offers a significant number of resettlement places to refugees as part of a planned and controlled migration programme.[74] However, under relatively recent reforms to its law, Canada now penalises those who arrive in Canada unlawfully. Under the Protecting Canada's Immigration System Act, the minister of public safety can designate the arrival of a group of individuals who entered or attempted to enter Canada in a manner that runs contrary to Canada's immigration laws, as a 'designated irregular arrival'.[75] Individuals who arrive as part of a designated irregular arrival who do not hold a visa to enter Canada ('designated foreign nationals')[76] will be subject to different detention rules and will have no access to the Refugee Appeal Division at the Immigration and Refugee Board of Canada. They will also be subject to restrictions on applying for permanent residence, travel and family sponsorship.[77] This represents a significant change in Canadian refugee policy which has historically been regarded as generous and liberal. As in Australia, policy change has been heavily influenced by a discourse by government and the media which has focused on the 'illegal nature' of boat arrivals.[78] The Canadian scholar Labman has written extensively on that country's refugee policy and says that Canada uses resettlement to 'soften the blow' of restrictive asylum legislation and 'divides refugee flows into two categories of deserving and undeserving'.[79] She discusses the 'increasing tendency of the Canadian government to position resettlement against in-country asylum rather than present the two streams of refugee protection in their traditionally complementary roles'.[80] Of concern is that the Canadian authorities are increasingly utilising the 'queue' terminology to justify restrictive legislation for those seeking to apply onshore via boat.[81]

The resettlement policy of the US also prioritises resettlement and deters onshore asylum-seekers. Although it is widely regarded as having a generous resettlement policy, it has a long history of interdicting Cuban, Haitian, Chinese, and other asylum-seekers and migrants at sea.[82] It has also tightened its asylum criteria in recent years.[83] Further, some commentators note that resettlement priorities are highly politicised. For instance, S.B. Ray notes that the greatest beneficiaries of the US resettlement programme have traditionally been refugees from countries where the US has engaged in war (such as Vietnam and Iraq) or nationals of enemy nations.[84] Thus, the US resettlement programme has been criticised for prioritising foreign policy considerations over refugee protection needs.[85]

Having noted the above, it should be recognised that neither Canada nor the US (nor indeed any other country in the world) sets off onshore asylum arrival places against their resettlement programme so as to penalise 'queue-jumping' spontaneous arrivals.

Further, Australia is unique in that any boat arrivals taken to offshore processing locations, and recognised as refugees there, are resettled outside Australia. That is, whilst there may be issues with deterrence in Canada and the US, they are not seeking to *substitute* resettlement for in-country asylum in the same way as Australia.

I will now turn to deconstruct the use of resettlement by Australia from an ethical perspective.

## IV.   Questioning the ethics of resettlement

### (A)   *Normative framework: the collective v the individual*

As noted above, UNHCR encourages resettlement as a responsibility sharing mechanism. In this way, the international refugee protection regime is being framed as a 'global public good'[86] which is supposed to be shared equitably amongst states. As Astri Suhrke points out, 'arrangements that distribute refugees or asylum seekers according to principles of need and equity suggest benefits to all sides'.[87] However, as Alexander Betts notes, there is no clearly defined normative framework for dealing with refugees who remain in source regions in the global south.[88] As such:

> The absence of clear norms on burden-sharing thereby contributes to a situation in which the states with the least capacity to contribute to refugee protection have the greatest responsibility.[89]

Astri Suhrke has also questioned the capacity for burden-sharing schemes to create greater equity in the asylum burden:

> Sharing schemes may … become a mechanism for states to fix their commitments at very low levels, thereby institutionalising a burden-shift among regions and restricting the rights of refugees.[90]

In addition to this, the notion of asylum as a collective responsibility may act to limit the individual agency of asylum-seekers. Under international human rights principles, asylum-seekers have the right to seek asylum.[91] The Refugee Convention also obliges states not to return refugees back to a place of harm under the non-refoulement principle.[92] Thus, arguably, asylum-seekers have a right to seek asylum in a country such as Australia, without having to wait to be selected for resettlement. However, the notion that there is a right to seek asylum in a country of one's *choosing* is a contested one.[93] As Kneebone notes, the right to seek asylum has tended to be interpreted by states as 'conferring an obligation to do so in the first "safe" place of asylum'.[94] This approach is strongly reflected in Australian policy which penalises secondary or irregular movements.

The notion that asylum-seekers can and should be able to exercise individual agency by seeking asylum in a country of their choosing illustrates the choice paradigm at the centre of contemporary refugee protection: that of the individual agency of asylum-seekers which is set against the state interest in selecting refugees via resettlement. It can be argued that asylum-seekers as individuals with agency should be permitted to exercise that agency by seeking asylum in a country of their choice (for instance, where they already have family or ethnic connections). This does not necessarily require states to give *effect* to that choice by granting such persons refugee status, but it does suggest that the exercise of agency by states (in selecting certain refugees via resettlement) is not absolute, and must also be considered against the exercise of agency by individual refugees. In examining any conflict between state selectivity and individual agency, it may be the case that prioritising resettlement over spontaneous arrivals reduces asylum-seekers' agency. Arguably then, an emphasis on resettlement as the primary means of obtaining refugee protection fails to adequately reflect the right of refugees to seek asylum.

On the issue of individual choice and burden-sharing, Joan Fitzpatrick seems to suggest that burden-sharing (if it results in increased protection for a larger number of refugees) may be morally acceptable even if this results in dilution of individual preference:

> From a moral perspective, one might criticise burden-sharing arrangements for treating asylum seekers as an undifferentiated mass rather than as persons with discrete interests and preferences. Yet of all the measures that objectify asylum seekers, effective burden-sharing measures that increased overall opportunities for safe haven would be the easiest to defend in moral terms.[95]

Thus, in an ideal world, a programme of resettlement which reasonably meets demand and is based on equitable principles, may be ethically acceptable. However, the way in which resettlement is actually practiced by states (as discussed above) suggests that this ideal is not being met as it does not increase overall opportunities for refugee protection globally. Indeed, it could be argued that Australia's use of resettlement reduces the overall opportunities for refugee protection as it penalises large numbers of asylum-seekers who arrive by boat – thereby excluding significant numbers of refugees from the Australian refugee protection system. In this context, dilution of individual agency may suggest an ethical repudiation of resettlement, particularly given the terms of the Refugee Convention which relies on presence onshore. Even if this is not so, it appears to be clear that state selectivity in using resettlement to *punish* those who choose to seek asylum on the shores of asylum-host states is ethically unsustainable – a point to which I will come later in the article.

## (B) *Ethics of immigration v. ethics of refugee policy*

Before examining the specific ethical arguments surrounding resettlement, the particularities of refugee policy in the context of the broader issue of immigration must be noted. There is a significant body of literature which discusses matters related to resettlement, such as the ethics of immigration, the duty to rescue and global justice.[96] These works make various arguments for a duty to assist those in need – whether due to economic disparities or humanitarian reasons. For instance, Joseph Carens has written quite extensively on the ethics of immigration.[97] More generally, there are excellent works on issues of distributive justice by writers such as John Rawls.[98] However, there are comparatively few works written on refugees specifically, and not a great many on the ethics of granting resettlement – that is, whether it is ethical for a state to choose those refugees it wishes to grant protection to, the extent to which resettlement priorities should be framed by regional priorities and whether it should be used as a reason for punitive measures against spontaneous arrivals. Matthew Gibney has written a valuable and erudite text on some ethical aspects of asylum in which he makes some interesting statements on resettlement.[99] Apart from this, whilst I refer to the general ethical literature on immigration and related matters, I acknowledge some caution must be used in applying that analysis wholesale to the asylum context where the relevant legal issues and political questions are quite different. This is due to the fact that, at least in theory, asylum constitutes an exception to the normal immigration controls exercised as a central part of state sovereignty.[100] That is, asylum-seekers have a right to seek asylum, which differentiates them from other types of migrants (because refugees *are* in a special position vis-à-vis a destination state, as recognised in international law).

I now turn to analyse resettlement from an ethical perspective. In doing so, I will examine two main questions:

- Is resettlement as a concept ethical?
- Should resettlement be utilised to prevent and penalise spontaneous arrivals attempting to seek asylum in a country?

### (C) *Is resettlement as a concept ethical?*

In answering this question, I will be asking whether resettlement caters for those in greatest need of refugee protection and how we can and should define 'need'. Should states be permitted to select only those refugees they wish to integrate into their society? Or should they accept all on the basis of need? Then I will move on to examine more closely the various ethical positions taken when defining the need for protection and the duty to rescue.

### (i) *Liberalism v. communitarianism – open borders and state control*

Under a liberalist view of asylum, immigration restrictions are inconsistent with basic liberal egalitarian ideals, including freedom, equal opportunity and moral equality. As such, writers such as Joseph Carens argue that liberal states have a prima facie duty to maintain open borders.[101] In contrast, a number of commentators argue that state self-interest in controlling borders and limiting numbers of asylum-seekers should be considered in ethical discussions of refugee policy as a means of reaching a realistic or 'non-ideal' ethical position. Michael Walzer presents what is known as the communitarian view of immigration centred on the moral importance of communal self-determination. Walzer understands political membership as a social good, constituted by the shared understandings of a political community. Walzer argues that states should be able to control immigration:

> The politics and the culture of modern democracy probably require the kind of largeness, and also the kind of boundedness, that states provide...At some level of political organisation, something like the sovereign state must take shape and claim the authority to make its own admissions policy, to control and sometimes restrain the flow of immigrants.[102]

There is also an argument that admission of non-citizens into a community depends on an acceptance of that decision by the society of the host country. As Walzer points out, 'the sharing of sensibilities and intuitions among the members of a historical community is a fact of life'.[103] He also notes that the nature of adjustments to distributive decisions in political communities will depend upon understandings shared among the citizens about the value of cultural diversity, local autonomy and similar factors.[104] Walzer therefore notes that:

> The community itself is a good – conceivably the most important good – that gets distributed. But it is a good that can only be distributed by taking people in, where all the senses of that latter phrase are relevant: they must be physically admitted and politically received. Hence membership cannot be handed out by some external agency; its value depends upon an internal decision.[105]

Applying this to the Australian situation, it appears that the current offshore processing regime and resettlement policy is supported by both of the major political parties (with some only minor differences in policy detail),[106] in addition to receiving support in the electorate.[107] Arguably, then, the Australian political community has made a distributive decision about membership which prioritises selection via resettlement.

The validity of this approach can be questioned from two angles. First, the ethical analysis of immigration and the importance of community made by writers such as Walzer cannot be imported wholesale into the refugee context. As discussed above, refugees are distinct from immigrants for several reasons. Therefore, although Australia may wish to control intake by selecting refugees via resettlement, this cannot be paired with exclusion of other refugees as the Australian community (via its government) has accepted responsibilities by signing the Refugee Convention. The second related question is the extent to which we should ethically validate the practice of states that runs counter to its international responsibilities. Even if we accept that state interest and the will of a democracy to limit refugee applications may be a legitimate factor in ethical debates, it does not justify breaches of individual rights (such as those taking place in Nauru and Papua New Guinea). That is, if resettlement is operated so it has an undesirable side-effect (that being the breach of the fundamental human rights of persons in offshore locations) then it cannot be classed as acting for the greater global good. Putting it another way, a state cannot ethically support a policy of resettlement by reference to values of fairness, distribution of justice and need if this is coupled with a policy of unfairness and injustice to those who choose *not* to use that resettlement avenue.

In questioning the ethics of resettlement as a concept in this context, the approaches taken by consequentialist theories (in particular, utilitarianism) are of interest. As Scheffler explains: '[c]onsequentialism in its purest and simplest form is a moral doctrine which says that the right act in any given situation is the one that will produce the best overall outcome, as judged from an impersonal standpoint which gives equal weight to the interests of everyone ... ' Utilitarianism is the most recognised form of consequentialism, this says that: ' ... the proper action is the one which maximizes overall human happiness'.[108]

According to these theories, one should examine the consequences of an action and its effect on the common good, rather than on individual rights. Using this approach, it can be argued that resettlement as a notion is ethically valid because (when utilised in an ideal way), it allows states a level of control over the intake process (via quotas and selection); the consequence of this is that they will be more likely to give protection to a higher number of refugees than they would otherwise. That is, in an ideal setting, with states acting for the common good, states would properly share the global asylum 'burden' by taking resettlement refugees according to refugee need, and resettlement would ideally result in the protection of the greatest number of refugees. This is on the basis that states are more likely to increase refugee places if they are able to do so in a controlled manner according to national priorities. However, in reality, this is not how resettlement works. As noted above, overall opportunities for refugee protection are not maximised despite Australia's emphasis on burden-sharing via resettlement. Compared to the refugees hosted in the South Asian region, such as Malaysia and Pakistan, Australia hosts a relatively small number.[109] In such a situation, the emphasis is also on the consequences for the greater good (overall refugee protection spaces being provided) rather than on individual refugee agency and choice (the right of refugees to travel to their preferred country of asylum and seek refugee status there).

I will now turn to examine the concept of need and how resettlement is said to meet that requirement.

(ii)  *Need part 1: proximity and the duty to rescue*

Countries such as Australia justify their prioritisation of resettlement over spontaneous arrivals by stating that resettlement serves those refugees in greatest need of protection. This resettlement narrative posits refugees in camps in source regions as the 'deserving refugees'. Indeed, some commentators argue that the Refugee Convention operates to prioritise those that can pay to leave their country of origin:

> The Convention-based system, as it currently operates, gives priority to those present, on the basis of their mobility (and capacity to pay), not to those with the greatest need. Women and children predominate in refugee camp populations, suffer most human rights abuses, and are most vulnerable in refugee situations...women, especially those caring for children, are less mobile and less able to organise international travel in many refugee producing countries.[110]

Whilst those who are resettled via UNHCR are undoubtedly in great need of protection, evidence shows that state resettlement decisions are influenced by domestic political and community concerns, such as the ability of selected refugees to integrate into the host society.[111] As discussed above, resettlement priorities set by countries such as the US and Australia have been strongly influenced by political and foreign policy considerations. Thus, it can be argued that resettlement is not solely a humanitarian act and is influenced greatly by factors other than refugee need.

In discussing this issue, we must also ask whether the need of those refugees waiting for resettlement is greater than those who choose to seek asylum onshore in countries such as Australia. It could be argued that Australia has a greater ethical obligation to those asylum-seekers who reach its shores and who have nowhere else to go. The ethical analysis carried out on the relevance of proximity and the duty to rescue is helpful here. Kamm has argued that geographical distance can indeed matter: that in some circumstances, a duty to rescue people who are far from us may be less than our duty to rescue people who are near us. Kamm recognises that where there is a distant person in need and there is 'some particular agent whose act would be instrumentally determinate to ending peril' then there may be a duty to act.[112] However, Kamm then argues that 'as the costs involved in acting go up, a duty to aid a distant person may be defeated whereas a duty to aid a near person would not be'.[113] Her reasoning for this comes from her earlier premise that:

> ... in a context where the cost of aid to the agent is low and the effects of not aiding are great to a stranger, the duty to aid a stranger who is near and the duty to aid a stranger who is far may be equally strong.[114]

Others have suggested that geographical distance is not relevant to such situations. Peter Singer famously used an example of a drowning child to illustrate various duties to rescue.[115] He concludes that geographical distance may not matter morally, so, for instance, we cannot discriminate against someone merely because s/he is far away from us.[116] Bauhn also appears to agree with Singer, stating that:

> To the extent that the rights of the distant needy and the near needy are equally deserving of our support, and to the extent that neither rescue operation requires that we sacrifice any part of our own basic well-being, it would seem reasonable to conclude that our duty to rescue the distant needy is as strong as our duty to rescue the near needy. Hence, I believe that Singer is right when he holds that geographical distance, taken by itself, does not matter morally.[117]

Whilst that may be the case, I would submit that there is a greater ethical obligation on states to 'rescue' the needy refugee who is attempting to seek refuge on our shores, rather than those hosted in third countries. Taking the example of boat arrivals to illustrate this: if persons leave their country of residence and attempt to seek Australia's protection by travelling in a boat on the high seas, they become vulnerable to danger on the seas in a space where protection is not forthcoming unless a state accepts them into their territory and treats them in accordance with the obligations set out in the Refugee Convention and other treaties. Further, it is arguable that the refugees awaiting resettlement in Africa can also be helped by other countries, not just Australia. In contrast, those asylum-seekers leaving Indonesia in a boat and seeking refugee status on the shores of Australia can only be assisted *by Australia*.

In such situations, Australia would be under a duty to aid and protect.

A counterargument to this is that the burden of dealing with those refugees should be shared with all countries within the South-East Asian region. Indeed, this is central to the agenda of the Australian government via its push for a regional resettlement framework. Whilst this may be the case, asylum-seekers at sea in or near Australian territorial waters would clearly engage only the obligation of *Australia* at first instance.

It should also be noted that although Singer's ethical analysis of the duty to rescue is of interest, it was written in response to starvation situations where there is no clear international legal obligation on states to act. In contrast, international refugee law does place binding obligations on states via the 1951 Refugee Convention. To that extent, whilst Singer's analysis is helpful, his analysis cannot be applied directly to refugee policies without taking account of those international obligations. To this end, it is arguable that Australia's relational duty to those seeking asylum onshore is greater than others in the region because Australia is a party to the 1951 Refugee Convention and has an obligation to deal with those asylum-seekers according to that treaty. To use the language of rescue, state parties to the Refugee Convention have a special relationship with the rescuee which places upon them a higher obligation to assist. Bauhn has elucidated this, noting that a person with a relational duty may have a special duty to rescue – for instance, a lifeguard employed to maintain the safety of a certain pond has a special responsibility to rescue a child about to drown there that nobody else has.[118] By analogy, one could argue that Australia's international obligations under the Refugee Convention to deal equitably and fairly with those seeking asylum onshore render Australia's position akin to that of a lifeguard and his/her duty to rescue that drowning child. That is, it puts Australia under a unique relational duty to assist persons attempting to seek asylum on the Australian territory. This is particularly so in the South-East Asian region where key countries such as Malaysia and Indonesia are not signatories to the Refugee Convention and where those countries who are (such as Papua New Guinea and Nauru) do not comply with many of the convention's obligations. Thus, it is arguable that Australia has greater relational obligations to refugees in the South-East Asian region as it is the only country which is a party to the Refugee Convention and which has a developed asylum processing system, with judicial and merits review. Its relational obligations are therefore heightened by the lack of relational obligations on the part of other countries in the region.

(iii)   *Need part 2: humanitarianism*

Some ethics writers adopt what is known as a humanitarian approach to immigration which is focused on refugee policy (not simply immigration generally) and is centred on the concept of need. This is a pragmatic approach which posits that in some circumstances states should open their borders to persons in need.

Matthew Gibney sets out one of the most robust arguments adopting this approach. He points out that there are a number of powerful advantages in recognising resettlement as a way for states to fulfil some of their responsibilities under a humanitarian principle.[119] For instance, resettlement programmes reduce the overall financial and political costs of refugee intakes: the costs of processing onshore applications are lessened or avoided, and the programmes allow states to manage their refugee commitments with 'greater predictability and less risk'.[120] Matthew Gibney also argues that requiring states to abandon non-arrival (deterrent) measures completely is unrealistic, given that the consequences of doing so are uncertain.[121]

Upon this basis, we can argue that states have an ethical obligation to accept refugees via resettlement given they are able to select and control the process (thereby keeping their costs – political and financial – of assistance low). In contrast, the political and financial costs of prioritising those who seek asylum on our shores is higher, That is, states view spontaneous arrivals as electorally unpopular and of high financial cost. There are two problems with this argument. First, such analysis is premised on the assumption that states will indeed feel ethically obliged to offer significant places for resettlement where the costs of doing so are low – for instance, where they can select those who will integrate well into the Australian community and where the processing is primarily carried out by UNHCR (and the decision to accept the refugee is made by Australia). As detailed in Part II of this article, the reality is very different and only a small number of countries in the world offer resettlement and the number of places offered is far below demand. Second, although it reflects the reality of states' self-interest, it entrenches refugee protection as a discretionary act. As Baglay has pointed out:

> humanitarianism allows a nation to stay in control of admission ... Humanitarianism does not specify the exact circumstances and number of people to be assisted, therefore allowing for fluctuations in humanitarian admissions concomitant with public sentiment and perceived national interests.[122]

I now move beyond questioning resettlement as a concept to discuss the specific question of whether resettlement can be used to penalise spontaneous arrivals on state territory.

### (D) *Should resettlement be utilised to prevent and penalise spontaneous arrivals attempting to seek asylum in a country?*

As discussed in Part III, a failure by asylum-seekers to use resettlement or other 'lawful' migration avenues is penalised in a number of ways. Such use of resettlement by Australia in the Asia Pacific is problematic on an ethical basis for a number of reasons.

First, the prioritisation of resettlement may result in some persons who are in 'need' to be 'rescued' (given protection), but this would come at an extremely high cost to the individual rights of other persons who receive punitive treatment for *not* using a planned process (i.e. those coming by boat). This is significant because, using a deontological approach, any benefit of resettlement must be weighed against the harm which would result to the excluded boat arrival asylum-seekers. In the case of Australia, it can be argued that if resettlement can only be carried out by deterring onshore asylum-seekers and detaining them in unsafe situations, then (using a non-consequentialist approach), this would be undesirable as it would result in great harm to an underprivileged segment of society.

Second, the use of resettlement as a deterrent or punishment by a state contradicts the humanitarian and ethical norm of resettlement as the best means of providing for refugee 'need'. Whilst it is acknowledged that the stated rationale for Australia's deterrence of boat arrivals is a humanitarian one (a means of preventing asylum-seekers undertaking dangerous sea voyages), it largely serves a domestic political value by dampening electoral concerns about 'boat people' and enhances national security values. Further, using a Kantian deontological framework, we can argue that it is ethically unacceptable to use any person as a tool to achieve something else. Thus, it is ethically unacceptable for Australia to punish boat arrivals as a means of requiring refugees to utilise resettlement as the only avenue for refugee protection. In this regard, regionalised arrangements to 'swap refugees' and to resettle recognised refugees in third states may increase protection in a broad sense by increasing resettlement, but at the cost of rights of other refugees. In this sense, regionally focused resettlement may be an acceptable regional solution if based on protection needs but not as a tool of deterrence and penalisation.

A third issue is that regionalised resettlement policies via swap deals and other policies may be problematic on an ethical basis because they draw the focus away from the UNHCR's *global* protection priorities. It would be particularly concerning if resettlement was no longer offered in any significant numbers to those falling *outside* this regional strategic pool of applicants in South-East Asia (such as those in South America or the Middle-East). It also changes the core norm underlying resettlement from one that is humanitarian in nature to one of deterrence, that is, using resettlement to reduce the regional demand for people smugglers. There is a danger that a regionalised resettlement focus may be used as a justification for greater deterrence policies towards those asylum-seekers who attempt to obtain protection from Australia as an 'unauthorised' boat arrival.

## V.  Conclusion

The high numbers of refugees in today's world pose difficult legal and moral challenges to many countries, including Australia. This article illustrates that although resettlement is supported by the rhetoric of burden and responsibility sharing, it is used by some resettlement states to avoid responsibility for onshore arrivals. Australian policy reflects a two-tiered system which prioritises the selection of refugees from overseas as part of a managed, 'orderly' resettlement programme and penalises those who flee their countries of origin and come to Australian shores to apply for asylum. One of the most fundamental questions Australia must therefore address is how to properly balance the desire to offer protection to refugees via resettlement, with the moral and legal obligation to give protection and assistance to those refugees who arrive by boat.

In an ideal world, states would take a proportion of refugees according to need and a good-faith assessment of their economic capacity to provide for those refugees. However, as discussed earlier in this article, resettlement places offered by industrialised nations are not sufficient to meet the worldwide demand for those places.[123]

From a utilitarian viewpoint, resettlement may be preferable to prioritising onshore arrivals as it allows states to control the intake process and reduces the cost of processing onshore asylum claims. Resettlement serves the self-interest of states in that it allows them to select refugees in an ordered and controlled fashion. Thus, at least theoretically, it allows states to give protection to a greater number of people than would otherwise be the case. However, this rests on a number of assumptions and values: that the process used to prioritise and choose persons for resettlement is fair, and that those states will offer resettlement places in a way which sufficiently meets protection needs. It also operates with an expectation that given this orderly system, asylum-seekers should not exercise their individual agency by travelling to Australia to make an onshore refugee claim. Such an effect on individual agency may be a negative one if refugees are forced to live in countries in which they subsist but cannot flourish, where they may not fear persecution but are also not welcomed or integrated into the community. It must also take account of the reality that states act in their own interests and will give resettlement places to those people deemed to be capable of fitting within their existing political and cultural community.

In conclusion, there are significant ethical questions raised about resettlement as a concept. The preceding discussion demonstrates that there may be no clear answer to the ethical debate about the acceptability of resettlement as a concept. Whilst this may be so, it does appear clear that any prioritisation of resettlement by asylum host countries which prevents or penalises access to refugee status for those wishing to claim asylum *outside* the parameters of that resettlement construct is ethically unacceptable.

## Acknowledgements

Many thanks to Dr Alexander Betts, Leopold Muller Associate Professor in Refugee and Forced Migration Studies and Director, Refugee Studies Centre, University of Oxford, for his insightful comments on an earlier draft of this article and to Professor Susan Kneebone for her invitation to present this article at the 'Comparative Regional Protection Frameworks for Refugees: Norms and Norm Entrepreneurs' Roundtable, Refugee Law Initiative, University of London, 2013. I am also grateful to the anonymous reviewers for their helpful comments on this article.

## Disclosure statement

No potential conflict of interest was reported by the author.

## Notes

1. UNHCR, *Global Trends 2014* (Geneva: UNHCR), 2, http://www.unhcr.org/558193896.htmll.
2. Ibid.
3. Ibid., 2. This figure has hovered around the 80% level for many years.
4. UNHCR, *Resettlement Handbook*, revised ed. (Geneva: UNHCR, 2011), 3, http://www.unhcr.org/3c5e542d4.html.
5. UNHCR, 'Global Consultations on International Protection/Third Track: Strengthening and Expanding Resettlement Today: Dilemmas, Challenges and Opportunities', UN Doc. EC/GC/02/7, II A 5, 25 April 2002.
6. UNHCR, 'UNHCR Urges More Countries to Establish Refugee Resettlement Programmes', Press Release, 5 July 2010, http://www.unhcr.org/4c31cd236.html.
7. See UNHCR, 'Projected Global Resettlement Needs, 20th Annual Tripartite Consultations on Resettlement', Geneva, 24–26 June 2014, 7–8, http://www.unhcr.org/543408c4fda.html; UNHCR, *Progress Report on Resettlement*, EC/65/SC/CRP.11, 6 June 2014, 3, http://www.unhcr.org/53aa90bf9.html; UNHCR, 'What We Do: Resettlement', http://www.unhcr.org/pages/4a16b1676.html.

8. UNHCR, 'Syrian Regional Refugee Response', http://data.unhcr.org/syrianrefugees/regional. php, statistics current as at 4 October 2015. The UNHCR also reports that in 2014 Lebanon hosted the largest number of refugees in relation to its national population, with 232 refugees per 1000 inhabitants: UNHCR, 'Global Trends 2014', 3.

9. UNHCR, 'Factsheet: Resettlement and Other Forms of Admission for Syrian Refugees', 7 October 2015, http://www.unhcr.org/52b2febafc5.html. Of this number, Australia has agreed to offer 12,000 resettlement places to refugees from Syria. This will be in addition to the normal yearly resettlement quota of 13,750.

10. UNHCR, '2015 UNHCR Country Operations Profile – Pakistan', http://www.unhcr.org/pages/ 49e487016.html.

11. UNHCR, '2015 UNHCR 2015 UNHCR Subregional Operations Profile – South-East Asia – Malaysia', http://www.unhcr.org/cgi-bin/texis/vtx/page?page=49e4884c6&submit=GO.

12. In 2011–2012 a total of 42,928 people lodged applications under the offshore programme component and in 2012–2013 that figure was 50,444: Department of Immigration and Border Protection, 'Fact Sheet 60 – Australia's Refugee and Humanitarian Programme', https://www. immi.gov.au/media/fact-sheets/60refugee.htm.

13. Department of Immigration and Border Protection, 'Information Paper – Humanitarian Program', December 2013, 3, http://www.immi.gov.au/media/publications/refugee/ref-hum-issues/pdf/humanitarian-program-information-paper-14-15.pdf.

14. United Nations High Commissioner for Refugees, *2012 Global Trends – Displacement: the New 21st Century Challenge* (Geneva: UNHCR, 2013), 19.

15. See discussion at III(D).

16. For example, by way of grant of a visa.

17. See discussion in Australian Parliamentary Library, 'Refugee Resettlement to Australia: What Are the Facts?', 6 December 2011.

18. See for instance, the large numbers of Syrian refugees residing in urban environments: UNHCR, *Syrian Regional Response Plan 2014*, 35, http://www.unhcr.org/syriarrp6/docs/ Syria-rrp6-full-report.pdf.

19. Convention Relating to the Status of Refugees, 28 July 1951, 189 UNTS 150 (entered into force 22 April 1954); Protocol Relating to the Status of Refugees, 31 January 1967, 606 UNTS 267.

20. UNHCR, 'Resettlement Handbook', 47.

21. Ibid., 45. See also UNHCR, 'Global Consultations on International Protection/Third Track: Strengthening and Expanding Resettlement Today: Dilemmas, Challenges and Opportunities', 25 April 2002, EC/GC/02/7, II A 5, http://www.unhcr.org/refworld/docid/3d62679e4. html.

22. UNHCR, 'Resettlement Handbook', 37.

23. Ibid., 354.

24. Ibid., 47.

25. Thais Bessa, 'From Political Instrument to Protection Tool? Resettlement of Refugees and North-South Relations', *Refuge* 26, no. 1 (2009): 91, 93.

26. See discussion in UNHCR, 'Resettlement Handbook', 47.

27. UNHCR, *Global Trends 2011* (Geneva: UNHCR, 2012), 17, http://www.unhcr.org/4fd6f87f9. html.

28. J. van Selm, 'Great Expectations: A Review of the Strategic Use of Resettlement', UNHCR Policy Development and Evaluation Service, PDES/2013/13, August 2013, Introduction, 5.

29. Ibid., Executive Summary, 1.

30. *Australian Treaty Series* (1954), No. 5. Australia's ratification came into effect on 22 April 1954. It acceded to the Protocol Relating to the Status of Refugees on 13 December 1973, with effect from that date: *Australian Treaty Series* (1973), No. 37.

31. Article 33(1) of the Refugee Convention provides: 'No Contracting State shall expel or return ("refouler") a refugee in any manner whatsoever to the frontiers of territories where his life or freedom would be threatened on account of his race, religion, nationality, membership of a particular social group or political opinion.'

32. These rights include freedom of religion (Article 3), freedom of association (Article 15), access to courts (Article 16), and rights to wage-earning employment (Article 17), welfare, including housing (Article 21), public education (Article 22), public relief (Article 23) and social security (Article 24): see Refugee Convention, above n.19.

33. For instance, Australia resettled some 170,700 displaced persons and a further 11,000 arrivals from the end of World War II to 1954: see R. Germov and F. Motta, *Refugee Law in Australia* (Oxford: Oxford University Press, 2003), 33.

34. See Barry York, 'Australia and Refugees, 1901–2002: An Annotated Chronology Based on Official Sources' (Chronology, Parliamentary Library, Parliament of Australia, 2003), 2.

35. Ibid., 2.

36. Graeme Hugo, 'From Compassion to Compliance? Trends in Refugee and Humanitarian Migration in Australia', *GeoJournal* 56, no. 1 (2002): 27, 28.

37. See Richard Towle, 'Processes and Critiques of the Indo-Chinese Comprehensive Plan of Action: An Instrument of International Burden-Sharing?', *International Journal of Refugee Law* 18, no. 3–4 (2006): 537, 539–40.

38. Susan Kneebone, 'The Australian Story: Asylum Seekers Outside the Law', in *Refugees, Asylum Seekers and the Rule of Law: Comparative Perspectives*, ed. Susan Kneebone (Cambridge: Cambridge University Press, 2009), 176.

39. York, 'Australia and Refugees, 1901–2002', 30–49. For instance, the humanitarian intake from Africa almost doubled during the course of the 1990s, with the Minister for Immigration in charge during that period, Philip Ruddock, indicating a strong interest in that region: Elibritt Karlsen, Janet Phillips, and Elsa Koleth, 'Seeking Asylum: Australia's Humanitarian Program' (Background Note, Parliamentary Library, Parliament of Australia, 2010, updated 21 January 2011), 5, http://www.aph.gov.au/binaries/library/pubs/bn/sp/seekingasylum.pdf.

40. Karlsen, Phillips, and Koleth, 'Seeking Asylum', 5.

41. In August 2001, a Norwegian-registered container ship called the *MV Tampa* rescued 433 asylum-seekers from a sinking Indonesian vessel. The Australian government refused to allow the asylum-seekers to enter Australian territory: see discussion by A. Edwards, 'Tampering with Refugee Protection: The Case of Australia', *International Journal of Refugee Law* 15, no. 2 (2003): 192, 192–3.

42. See Tara Magner, 'A Less than "Pacific" Solution for Asylum Seekers in Australia', *International Journal of Refugee Law* 16, no. 1 (2004): 53.

43. A 'protection visa' is the name given to the visa granted to persons recognised as a refugee or eligible for complementary protection under s36 of the Migration Act 1958 (Cth).

44. The Minister for Immigration and Citizenship, or his delegate, is responsible for deciding whether to grant or refuse a visa according to the Australian visa criteria, see Migration Act 1958 (Cth) s65; Migration Regulations 1994 (Cth) Sch 2, paras 200.223, 201.223, 203.223, and 204.223. One consideration is whether the grant of the visa will be 'consistent with the regional and global priorities of the Commonwealth in relation to the permanent settlement of persons on humanitarian grounds'.

45. Department of Immigration and Border Protection, 'Fact Sheet 60 – Australia's Refugee and Humanitarian Programme'. In 2012–2013 this figure was set at a higher level of 20,019, but has been brought back to 13,750 for the financial years 2013–2014, 2014–2015 and 2015–2016.

46. See Department of Immigration and Border Protection, 'Fact Sheet 60'.

47. People who wish to be considered for a Special Humanitarian Programme (SHP) visa must be living outside their home country and be proposed for entry by an Australian citizen, permanent resident, eligible New Zealand citizen, or an organisation operating in Australia: see Department of Immigration, Offshore Resettlement, https://www.immi.gov.au/visas/humanitarian/offshore/.

48. See R. Illingworth, 'Durable Solutions: Refugee Status Determination and the Framework of International Protection', in *The Refugees Convention 50 Years On: Globalisation and International Law*, ed. S. Kneebone (Aldershot: Ashgate, 2003), 91, 105.

49. J. McAdam 'Editorial: Australia and Asylum Seekers', *International Journal of Refugee Law* 25, no. 3 (2013): 435, 439.

50. Refugee Council of Australia, 'Myths and Facts about Refugees and Asylum Seekers', http://www.refugeecouncil.org.au.

51. 'Enough Is Enough: It's Time For a New Approach' (A joint statement by Australian non-government organisations on the first anniversary of the report on the Expert Panel on Asylum Seekers, 13 August 2013), http://www.refugeecouncil.org.au/n/mr/130813-NewApproach.pdf. Signatories to the letter included the Refugee Council of Australia, the

Asylum Seeker Resource Centre, the Human Rights Law Centre and the Refugee and Immigration Legal Service.

52. Minister for Immigration and Border Protection (Peter Dutton), 'Restoring Integrity to Refugee Intake', Press Release, 12 May 2015, http://www.minister.border.gov.au/peterdutton/2015/Pages/restoring-integrity-to-refugee-intake.aspx.

53. Department of Immigration and Border Protection, 'Offshore Refugee and Humanitarian Visas: Creating a Simpler Framework' (Discussion Paper – January 2015), 7.

54. Migration Act 1958 (Cth), s85.

55. The Minister for Immigration may 'lift the bar' under s46A Migration Act to permit an unauthorised maritime arrival to lodge a valid application for a protection visa.

56. Migration Act 1958 (Cth), s35A; Migration Regulations 1994, Temporary Protection (Class XD) Visas.

57. Migration Act 1958 (Cth), s5AA defines an 'unauthorised maritime arrival' as a person who enters Australia by sea at an excised offshore place, or any other place, and becomes an unlawful non-citizen as a result. Due to the controls operated in international airports in the region, those arriving by plane generally hold a valid visa and are able to claim asylum. It is those arriving by boat on unauthorised voyages ('boat people') who do not hold such visas and who are therefore delineated as 'unlawful non-citizens' under the Act.

58. Migration Act 1958 (Cth), ss46A; 189; 196, 198A.

59. This applies to unauthorised arrivals who arrive after 13 July 2013.

60. See for example UNHCR, 'UNHCR Mission to Manus Island, Papua New Guinea: 15–17 January 2013', 4 February 2013; UNHCR, 'UNHCR Monitoring Visit to the Republic of Nauru: 7 to 9 October 2013', 26 November 2013. Both available at http://www.unhchr.org. au. See also Amnesty International, 'This is Breaking People: Human Rights Violations at Australia's Manus Island Asylum Seeking Processing Centre, Papua New Guinea', December 2013, http://www.amnesty.org.au/images/uploads/about/Amnesty_International_Manus_Island_report.pdf.

61. 'UNHCR Mission to Manus Island, Papua New Guinea; UNHCR, 'UNHCR Monitoring Visit to the Republic of Nauru'.

62. Amnesty International, 'This is Breaking People', 3.

63. 'UNHCR Statement on Australia-Cambodia Agreement on Refugee Relocation', 26 September 2014, http://www.unhcr.org/542526db9.html; Maria O'Sullivan, 'Explainer: Does Cambodia Refugee Deal Comply with the Convention?', The Conversation, 30 September 2014, http://theconversation.com/explainer-does-the-cambodia-refugee-deal-comply-with-the-convention-29639.

64. See The Report of the Expert Panel on Asylum Seekers, 13 August 2012, 56–57, http://expertpanelonasylumseekers.dpmc.gov.au/report ('Expert Panel Report').

65. The Bali Process on People Smuggling, Trafficking in Persons and Related Transnational Crime ('Bali Process'), see http://www.baliprocess.net.

66. Arrangement between the Government of Australia and the Government of Malaysia on Transfer and Resettlement (25 July 2011).

67. 'Joint Statements by the Prime Ministers of Australia and Malaysia on a Regional Cooperation Framework', Media Release, 7 May 2011, http://www.aph.gov.au/.

68. Department of Immigration 'Information Paper'. This increase was enacted in response to recommendations of the Expert Panel Report, see n.64.

69. Plaintiff M70/Plaintiff M106 [2011] HCA 32.

70. A. Rourke, 'Australian Vessels Rescue Refugees: Rescue Ships Save More than 120 Afghan Asylum Seekers after a Second Boat in a Week Capsizes off Indonesia', The Guardian, 27 June 2012, http://www.theguardian.com/world/2012/jun/27/australian-indonesian-vessels-rescue-refugees.

71. 'Expert Panel Report': 14.

72. Ibid., 39 (emphasis added).

73. Paul Farrel, 'Asylum Seekers Registered with UNHCR in Indonesia Blocked from Resettlement', The Guardian, 18 November 2014, http://www.theguardian.com/australia-news/2014/nov/18/asylum-seekers-registered-with-unhcr-in-indonesia-blocked-from-resettlement. The policy will take effect retrospectively to cover those refugees who have registered with UNHCR from 1 July 2014.

74. See S. Labman, 'At Law's Border: Unsettling Refugee Resettlement' (PhD Thesis, December 2012), https://circle.ubc.ca/bitstream/handle/2429/43703/ubc_2013_spring_labman_shauna. pdf?sequence=1.

75. Protecting Canada's Immigration System Act, S.C. 2012, c. 17, Section 20(1).

76. Ibid., c. 17, Section 20(2).

77. Canadian Government, 'Backgrounder, Designating Human Smuggling Events', http://www. cic.gc.ca/english/department/media/backgrounders/2012/2012-06-29f.asp.

78. For instance, the Public Safety Minister Vic Toews said on the day the *Sun Sea* (a boat containing 490 asylum-seekers from Sri Lanka) arrived that his government 'must ensure that our refugee system is not hijacked by criminals or terrorists': 'Tamil Asylum Ship Docks in Canada', *Sunday Express*, 14 August 2010, http://www.express.co.uk/news/world/193130/ Tamil-asylum-ship-docks-in-Canada.

79. Shauna Labman, 'Queue the Rhetoric: Refugees, Resettlement and Reform', *University of New Brunswick Law Journal* 62 (2011): 57.

80. Ibid., 55.

81. Public Safety Canada, 'Canada's Generous Program for Refugee Resettlement is Undermined by Human Smugglers Who Abuse Canada's Immigration System', 21 October 2010, http:// archive.today/e5fyO.

82. Human Rights First, 'How to Repair the U.S. Asylum and Refugee Resettlement Systems—A Human Rights First Blueprint' (2012), 5, http://www.humanrightsfirst.org/wp-content/ uploads/pdf/asylum_blueprint.pdf.

83. Donald Kerwin, 'The Faltering US Refugee Protection System: Legal and Policy Responses to Refugees, Asylum-Seekers, and Others in Need of Protection', *Refugee Survey Quarterly* 31, no. 1 (2012): 13.

84. S.B. Ray, 'Optimal Asylum', *Vanderbilt Journal of Transnational Law* 46 (2013): 1215, 1223.

85. Ray, 'Optimal Asylum', 1229; Matthew Gibney, *The Ethics and Politics of Asylum: Liberal Democracy and the Response to Refugees* (Cambridge: Cambridge University Press, 2004), 159–60.

86. See Astri Suhrke, 'Burden-Sharing during Refugee Emergencies: The Logic of Collective versus National Action', *Journal of Refugee Studies* 11, no. 4 (1998): 396; Alexander Betts, *Protection by Persuasion: International Cooperation in the Refugee Regime* (Ithaca: Cornell University Press, 2009); Eiko Thielemann 'Toward a Common Asylum Policy: Public Goods Theory and Refugee Burden Sharing' (Paper prepared for the European Consortium for Political Research Standing Group on EU Politics, Third Pan European Conference, Istanbul, 21–23 September 2006), ttp://www.jhubc.it/ecpr-istanbul/virtualpaperroom/032.pdf.

87. Suhrke, 'Burden-Sharing', 398.

88. Betts, 'Protection by Persuasion', 12.

89. Ibid., 12–13.

90. Suhrke, 'Burden-Sharing', 413.

91. Article 14 of the Universal Declaration on Human Rights provides that '[e]veryone has the right to seek and to enjoy asylum from persecution in other countries': UNGA Res. 217A (III), 10 December 1948.

92. Refugee Convention, Article 33.

93. Susan Kneebone, 'The Legal and Ethical Implications of Extra-territorial Processing of Asylum Seekers: The Safe Third Country Concept', in *Moving On: Forced Migration and Human Rights*, ed. J. McAdam (Oxford: Hart Publishing, 2008), 139–40; Matthew Gibney, 'Forced Migration, Engineered Regionalism and Justice between States', in *New Regionalism and Asylum Seekers: Challenges Ahead*, ed. Susan Kneebone and Felicity Rawlings-Sanaei (Oxford: Berghahn, 2007), 71–2.

94. Kneebone, 'Legal and Ethical Implications', 141.

95. Joan Fitzpatrick, 'Ethical Refugee Policy and the Moral Relevance of Numbers: Response to Adelman and Churgin', *International Migration Review* 30, no. 1 (1996): 325.

96. K. Nielsen, 'Ideal and Non-Ideal Theory: How Should We Approach Questions of Global Justice', *International Journal of Applied Philosophy* 2, no. 3 (1985): 33–41, discusses distributive obligations of affluent nations vis-à-vis poor states. See also S.C. Neff, 'Rescue across State Boundaries: International Legal Aspects of Rescue', in *The Duty to Rescue: The Jurisprudence of Aid*, ed. M.A. Menlowe and A. McCall Smith (Brookfield, VT: Dartmouth, 1993), 159–204.

97. Joseph Carens, 'Realistic and Idealistic Approaches to the Ethics of Migration', *International Migration Review* 30, no. 1 (1996): 156; J. Carens, *The Ethics of Immigration* (Oxford: Oxford University Press, 2013).

98. For example, John Rawls, *A Theory of Justice*, revised ed. (Boston, MA: Harvard University Press, 2009); John Rawls, 'The Law of Peoples', *Critical Inquiry* 30, no. 1 (1993): 1.

99. Gibney, 'The Ethics and Politics of Asylum'.

100. See Matthew Gibney, 'Asylum: A Principled Hypocrisy', in *Migration: A COMPAS Anthology*, ed. B. Anderson and M. Keith (Oxford: COMPAS, 2014), http://compasanthology.co. uk/asylum-principled-hypocrisy/.

101. Carens, *The Ethics of Immigration*, Ch. 11. See also J. Carens 'Aliens and Citizens: The Case for Open Borders', *The Review of Politics* 49, no. 2 (1987): 251.

102. Walzer, 'Spheres of Justice', 39.

103. Ibid., 28.

104. Ibid., 29.

105. Ibid., 29.

106. See, for example, Melissa Phillips, 'Immigration', *Election Watch 2013*, http://electionwatch. edu.au/australia-2013/policy/immigration; 'Labor Caucus Rejects Calls to Abandon Support for Offshore Processing', *The Guardian*, 17 June 2014, http://www.theguardian.com/world/ 2014/jun/17/labor-caucus-rejects-calls-to-abandon-support-for-offshore-processing.

107. See, for example, '2014 Lowy Institute Poll Finds Strong Support for Government Policy on Turning Back Boats', Press Release, 6 June 2014, http://www.lowyinstitute.org/news-and-media/press-releases/2014-lowy-institute-poll-finds-strong-support-government-policy-turnin g-back-boats.

108. S. Scheffler, 'Introduction', in *Consequentialism and its Critics*, ed. S. Scheffler (1988), 1, cited in Brilmayer, 'Rights and Choice in Law', *Yale Law Journal* (1989): 1287.

109. See discussion in Part III.

110. A. Millbank, 'The Problem with the 1951 Refugee Convention' (Australian Parliamentary Library, Research Paper 2, 2000-01), http://www.aph.gov.au/About_Parliament/Parliamenta ry_Departments/Parliamentary_Library/pubs/rp/rp0001/01RP05.

111. See Gibney, 'The Ethics and Politics of Asylum', 159–60, 191.

112. F.M. Kamm, 'The New Problem of Distance in Morality', in *The Ethics of Assistance: Morality and the Distant Needy*, ed. Deen K. Chatterjee (Cambridge: Cambridge University Press, 2004), 70.

113. Ibid.

114. Ibid., 62.

115. Peter Singer, 'Famine, Affluence, and Morality', *Philosophy and Public Affairs* 1, no. 1 (1972): 229, 231–2.

116. Ibid., 232.

117. Per Bauhn, 'The Duty to Rescue and the Duty to Aid the Starving', *International Dialogue, A Multidisciplinary Journal of World Affairs* 3 (2013): 7.

118. Per Bauhn, 'The Extension and Limits of the Duty to Rescue', *Public Reason* 3, no. 1 (2011): 40.

119. Gibney, 'The Ethics and Politics of Asylum', 239.

120. Ibid.

121. Ibid., 238.

122. Sasha Baglay, 'Review: Humanitarianism, Identity and Nation: Migration Laws of Australia and Canada', *Osgoode Hall Law Journal* 44, no. 3 (2006): 390.

123. UNHCR, 'Global Trends 2011', 17. UNHCR also notes that '[o]f the 14.4 million refugees of concern to UNHCR around the world, less than one per cent is submitted for resettlement', UNHCR Webpage 'Resettlement', http://www.unhcr.org/pages/4a16b1676.html.

# Rights, needs or assistance? The role of the UNHCR in refugee protection in the Middle East

Dallal Stevens

*School of Law, University of Warwick, UK*

This article examines the meaning of 'protection' as applied by the United Nations High Commissioner for Refugees in its policy in the Middle East, with particular reference to Jordan and Lebanon. It traces the move by human rights and development agencies to adopt a 'rights-based approach' in their activities, and critiques the adoption of such an approach by the United Nations High Commissioner for Refugees (and non-governmental organisations) in the definition of '(international) protection'. The article then proceeds to explore how this interpretation of protection manifests itself in the context of Iraqi and Syrian flight to neighbouring states. It concludes by arguing that the language of protection continues to be confusing and that a rights-based definition not only does not reflect the reality of assistance on the ground, but may, in fact, impede the willingness of states in the region to support refugees in the long term.

## 1. Introduction

This article focuses on the concept of protection (the norm of protection) as administered by the United Nations High Commissioner for Refugees (UNHCR) and non-governmental organisations (NGOs) (the norm entrepreneurs) in the context of the Middle East and the recent flight of Iraqis and Syrians to neighbouring Arab states.[1]

From the outset, it is important to clarify the area of concern to this analysis, both in terms of 'territory' and 'space', and the actors involved. Generally speaking, the territory of 'the Middle East' includes Bahrain, Egypt, Iran, Iraq, Israel, Jordan, Kuwait, Lebanon, Oman, Palestine, Qatar, Saudi Arabia, Syria, Turkey, the United Arab Emirates and Yemen. Some definitions include Cyprus and Northern Cyprus. For the purposes of this article, the discussion will revolve around the Levant region – that is, Jordan, Lebanon and Syria – in view of the large-scale migration that has recently occurred in these countries. It is also advisable to consider the forum – or space – of protection in the hosting state – that is, camp, informal settlements, rural or urban areas, or family hosts. In the Levant countries, asylum seekers and refugees are to be found in all five, creating a complex scenario for those trying to reach potential beneficiaries of the refugee protection framework. The forum will inevitably result in different outcomes; those in urban settings, for example, will not be assisted in the same way as those residing in camps.

Consequently, there is scope for considerable variation in approach. A great deal depends on conditions in the state concerned, as well as the context in which asylum and refugee policy functions. As with other parts of the world, the provision of protection in the Middle East is undertaken by a range of actors: states, the UNHCR, the United Nations Relief and Works Agency for Palestinian Refugees in the Near East (UNRWA) and NGOs. It is worth noting that Middle Eastern countries face a variety of immigration, emigration and displacement issues such that it is impossible and ill-advised to over-generalise about the implications for the region as a whole. Nonetheless, the discussion of protection herein is of wide application due to its normative status.

The majority of countries in the region are not party to the 1951 UN Convention relating to the Status of Refugees/1967 Protocol (the 'Refugee Convention').[2] They are therefore not bound by the Convention's legal definition of refugee. Rather, the non-party states, as well as some state parties – such as Egypt and Yemen – have handed over responsibility for refugee status determination, often through Memoranda of Understanding, to the UNHCR.[3] They also rely heavily on the UNHCR and partner NGOs to provide protection to asylum seekers and refugees. Israel and Cyprus, by contrast, do undertake refugee status determination. These variations raise interesting questions as to the meaning and content of 'protection' provided in the region. Due to the fact that the Refugee Convention is not binding on the non-state parties, one could start by assuming a simple understanding of 'protection' as the provision of a place of safety for those forced to leave their country of residence and enter another. While this might conceivably be the view of the state, it ignores the fact of the UNHCR presence and the central and powerful role it plays in both refugee determination and protection provision. To a large extent, the UNHCR has considerable latitude, within its mandate, to orient policy in a direction of its own choosing. It will draw on a range of instruments and initiatives to inform action on the ground, including its own Statute and guidance, as well as any applicable Memorandum, producing, in effect, a multi-dimensional protection regime that includes, *inter alia*, refugee law and policy, human rights, humanitarianism[4] and development approaches.

This article considers the background to the concept of protection before examining how it has been, and is being, conceived by the UNHCR. The discussion addresses one particular aspect of the refugee protection framework: the adoption by the UNHCR in its policy – and indeed by many NGOs working with refugees – of a 'rights-based approach' to refugee protection and assistance. It examines whether the language of 'rights' in this context has any bearing upon the treatment of Iraqi and Syrian refugees in their host states, the enhancement of protection, or the satisfaction of their needs. It argues that the language of protection as 'rights-based' is confusing and not only does not reflect the reality of assistance on the ground, which is oriented towards needs, but may, in fact, impede the willingness of states in the region to support refugees in the long term.

## 2. The concept of protection

The question of what is actually being provided to assist the refugee is central to this analysis. While it is clearly important to identify 'who' is making provision and 'where' that provision is made, as outlined in the introduction, the main objective for all actors is, ostensibly, to protect refugees. Yet, notwithstanding the ubiquity of the terms 'protection' or 'refugee protection', consensus as to the meaning of such concepts remains, it is contended, somewhat elusive.[5] This, despite the significance of protection and the fact that it is core to the UNHCR's mandate and the Refugee Convention,[6] as well as to the activities of many of the NGOs based in the Middle East. It is therefore crucial to understand what is meant by protection in this context before proceeding. Three aspects of protection will now be addressed: the legal basis for 'refugee protection'; the 'rights-based approach'; and the link between protection and humanitarianism.[7]

To what, then, does the term 'protection' refer? Arthur Helton has posited that:

> [w]hen we speak of 'protection', we mean *legal* protection. The concept must be associated with entitlements under law and, for effective redress of grievances, mechanisms to vindicate claims in respect of those entitlements. An inquiry, then, into whether a population has 'protection' is an examination of the fashion in which the pertinent authorities comply with the entitlements of individuals under international law, and the manner in which these legal precepts are implemented and respected.[8]

Helton was prompted to provide his assessment of the meaning of protection due to the lack of a formal definition, despite the norm of protection being so core to the fundamental rationale of refugee law. Though there are 15 usages of the term in the text, the Refugee Convention does not actually define 'protection'.[9] Perhaps the most important reference to protection is in Article 1A(2)[10] of the Convention. This has long been recognised from the drafting history as having a limited meaning, and refers to 'diplomatic protection' – that is, the protection owed by a state to its citizens abroad.[11] However, such an interpretation is no longer considered appropriate for contemporary refugee law. Rather, as Zimmerman and Mahler suggest, Article 1A(2) should be understood to mean that in order for a person not to qualify as a refugee, the home state must be able and willing to ensure that he or she is not exposed to persecution.[12]

## 2.1 *Standards of protection*

The contemporary understanding of the term 'protection' in the context of the Convention now extends beyond the failings of the home state and is frequently used in an additional sense: to describe the standards to which the refugee is legally entitled in the country of refuge. More usually, such protection is referred to as 'rights', and while a number of the Convention's Articles talk of rights,[13] it is usual to include human rights obligations arising under other instruments. As Helton notes, the 'concept of "protection" ... can be taken to mean the act of respecting and upholding fundamental human rights, such as the core rights declared in the Covenants on Civil and Political Rights, and on Economic, Social and Cultural Rights'.[14] There is an implicit assumption that the state parties, and any other actor interested in refugee issues, understands what refugee protection means – namely, the rights and obligations set out in the Convention and in other human rights agreements are constitutive of refugee protection. This is certainly a useful starting point, but the nature of protection provided to refugees is often context-driven. For example, it is well recognised that 'protection needs' may vary in cases of mass influx, as distinct from individualised persecution, or generalised violence and armed conflict; and they may be dependent on who the protector is or where that protection is being provided.[15] In addition, over time, the terminology changes: for example, ExCom Conclusion 22 (1981) refers to 'measures of protection' being on the one hand, 'admission and *non-refoulement*' and on the other, 'treatment' in accordance with 'minimum basic human standards', which it lists[16]; ExCom Conclusion 52 (1988), by contrast, mentions 'protection' *and* 'a basic standard of treatment', almost as if they are separate.[17] With such a range of parameters, uniformity and consistency are not possible and compromise is often an accepted part of the process.[18]

In contrast to the Refugee Convention, which binds state parties, 'international protection' was described in some detail in Paragraph 8 of the Statute of the UNHCR. There, we are told that the High Commissioner would provide for the protection of refugees falling under the competence of his office by undertaking a number of activities, such as promoting the conclusion and ratification of international conventions for the protection of refugees; promoting through special agreements with governments the execution of any measures calculated to improve the situation of refugees; and promoting the admission of refugees. Naturally, this definition was a product of the negotiations at the time. The list in Paragraph 8 arguably does not conform to the present view of all aspects to protection; nor does it take account of the changes in the UNHCR's own thinking about protection in the decades following the Statute coming into force. Significantly, the agency was accorded a humanitarian role and the position of the United States, which would have limited the concept of protection to 'legal protection', did not triumph.[19] As with the meaning of 'protection' under the Refugee Convention, 'international' protection has been subject to interpretation and debate.

## 2.2 The UNHCR and the concept of protection

Within a decade of its founding, the UNHCR had developed its role as an operational agency and was increasingly organising relief efforts.[20] Crucial to this expanding role was the emergent support from the United States in recognition of the enduring need for an effective body able to provide relief and assistance to refugees on a global scale. At the same time, the High Commissioner utilised his 'good offices' to adopt a more flexible approach to those in need of assistance when encouraged to do so by the international community.[21] As the years passed, the UNHCR continued to develop its capacities in response to the various causes of mass flight as well as to global politics.[22] Two notable features of its development are the widening competence and transformation 'from a refugee organization into a more broadly-based humanitarian agency'.[23] Thus, it has expanded its mandate and assumed responsibility for millions of displaced people in addition to refugees (namely, stateless people, the internally displaced and victims of natural disasters). Laura Barnett has suggested that the UNHCR has 'shifted towards an operational approach, fostering local civil society, building democratic governance, and working for conflict prevention'.[24] Such dramatic organisational change is particularly relevant to the Middle East where the UNHCR has a very high profile and potentially influential role. But it does not come without criticism.[25]

The 1994 Note on International Protection is particularly helpful in revealing how the UNHCR perceived the broadening of its mandate and the shift towards humanitarianism, particularly in so far as protection is concerned. It explains that the UNHCR has:

> adopted the usage of regional instruments such as the OAU Refugee Convention and the Cartagena Declaration, using the term 'refugee' in the broader sense, to denote persons outside their countries who are in need of international protection because of a serious threat to their life, liberty or security of person in their country of origin as a result of persecution or armed conflict, or serious public disorder.[26]

This reference to armed conflict is pertinent to many of the forced displacements that have occurred in the Middle East in recent times and allows for a generous approach to be adopted.[27] In addition, the note provides a description of 'international protection' that moves us beyond the formulation of Paragraph 8 of the Statute, which tells us simply what the UNHCR will do to 'provide for protection' without defining 'protection' itself. Most notable is the cross reference in the note to the Preamble of the 1951 Refugee Convention: the overall objective of international protection is stated as being the assurance of the widest possible exercise of fundamental rights and freedoms, which all human beings should enjoy without discrimination.[28] 'International protection is thus premised on human rights principles'[29] and it is interesting to note the change from 'treatment' and 'basic human [or humanitarian] standards' of earlier ExCom conclusions.[30] According to the note, it:

> begins with securing admission, asylum, and respect for basic human rights, including the principle of *non-refoulement*, without which the safety and even survival of the refugee is in jeopardy; it ends only with the attainment of a durable solution, ideally through the restoration of protection by the refugee's own country.[31]

Significantly, the note moves beyond the fulfilment of rights to an acceptance that international protection must also address the issue of 'needs' more directly: protection, it claims, 'involves seeking … to meet the whole range of needs that result from the absence of national protection'.[32] 'Material assistance', it suggests, 'is often essential for refugees' survival' and is therefore often 'a *sine qua non* of international protection'.[33] But what are such *needs*? While there appears to be a correlation between *rights* and needs,[34] there is also recognition that 'the refugee … [must] have some means of subsistence, as well as shelter, health care and other basic necessities', suggesting a closer alignment between welfare and needs.[35] This adoption of the language of 'needs' may seem unsurprising to some since the Statute stresses that the work of the High Commissioner is 'humanitarian and social', indicative of a welfare orientation, but the point is that it does not define either 'protection' or what it means to be 'humanitarian and social'. The note removes any uncertainty by clearly stating that the UNHCR perceives protection as being about addressing the needs of the (broadly defined) refugee as well as assisting him or her to fulfil their basic rights. To repeat: 'Since material assistance is often essential for refugees' survival, it can also be a *sine qua non* of international protection.'[36]

## 2.3 *Evolving UNHCR approaches to 'protection'*

By 1999, however, there appears once more to be a subtle change in UNHCR definitions of 'international protection'. For example, in the field guide for NGOs, *Protecting Refugees*, a much reduced definition is employed. It states simply that:

> Since, by definition, the basic rights of refugees are no longer protected by the governments of their home countries, the international community then assumes the responsibility of ensuring that those basic rights are respected. The phrase 'international protection' covers the gamut of activities through which refugees' rights are secured.[37]

No explicit mention here, then, of *needs*; rather, the focus is clearly on *rights*. Furthermore, the broad-based nature of the statement is striking: any action that secures rights is deemed protection. Perhaps in recognition of the lack of specificity in the words 'gamut of activities', the materials of the *Reach Out Refugee Protection Training Project* (an initiative between NGOs, Red Cross/Red Crescent and the UNHCR to train humanitarian staff in the basic elements of refugee protection) provide the following UNHCR 'working definition' of protection that strives to be both comprehensible and comprehensive:

> Protection encompasses all activities aimed at ensuring the enjoyment, on equal terms of the rights of women, men, girls and boys of concern to the UNHCR in accordance with the

letter and spirit of the relevant bodies of law (international, humanitarian, human rights and refugee law). It includes interventions by States or UNHCR on behalf of asylum-seekers and refugees to ensure that their rights, security, and welfare are recognized and safeguarded in accordance with international standards. Such interventions will, amongst others, be deemed to: ensuring [*sic*] respect for the principle of *non-refoulement*; promoting admission to safety and access to fair procedures for the determination of refugee status; upholding humane standards of treatment; realizing the right to assistance and services; promoting non-discrimination, and the implementation of durable solutions.[38]

Once more, we find here a re-articulation by the UNHCR of its protection function in a manner that seeks to combine rights, process, welfare and the quest for durable solutions. While this description seems comprehensive and reflective of the UNHCR's multidimensional approach to protection, the humanitarian role – in the sense of addressing immediate suffering – is only met by the 'right to assistance and services' and the safeguarding of 'welfare'. In many ways, the definition reveals the difficulties faced by the UNHCR in establishing a policy that is not only 'working' but 'workable'. Consequently, the urge to define and redefine continues.

A recent description of protection, as seen through the eyes of the UNHCR's Director of International Protection, Volker Türk, provides useful insight into the UNHCR's current thinking about its role and the meaning of protection in the twenty-first century. And, here, again, it is important to quote a significant portion of the statement vis-à-vis protection:

> [P]rotection ... means that refugees, the stateless, IDPs, and other persons of concern are able to enjoy the widest possible array of human rights and fundamental freedoms without discrimination. This focus must permeate all our interactions with persons of concern. It must also provide the overall strategic direction to our operations and inspire the design, coordination and delivery of services. A rights-based approach is ... inherent to UNHCR's protection mandate.
>
> ... it means delivering concrete, quality protection services ... It also means advocating for and intervening on behalf of refugees and other persons of concern when they are at risk ... [and] it means integrating protection considerations into every service we deliver (mainstreaming protection).
>
> Protection activities and approaches are anchored in international norms and standards and yet must be delivered with a deep awareness of circumstances and contexts in which we work. The time has perhaps come to reframe protection as a broader governance issue.[39]

There are a number of points that are worth highlighting here: (1) the focus on the rights and freedoms of refugees and the emphasis on a 'rights-based approach' as being core to UNHCR's protection mandate (this is the expanded mandate and includes all persons of concern to the UNHCR); (2) the use of the first-person personal pronoun in the statement is interesting; this is about UNHCR's conceptualisation of the protection it offers rather than a clarification of the meaning of protection for other organisations or even states; (3) the suggestion by Türk that protection should be reframed as governance (though he does not explain in detail his understanding of 'governance' here or the implications of such reframing). Clearly, 'protection' is expected to achieve much and the UNHCR is prepared, through these stated objectives, to shoulder enormous obligations and responsibility for refugees beyond its earlier competences of both legal protection and its express humanitarian role.

This article will now focus on the first issue underlined above: the emergence of what might be referred to as the norm of a 'rights-based approach' in the discourse of humanitarian organisations, especially in the context of development and humanitarianism. It will then explore the application of this norm by the UNHCR in its delivery of protection in Jordan and Lebanon.

### 3.   A rights-based approach

This section opens by outlining the background to the 'rights-based approach' movement before moving on to examine how the UNHCR has adopted and applied the framework.

That a rights-based approach is a 'good thing' might seem incontrovertible, but since its precise meaning and scope are not so clear-cut, due in part to the way that it is understood in different ways in different contexts, it is, arguably, a contested and contestable concept, requiring further exploration. Some important questions that need addressing but are often ignored include the following: why was the rights-based approach adopted? Is it simply rhetoric or an effective practical tool in the armoury of NGOs and human rights organisations? And, crucially for this article, what does it add to refugee protection? At a fundamental level, it is always advisable that there is clarity about key concepts or norms, particularly when those concepts have an effect in regions such as the Middle East where the UNHCR plays a major role as a norm entrepreneur. As Volker Türk rightly noted recently, '[i]t is … critical to delineate, realistically, in each context what protection in humanitarian settings can and must do, being clear about its potential, as well as its limitations'.[40]

The concept, or norm, of a human rights-based approach emerged as a fundamental feature of development and humanitarian programmes in the 1990s, particularly following UN reforms in 1997.[41] In 2003, the then UN Secretary-General, Kofi Annan, invited all UN agencies to 'mainstream human rights into their activities and programmes within the framework of their respective mandates'.[42] In an influential Statement of Common Understanding, three strands to the human rights-based approach were identified: (1) all programmes of development cooperation should further the realisation of international human rights; (2) be guided by the standards and principles of international human rights law; and (3) programmes of development cooperation should contribute to the capacity of duty-bearers to meet their obligations and of rights-holders to claim their rights.[43]

As can be seen, the statement made specific reference to *development* cooperation and *development* programming by UN agencies. It is therefore unsurprising that those working in development heeded Annan's call with enthusiasm, and that it is therefore in that context that we have seen the greatest adoption of the rights-based approach. Notwithstanding this apparent attempt at agreement, what the adoption of such an approach by agencies actually means in practice is not altogether certain. Arguably, the concept itself remains somewhat elusive due to the tendency for organisations to adopt alternative interpretations of a rights-based approach. As one commentator puts it, 'Agencies and organizations have often improvised in defining for themselves what constitutes a rights based approach.'[44] What adds to the confusion is that organisations do not simply draw upon human rights norms but also utilise other concepts from a range of disciplines – for example, ethics, good governance, development and social justice.[45] Thus, the outlining of basic principles, whilst important, is perhaps the easiest endeavour, but it can only provide a general framework that remains subject to frequent and further interpretation.

In the quest for consensus and clarification, reference is frequently made to a publication of The Office of the High Commissioner for Human Rights (OHCHR) entitled 'Frequently Asked Questions on a Human Rights-Based Approach to Development

Cooperation'. There, it is stated that '[a] human rights-based approach is a conceptual framework for the process of human development that is normatively based on international human rights standards and operationally directed to promoting and protecting human rights'.[46] It continues: 'Mere charity is not enough from a human rights perspective.'[47] That human rights and development are connected is deemed fairly obvious.[48] '[C]lose enough in motivation and concern to be compatible and congruous ... different enough in strategy and design to supplement each other fruitfully'.[49] They both seek to secure the freedom, well-being and inherent dignity and equality of all people.[50]

For its part, the Danish Institute of Human Rights (DIHR), in its 'inspirational' guide entitled *Applying a Rights-based Approach* aimed at civil society organisations working in the development context, identified four basic principles underpinning a rights-based approach:

- inalienability, indivisibility and interdependence of human rights;
- empowerment and participation;
- equality and non-discrimination;
- accountability.[51]

The origin of these four principles is obvious: they are derived from the UN Statement of Common Understanding set out above, which carefully listed the human rights principles that should guide all phases of an organisation's programming process: *universality and inalienability; indivisibility; interdependence and interrelatedness; non-discrimination and equality; participation and inclusion; accountability and the rule of law*.[52] In recognition of the difficulty of translating principles or values into practice, and to assist rights-based approach programming efforts, the DIHR identifies four further 'focus areas':

- 'the most vulnerable groups, including issues of gender discrimination';
- 'the root causes of poverty, deprivation and human rights violations';
- 'the relationship between rights-holders and duty-bearers'; and
- 'empowerment'.[53]

The Danish guide also emphasises the importance of the rights-holder and the duty-bearer – unsurprising, as these, too, are highlighted in the third principle of the Common Understanding. Fundamental to the approach, then, is that 'every human being is a rights-holder and that every human right has a corresponding duty-bearer'.[54] The rights-holder – in our context, the asylum seeker or refugee – is entitled to rights, and to claim them; the rights-holder 'is entitled to hold the duty-bearer accountable' but also 'has a responsibility to respect the rights of others'.[55]

A third articulation of a rights-based approach is also worth mentioning; it, too, shows how the principles of the Common Understanding, as well as subsequent agency definitions, have been adopted and translated into an aide-memoire: namely, PANEL, an acronym for 'participation, accountability, non-discrimination and equality, empowerment and legality'. This particular formulation has found favour with a number of organisations in the United Kingdom and Australia.[56]

While these examples show the manner in which the key points of a rights-based approach are underscored by different bodies, it is also striking how NGOs interpret statements of principle in their own way. The DIHR's list, for example, omits certain (significant) terms from the Common Understanding, such as interrelatedness, inclusion and the rule of law. Often, in the quest to fashion a set of norms and principles that are perceived as being comprehensible as well as workable by those working for NGOs, there is a tendency for definitions to become overly reductive. The danger, then, is that either the definition descends into a meaningless mantra or is too general and consequently subject to interpretation and reinterpretation. Clearly this can have significant consequences for agency activity on the ground and the translation of the conceptual to the practical.

## 4.   The UNHCR and a rights-based approach

As indicated, the rights-based initiatives of the 1990s and 2000s have been actively pursued by UN organisations, NGOs and donor governments, particularly with regard to development programming. It is also apparent that humanitarian and human rights organisations – as opposed to development organisations – have adopted the rights-based terminology when outlining their mandates. This is certainly true of the UNHCR. References to the 'rights-based approach' pervade the UNHCR's documentation relating to refugees and other persons of concern, but pinning down its meaning as understood by the agency is not so straightforward. Even the NGO training handouts produced by the organisation admit to the confusion between humanitarian assistance and development approaches.[57] One explanation provided by the *Handbook for the Protection of Internally Displaced Persons* states upfront that 'protection is about securing human rights (a rights-based approach)'.[58] The handbook proceeds to define a rights-based approach in a way that parallels earlier development definitions, though specific reference is not made to the DIHR's or other guides:

> A rights-based approach means that all of our policies, programmes and activities:
>
> • are based on rights, as provided in international law;
> • further the realization of rights; and
> • seek to strengthen the capacities of rights holders (women, men, girls and boys) to claim their rights, and the capacities of duty bearers (states and other authorities) to meet their obligations to respect, protect and fulfil those rights.[59]

Although this description relates to the context of internally displaced persons, its generality arguably permits wider application. In fact, Volker Türk talks about the promotion of 'accountability, equality and empowerment in [UNHCR's] operations' in his 2013 statement on international protection,[60] which is of direct concern to refugees as well as other persons of concern to the UNHCR; the handbook's definition quoted above also imposes obligations on UNHCR and its employees, while importantly placing the responsibility to respect, protect and fulfil rights squarely at the door of the state 'and other authorities'. The UNHCR defines its role as improving 'capacity' – whether it be of rights-holders or duty-bearers[61]; it is unclear whether it also considers itself a duty-bearer, in view of the scale of its operations and its impact on the individual seeking international protection.[62] Nonetheless, this approach allows the rights agenda to be brought into play in the protection of refugees, even where, as in the Middle East, the majority of countries have not actively signed up to the Refugee Convention and the obligations (rights) contained therein.

When we turn to a second document, *A Community-Based Approach in UNHCR Operations*, a new policy enters the arena: as the title declares, 'a community-based approach'.[63] The Director of International Protection cites the initiative favourably, noting that the UNHCR will focus on community-based protection to advance its work with the communities it serves.[64] 'A community-based approach', declares the document, 'is a way of working in partnership with persons of concern during all stages of UNHCR's programme cycle. It recognizes the resilience, capacities, skills and resources of persons of concern, builds on these to deliver protection and solutions, and supports the community's own goals.'[65] While it stresses that 'a community-based approach is integral to a rights-based approach, as they are founded on common principles and goals',[66] its distinctiveness is not necessarily clear. What more does it add, then, to the principles of participation and empowering individuals and communities to promote change and adherence to rights, principles recognised as foundational to a rights-based approach?[67]

It is noticeable that the text of *A Community-Based Approach* sets out to contrast a 'needs-based approach' from a 'rights-based approach', emphasising that persons of concern should no longer be viewed as beneficiaries of aid but as holders of rights with their own legal entitlements.[68] There is a new emphasis on the participatory role of the individual within his or her community, as well as, it seems 'an age, gender and diversity approach'.[69] Yet, confusingly, 'needs' have not disappeared altogether – '[l]ike all development', suggests the DIHR, '[a rights-based approach] implies an effort to improve the situation of people, focusing on their needs, problems and potentials'.[70] 'People are at the very centre of what we do', the UNHCR Director of International Protection informs us. 'To be effective, we need to understand their particular needs, not as homogeneous groups, but as individuals with specific backgrounds, aspirations and hopes.'[71]

It is very clear, then, that the UNHCR has adopted and developed a range of different approaches and concepts in fulfilment of its perceived role, and continues to do so. At times, these reveal a confusion of identity by the organisation as it grapples with complex situations and strives to be more solution-oriented; at others, it is clear that it is acting as a norm entrepreneur, seeking to encourage new ways of thinking. Change may be necessary, especially in the current climate of protracted displacement, limited options for displaced people, and a worrying lack of international solidarity, but the theoretical underpinnings or motivations of an organisation as important and influential as the UNHCR should always be scrutinised. The article will now consider how these various approaches to protection translate into practice in those Middle Eastern countries that have faced major refugee influxes in the past decade.

## 5. The language of protection in the Middle East: from needs, to rights, to community?

The 'rights-based approach' remains a focus around which other campaigns and initiatives revolve. It is imperative, consequently, to question whether such an approach makes a real difference to the refugee. One criticism that can be applied to those working in development, humanitarian assistance and human rights is that the linkage between the rights-based approach and programmatic work or activities on the ground is not always transparent.[72] Second, the emphasis on developing the capacity of rights-holders to claim rights against duty-bearers fails to recognise that this is not always feasible in every circumstance. Indeed, one can question the extent to which the UNHCR is genuinely inviting refugees to hold it to account when it has failed to meet its own or wider human rights standards. This is not to suggest that promoting rights is unimportant but the whole mission can be undermined by a failure to articulate unambiguously a uniform set of procedural and substantive principles, based in law, that are meaningful, implementable and that make a real difference to the 'rights-holder'. Such concerns are very much in evidence in the Middle East.

If we take by way of example the Regional Response Plan (RRP) which was developed in relation to Syrian refugees, we find how a rights-based approach is translating into practice. The first Syria RRP was published in March 2012 and was a strategic framework document prepared by the UNHCR 'to address the needs for protection and assistance of refugees fleeing from the Syrian Arab Republic into Jordan, Lebanon, Turkey and Iraq'.[73] The 2014 RRP, RRP6, is described as one of the largest appeals presented for a refugee emergency, comprising 100 partners, including the UNHCR, who work together to deal with the crisis in the region.[74] António Guterres, UN High Commissioner for Refugees, describes how the RRP6 is based on 'a shared analysis of regional developments with partners in the Syria Humanitarian Assistance Response Plan (SHARP)' and recognises that due to 'the scope and magnitude of the crisis, the humanitarian response must be closely aligned with development actions'.[75] The combination of humanitarianism and development is significant here and makes the region particularly apposite when considering the application of a rights-based approach by refugee-support NGOs and the UNHCR and the nature of protection.

The first four RRPs (all in 2012) each identify three regional strategic objectives: (1) 'Ensure that Syrians and other refugees and asylum-seekers fleeing from the Syrian Arab Republic have access to neighbouring territories in order to seek asylum and received protection, including protection from *refoulement*'; (2) 'Ensure that the basic needs of Syrians and other refugees fleeing from Syria are met with special attention to the most vulnerable'; (3) 'Undertake contingency measures for a potential mass influx'. RRP6, published in December 2013, has, in view of the longevity of the displacement, a somewhat altered focus. It rightly states that protection is its core objective; initially, in the 'Key Elements', there is no detailed explanation of the meaning ascribed to 'protection'. Rather, the document describes refugee protection within the context of the Syrian refugee crisis as focusing on:

> five priority *objectives*: access to territory and registration, prevention and response to Sexual and Gender-Based Violence, Child Protection – including strategic links between SGBV, Child Protection and Education – meaningful community participation and durable solutions (emphasis added).[76]

Clearly, those who have faced sexual or gender-based violence, and children, have been identified as the most vulnerable groups in need of protection. This focus on vulnerable groups can be traced to earlier explications of a rights-based approach, such as that of the DIHR discussed above.[77] Access and registration are also important, as is the involvement of the community (though whether host or refugee community or both is not outlined) and the quest for durable solutions. While there is no mention in 'Key Elements' of the *non-refoulement* obligation – this is perhaps deemed obvious – protection from *refoulement* is specifically mentioned elsewhere in the document in a section headed 'Protection'.[78] A 'fundamental tenet of protection', we are told, 'is that refugees should be able to secure entry to safe territory', and that 'the key protection response remains preservation of access for those fleeing conflict, and protection from *refoulement*'.[79] This is arguably the most comprehensible and apposite description – access to a place of safety and freedom from return – but, again, it does not tell us what 'protection' actually *is*.

It is very evident therefore, that RRP6 is a document addressing the immediate humanitarian *needs* of refugees and it includes protection as a component of such needs alongside essential services, food, health, education and material assistance to the most vulnerable.[80] In light of the discussion above, in which it was shown how both the UNHCR and many

NGOs endorsed a move away from a needs-based approach to a rights-based approach, and how a rights-based approach is perceived as fundamental to protection and the delivery of humanitarian assistance, it seems somewhat odd, and arguably confusing, that humanitarian needs receive such emphasis in RRP6, particularly considering the identification of protection as a humanitarian need. There are a number of explanations for this: the length and severity of the crisis has led to a reassessment of provision and priorities, with a complete rewrite of the RRP objectives; an important aspect of RRP6 is seen as the strengthening of local service delivery and resilience[81]; and organisations on the ground are beginning to have an eye to the future and are hoping to complement longer-term strategies for development in their handling of current displacement issues.[82] Indeed, it is very evident that Syrian displacement is regarded as having moved into what might be termed 'the development phase'. It is also true that civil society and NGOs working in the development field have seized upon a certain perspective of the rights-based approach – that is, its ability to regard the deprivation of needs as the denial of rights. Whatever the reason for the shift away from rights-speak and greater acknowledgement of refugees' needs, it should be welcomed as a more honest reflection of daily, monthly and yearly realities.

## 6. The reality of protection

The RRPs and NGO and academic reports of the past three years on the Syrian flight make grim reading.[83] Formerly, the migration of Iraqis across borders following hostilities between the United States and Iraq also raised serious concerns about the treatment of Iraqis in neighbouring countries, such as Jordan, Syria and Lebanon.[84] It is discernible from both these displacement events, and from the earlier discussion, that there is no single, uniform response that can be labelled 'protection'. Rather, 'protection' is a fluid concept with a tempo-spatial and human dimension – that is, what constitutes protection will be dependent on time, geography and personal circumstances. The nature of protection will differ in the short-term (say, 0–2 years), the mid-term (say, 2–5 years), and the long-term (5+ years). Likewise, spatial factors, such as region, country, urban or rural setting, family or local host, or camp, will also have a significant bearing on the type of protection. Circumstances of both the displaced and the population of the hosting state will influence decisions about service delivery and support. And, perhaps most crucially, who is seen as the lead protection provider – state or UNHCR – will have a huge bearing. If 'protection' is to be all-encompassing, delivery will be rare, and failure frequent.

If we take, then, a basic – yet fundamental – interpretation of protection as access to safe territory and freedom from *refoulement*, the record can be deemed generally good. This is so despite the fact that none of the countries under consideration in this piece are signatories to the Refugee Convention and may not even perceive those forced to seek asylum in their territory as legal refugees. The Arab states and Turkey have tended towards an open-door policy towards refugees in the region. The vast majority of Syrians, and other non-Syrians, have therefore succeeded in exercising their right to leave Syria and have entered another, neighbouring state. However, as might be anticipated, the picture is somewhat more nuanced. Asylum seekers and refugees are covered by the constitutional laws of Jordan and Lebanon, and by their immigration laws.[85] A Memorandum of Understanding handles the relationship between the UNHCR and each of the countries vis-à-vis refugees. The situation is therefore much more precarious and subject to change, as evidenced by the treatment of Palestinians.

In Jordan, Palestinian refugees from Syria are not registered with UNHCR, as they are deemed to be under the auspices of UNRWA and, since January 2013, they have been denied entry to Jordan, largely for political reasons.[86] In the case of Lebanon, similar concerns of the government have resulted in the withdrawal of the open door policy for Palestinians. Prevented from entering, there is little alternative but for these refugees to return to Syria, placing them at risk of harm.[87] Palestinians who have succeeded in gaining access to Lebanon are not being registered.[88] For both Jordan and Lebanon, there are a number of reports of removals and deportations though, as far as is known, the numbers are relatively low in view of the millions that have now fled Syria. Obviously, as the UNHCR is not in charge of border controls, it can only use its negotiating power to dissuade states from adopting restrictive entry practices, if and when this occurs.

Similarly to the Syrians, Iraqis crossing the border into Jordan and Lebanon following the Gulf Wars tended to be labelled 'guests' and were handled under the residency laws and bilateral agreements between neighbouring countries. In Jordan, this did not prevent their entry at first, but post-2005 and the bombing of three hotels in Amman, the capital, a visa regime was instituted which complicated the situation for Iraqis. There were reports of some deportations, but numbers have again been low. With promises by the government not to remove over-stayers alongside King Abdullah's General Pardon Law in June 2011, most Iraqis in Jordan, while faced with difficult circumstances, were generally 'safe' in so far as access to territory, permission to remain and freedom from *refoulement* are concerned.[89]

However, the notion of a 'safe haven' comprises more than simple access to territory. What happens in the place of safety also matters. And here the facts are more complex. What might be regarded as 'safe' one day, may be less so another. Thus, in an emergency situation, in the case of a mass influx of people, the priority is to address the immediate basic needs of shelter, food, water, medical aid and sanitation, for without these, life may be at risk. As time passes, the idea of what it is to be 'safe' often alters with the changing circumstances – the immediate needs may be essentially resolved, but other concerns arise.

Iraqis who fled after the second Gulf War were not housed in camps, many choosing to use their own resources in the first instance, before their finances were depleted. While their circumstances were undoubtedly very difficult, and many studies at the time drew attention to, *inter alia*, the lack of education, health care, and employment, as well as the constrained living conditions, the situation was not as dire as that faced by Syrian refugees. Broadly, Iraqis were 'safe' in the sense that the vast majority in Jordan did not face life-threatening circumstances, and, as time passed, some conditions improved, such as access to education and health care.

Syrians, in contrast to their Iraqi counterparts, tend not to be as wealthy or educated, and have left their homes with very few possessions. In Jordan, they might be accommodated in camps, or may make their way to towns or villages. With close family connections between the two countries, many are hosted by friends or family. In Lebanon, there are no official camps, due to the prohibition policy of the government. Syrians are therefore renting privately, staying with Lebanese hosts, living in unfinished buildings or informal shanty and camp-like settlements, or have made their way into UNRWA's camps for Palestinian refugees. Each of these places of residence raises concerns. The refugee camps in Jordan, such as Za'atari, have faced considerable problems – especially in the early days – with reports of violence, riots and rape.[90] A report by UNHCR and International Relief and Development found 50% of refugee dwellings to be inadequate, and as 80% of refugees live outside the camps, this is of great concern.[91] Conditions for refugees in Lebanon are also difficult, with refugees now comprising more than 25% of the Lebanese population.[92] Some have been attacked, with their makeshift homes destroyed[93]; many face terrible circumstances, especially in the winter months.[94] The failure of much-promised donor money to materialise has only exacerbated the situation, with UNHCR having to withdraw support for many families and assist only those determined to be priority cases.[95]

Both countries ostensibly do not permit employment without a work permit but the reality is that such permits are rarely issued and refugees are working illegally. This was the position for Iraqis and has not changed for Syrians. There are potentially serious consequences – fines, imprisonment, deportation – and while there appears to be tacit acceptance of the status quo by both governments, and enforcement is rare, a sense of fear and uncertainty is created amongst refugees, as well as resentment within the indigenous population which can be undercut by the low wages that refugees are willing to accept. History is also repeating itself in the report of rising negative coping strategies, such as child labour, early marriage[96] and increased survival sex work,[97] and an increase in domestic violence in the face of the considerable social and economic pressures of displacement.[98] Thus, while there is protection from the risk of persecution or serious harm in Syria, for growing numbers of the Syrian displaced, there is a lack of safety in the country of asylum.

This section has only touched on the very many issues confronted by the UNHCR and partner NGOs as they struggle to deal with the enormous refugee crisis in the Middle East. In this brief discussion, I have sought to show that what is arguably a simplistic rhetoric of protection and rights rarely translates directly to the field. There is no 'one size fits all' concept or interpretation. In the early days of a refugee influx, the UNHCR, humanitarian and aid organisations are fire-fighting, desperately trying to deal with the basic necessities for survival. Does the rights discourse have much bearing at this stage? Arguably not, other than as a reminder that the delivery of assistance by norm entrepreneurs should have the individual at its centre, that is, his or her human dignity should be paramount.[99] As an emergency slowly develops into protracted displacement, the needs of the refugees may alter but they continue to be important. Are they encouraged to see themselves as rights-holders who can enforce against the duty-bearer? Are they empowered participants in their futures? Is this realistic or appropriate in the Middle East? It is perhaps in recognition of this that the UNHCR started to talk about realising and maintaining 'protection space', a euphemism, I would suggest, for encouraging states – in this case non-signatory states – not to *refoule* and to respect the rights of asylum seekers and refugees, by talking, rather, in the language of needs.[100] That people are in *need*, are beneficiaries, is a fact. Needs can be dressed up as rights, and rights as needs, but, ultimately, success can only be measured by the transformation of people's lives for the better.

## 7.  Conclusions

This article has discussed how a rights-based approach has been adopted by a plethora of aid, development and human rights organisations, as well as the UNHCR, and is now a fundamental principle at the heart of policy and practice, including refugee protection. Years of appealing to the conscience of recalcitrant governments, through articulation of the suffering of people, have failed to improve the lives of many. The language of rights – with its apparent moral certainties and its threat of enforcement against the powerful – is an attractive option for the weary humanitarian. That said, the question remains: is it more empty rhetoric than a basis for meaningful action? The tendency of the last two decades has been to place a heavy burden on the power of rights enforcement to engender significant change for the individual, but the reality, as this article has argued, is that talking about rights does not necessarily achieve rights. This is especially true of refugee policy in the

Middle East where there will often be limits to persuading hosting states to enforce the full range of rights where their own resources are under pressure and they struggle to realise rights for their own nationals. Indeed, it is possible that too great an emphasis on rights could act to the detriment of asylum seekers and refugees, a scenario that is common for this region and beyond.

Equally, one can also argue that a great deal is also being carried under the banner of 'protection'. Not only is protection now heavily associated with rights, but many organisations, which, unlike the UNHCR, do not have a protection mandate, are assuming a protection role. For some, this is a dangerous step and not to be encouraged.[101] The word 'protection' arguably means much more to the public,[102] and perhaps also to government, than might be intended or achievable. In the Middle East, protection is deemed a 'core objective, but what is this 'protection'? As with rights, constant usage of the term does not make it materialise. Rather, as I have argued, there is lack of clarity, not helped by the shift between the language of 'needs' and 'rights' when describing protection, or from emphasis on organisational to community-based protection. In my view, this is patently exemplified in the cases of Iraqi and Syrian displacement, where change has been implemented not through protection as rights but through the desire to alleviate suffering and to engender human flourishing.

Sadly, as is well exemplified by the treatment of Iraqi and Syrian refugees, states, both within and outside the Middle East, are more than willing to ignore their responsibilities, notional or otherwise, and to pass the buck to the humanitarian actors. In the face of such immense human suffering, as now afflicts the region, this is the time to reinvigorate the international refugee regime, and place humanity and international solidarity, on which refugee protection is founded, truly at its core.[103] But this will only succeed if the meaning, expectations and practice of 'protection' are evident to all concerned.

## Acknowledgements

I am grateful to Susan Kneebone for her helpful comments on this article.

## Disclosure statement

No potential conflict of interest was reported by the authors.

## Notes

1. Here I employ the international relations understanding of 'norms' as 'a standard for appropriate behavior for actors with a given identity': Martha Finnemore and Kathryn Sikkink, 'International Norm Dynamics and Political Change', *International Organization* 52, no. 4 (1998): 887; Finnemore and Sikkink describe three stages in a norm's influence: norm emergence, norm cascade and internationalisation, ibid., 896. 'Norm entrepreneurs' are those actors who 'attempt to convince a critical mass of states (norm leaders) to embrace new norms' during the first stage of a norm's emergence: ibid., 895, 896–9.
2. *Convention Relating to the Status of Refugees*, 28 July 1951, 189 UNTS 150, (entered into force 22 April 1954); *Protocol Relating to the Status of Refugees*, 31 January 1967, 606 UNTS 267.

3.  The UNHCR is mandated to conduct refugee status determinations under its Statute – the 1950 Statute of the Office of the UNHCR, 14 December 1950, UNGA Res 428(v) (the UNHCR Statute), paras 6A(ii) and 6B.
4.  Ibid., [2]: 'The work of the High Commissioner shall be ... humanitarian and social ... '.
5.  I have discussed this in more detail elsewhere and build on my analysis here, extending the legal and conceptual to the practical. See Dallal Stevens, 'What Do We Mean By Protection?', *International Journal of Minority and Group Rights* 20, no. 1 (2013): 233–62.
6.  See below and the UNHCR Statute [8] for the original definition of 'international protection' to be applied by the UNHCR.
7.  For a history of humanitarianism see Michael Barnett, *Empire of Humanity – A History of Humanitarianism* (Ithaca, NY: Cornell University Press, 2011).
8.  Arthur Helton, 'What is Refugee Protection? A Question Revisited', in *Problems of Protection – the UNHCR, Refugees, and Human Rights*, ed. Niklaus Steiner, Mark Gibney and Gil Loescher (London: Routledge, 2003), 20.
9.  See, for discussion of the meaning of protection in the Refugee Convention, Andreas Zimmerman and Claudia Mahler, 'Article 1 A, para. 2', in *The 1951 Convention Relating to the Status of Refugees and its 1967 Protocol – A Commentary*, ed. Andreas Zimmerman (Oxford: Oxford University Press, 2011), 444–9; Susan Kneebone and Maria O'Sullivan, 'Article 1C' in ibid., 522–30.
10. Article 1A(2): 'owing to well-founded fear of being persecuted for reasons of race, religion, nationality, membership of a particular social group or political opinion, is outside the country of his nationality and is unable or, owing to such fear, is unwilling to avail himself *of the protection of that country*; or who, not having a nationality and being outside the country of his former habitual residence ... is unable or, owing to such fear, is unwilling to return to it' (emphasis added).
11. See Antonio Fortín, 'The Meaning of "Protection" in the Refugee Definition', *International Journal of Refugee Law* 12, no. 4 (2000): 548.
12. Zimmerman and Mahler, 'Article 1 A, para. 2', 445.
13. For example: Article 14 'Artistic rights and industrial property'; Article 15 'Right of association'. Article 12 on 'Personal status', Article 17 on 'Wage-earning employment', and Article 26 'Freedom of movement' refer to rights in their text.
14. Helton, 'What is Refugee Protection?', 22; see also James Hathaway, *The Rights of Refugees under International Law* (Cambridge: Cambridge University Press, 2005). One might also add a number of other treaties: *inter alia*, the 1969 American Convention on Human Rights, the 1981 African Charter on Human and Peoples' Rights, the 1950 European Convention on Human Rights, the 2000 EU Charter of Fundamental Rights.
15. For example, see Excom Conclusions on *Temporary Refuge* (No. 19 (XXXI) – 1980); *Protection of Asylum-Seekers in Situations of Large-Scale Influx* (No. 22 (XXXII) – 1981); and the UNHCR's current view about generalised violence and armed conflict: Volker Türk, UNHCR, 'Protection Gaps in Europe? Persons Fleeing the Indiscriminate Effects of Generalized Violence', 18 January 2011, http://www.refworld.org/pdfid/4d37d8402.pdf; Vanessa Holzer, *The 1951 Refugee Convention and the Protection of People Fleeing Armed Conflict and Other Situations of Violence* (UNHCR, Division of International Protection, September 2012).
16. Excom Conclusions on *Protection of Asylum-Seekers in Situations of Large-Scale Influx* (No. 22(XXXII) – 1981).
17. Excom Conclusions on *International Solidarity and Refugee Protection* (No. 52 (XXXIX) – 1988).
18. An interesting issue is whether the UNHCR has over-compromised. For example, the organisation has been criticised for its undue humanitarianism at the expense of its legal mandate: see Guy Goodwin-Gill, 'Refugee Identity and Protection's Fading Prospect', in *Refugee Rights and Realities: International Concepts and Regimes*, ed. Frances Nicholson and Patrick Twomey (Cambridge: Cambridge University Press, 1999), Ch. 9; and S. Alex Cunliffe and Michael Pugh, 'UNHCR as Leader in Humanitarian Assistance: A Triumph of Politics Over Law?', in ibid., Ch. 11.
19. UNHCR Statute: [2].
20. Gil Loescher, *The UNHCR and World Politics* (Oxford: Oxford University Press, 2001), Chs 4 and 5; Phil Orchard, *A Right to Flee: Refugees, States, and the Construction of International Cooperation* (Cambridge: Cambridge University Press, 2014), Ch. 7.

21. Ibid. High Commissioner Felix Schnyder stated in 1961 that 'in his opinion the "good offices" concept was elastic enough to permit him, when asked, to bring effective aid to nearly any group of refugees provided there was sufficient interest and support on the part of the international community': Press Release No. Ref. 638, 1 February 1961, cited in Despatch from the Mission in Geneva to the Department of State, No. 311, 6 April 1961, https://history.state.gov/historicaldocuments/frus1961-63v25/d311.

22. See Laura Barnett, 'Global Governance and the Evolution of the International Refugee Regime', *International Journal of Refugee Law* 14, nos 2–3 (2002): 238–62; Volker Türk, 'The Role of the UNHCR in the Development of International Refugee Law', in *Refugee Rights and Realities: International Concepts and Regimes*, ed. Frances Nicholson and Patrick Twomey (Cambridge: Cambridge University Press, 1999), Ch. 8.

23. Jeff Crisp, 'Mind the Gap! UNHCR, Humanitarian Assistance and the Development Process', *New Issues in Refugee Research*, Working Paper No. 43 (UNHCR, May 2001), 7.

24. Barnett, 'Global Governance and the Evolution of the International Refugee Regime', 251.

25. Most notably in relation to the Rwandan refugees, when the UNHCR was accused of being complicit in forced repatriation of innocent Rwandans by the Tanzanian government in 1996, and during the Yugoslavian War (1991–1999), when the UNHCR introduced the concept of 'preventative protection' during the Bosnian crisis (1992–1995), aimed at limiting the scale of the refugee crisis, but was, instead, accused of stopping the right to seek asylum. The UNHCR has also been accused of departing too far from its original legal mandate for refugees thereby undermining their protection.

26. UNGA, *Note on International Protection 1994, A/AC.96/830*, 7 September 1994: [32].

27. Though it should be noted that the Memoranda of Understanding between the UNHCR and state in question might apply a definition of 'refugee' that is based on Article 1A(2) of the Refugee Convention and is therefore much more restrictive. Furthermore, any attempt to resettle refugees to Northern states is likely to require a status determination based on Article 1A(2) before resettlement would be entertained.

28. UNGA, *Note on International Protection 1994*, [11].

29. Ibid.

30. See text in notes 16 and 17 above.

31. Ibid., [12].

32. Ibid. This emphasis on needs correlates with the move towards an increasing humanitarian role adopted by the UNHCR in the 1990s: see for example, Goodwin-Gill, 'Refugee Identity and Protection's Fading Prospect'; and, generally, Loescher, *The UNHCR and World Politics*.

33. UNGA, *Note on International Protection 1994*, [14].

34. As stated above, international protection 'involves seeking ... to meet the whole range of needs that result from the absence of national protection', ibid., [12].

35. Ibid., [9].

36. Note that broader definitions have been adopted where the protection of the 'individual' is concerned as opposed to the refugee. See for example the definition of 'protection' in Office for the Coordination of Humanitarian Affairs (OCHR), *Glossary of Humanitarian Terms in relation to the Protection of Civilians in Armed Conflict* (New York: OCHR, 2003), 25: 'A concept that encompasses all activities aimed at obtaining full respect for the rights of the individual in accordance with the letter and spirit of human rights, refugee and international humanitarian law. Protection involves creating an environment conducive to respect for human beings, preventing and/or alleviating the immediate effects of a specific pattern of abuse, and restoring dignified conditions of life through reparation, restitution and rehabilitation.' By contrast, the International Committee of the Red Cross (ICRC) has stated that: 'The concept of protection encompasses all activities aimed at ensuring full respect for the rights of the individual in accordance with the letter and the spirit of the relevant bodies of law (i. e. human rights, humanitarian and refugee law)' (IASC, *Growing the Sheltering Tree – Protecting Rights through Humanitarian Action* (2002), 11).

37. UNHCR, *Protecting Refugees – A Field Guide for NGOs* (September 1999), http://www.refworld.org/docid/3c03682d4.html, 18.

38. *Reach Out Refugee Protection Training Project*, Handouts on Refugee Protection (2005), http://www.unhcr.org/pages/4a16bb8a6.html, 39, quoting UNHCR, Department of International Protection, *Designing Protection Strategies and Measuring Progress: Checklist for UNHCR Staff* (2002).

39. 64th Session of the Executive Committee of the High Commissioner's Programme, Agenda Point 5(a), Statement by Volker Türk, Director of International Protection, 3 October 2013, http://www.unhcr.org/524d26059.html, 1–2.

40. 65th Session of the Executive Committee of the High Commissioner's Programme, Agenda Point 5(a), Statement by Volker Türk, Director of International Protection, 3 October 2014, http://www.unhcr.org/542e605d9.html, 2.

41. For example, Shannon Kindornay, James Ron, and Charli Carpenter, 'Rights-based Approached to Development: Implications for NGOs', *Human Rights Quarterly* 34, no. 2 (2012): 472–506; Elvira Domínguez Redondo, 'The Millennium Development Goals and the Human Rights Based Approach: Reflecting on Structural Chasms with the UN System', *International Journal of Human Rights* 13, no. 1 (2009): 29–43.

42. UNICEF, *The State of The World's Children* 2004, Annex B, 91; and see *The Human Rights Based Approach to Development Cooperation – Towards a Common Understanding Among the UN Agencies* (Interagency Workshop on a Human Rights-Based Approach in the Context of UN Reform 3–5 May 2003), available in OHCHR, 'Frequently Asked Questions on a Human Rights-Based Approach to Development Cooperation', http://www.ohchr.org/Documents/Publications/FAQen.pdf, Annex II.

43. *The Human Rights Based Approach to Development Cooperation Towards a Common Understanding among UN Agencies ("Common Understanding")* (outcome document from an Interagency Workshop on a Human Rights Based Approach in the Context of UN Reform, 3–5 May 2003): 1.

44. UNAIDS, *Issue Paper: What Constitutes a Rights-based Approach? Definitions, Methods, and Practices*, http://data.unaids.org/Topics/Human-Rights/hrissuepaper_rbadefinitions_en.pdf.

45. Ibid.

46. OHCHR, 'Frequently Asked Questions on a Human Rights-Based Approach to Development Cooperation', http://www.ohchr.org/Documents/Publications/FAQen.pdf, 15.

47. Ibid.

48. The OHCHR describes the concern of human development as being the: 'realization by all of basic freedoms, such as having the choice to meet bodily requirements or to escape preventable disease. It also includes enabling opportunities, such as those given by schooling, equality guarantees and a functioning justice system', ibid., 7.

49. UNDP, *Human Development Report 2000*: *Human Rights and Human Development* (New York: UNDP, 2000), 19.

50. Ibid., 1.

51. Jakob Kirkemann Boesen and Tomas Martin, *Applying a Rights-Based Approach – An Inspirational Guide for Civil Society* (The Danish Institute for Human Rights, 2007), 15.

52. *The Human Rights Based Approach to Development Cooperation.*

53. Kirkemann Boesen and Martin, *Applying a Rights-Based Approach*, 17.

54. Ibid., 11.

55. Ibid.

56. For example, the Scottish Human Rights Commission and the Australian Human Rights Commission.

57. UNHCR, *Reach Out*: *A Refugee Protection Training Project* – Handouts on Refugee Protection (2005), 19, http://www.unhcr.org/cgi-bin/texis/vtx/home/opendocPDFViewer.html?docid=4371d8362&query=rights-basedapproach%20refugees.

58. *Handbook for the Protection of Internally Displaced Persons* (Global Protection Cluster Working Group), http://www.unhcr.org/4c2355229.pdf, 6.

59. Ibid., 11.

60. Statement by Volker Türk, above note 40, 2.

61. The 2013 statement by Türk includes a section on 'Promoting more Government ownership and capacity in asylum/protection systems', above note 40, 4–5.

62. Elsewhere, in similar statements, the duty-bearer is described as 'the State and its agents'.

63. http://www.refworld.org/pdfid/47da54722.pdf.

64. Statement by Volker Türk, above note 40.

65. UNHCR, *A Community-Based Approach in UNHCR Operations* (January 2008), http://www/efworld.org/pdfif/47da54722.pdf, 14.

66. Ibid., 17.

67. Ibid., 16.

68. Ibid., 17. It is also interesting to note the different accounts of needs-based approach, rights-based approach and the charity approach that are listed in the DIHR's guide, *Applying a Rights-Based Approach*, 10.
69. Statement by Volker Türk, above note 40, 7.
70. Kirkemann Boesen and Martin, *Applying a Rights-Based Approach*, 10.
71. Statement by Volker Türk, above note 40, 5.
72. There have been numerous critiques of the human rights movement in the humanitarian and development contexts. See for example, David Kennedy, *The Dark Side of Virtue* (Princeton, NJ: Princeton University Press, 2005), Ch. 1; Andrea Cornwall and Celestine Nyamu-Musembi, 'Putting the "Rights-based Approach" to Development into Perspective', *Third World Quarterly* 25, no. 8 (2004): 1415–37; see also UNAIDS, *Issue Paper: What Constitutes a Rights-based Approach?* A more positive commentary is provided by Paul Gready and Jonathan Ensor, eds, *Reinventing Development? Translating Rights-based Approaches from Theory into Practice* (London: Zed Books, 2005).
73. See http://data.unhcr.org/syrianrefugees/download.php?id=4346.
74. *2014 Syria Regional Response Plan – Strategic Overview*, Foreword, 4, http://www.unhcr.org/syriarrp6/.
75. Ibid., Foreword, 5.
76. Ibid., Strategic Overview, 10.
77. Kirkemann Boesen and Martin, *Applying a Rights-Based Approach*.
78. *2014 Syria Regional Response Plan*, 17.
79. Ibid.
80. Ibid., 10, and see also the table of contents where protection is a sub-heading of 'Humanitarian needs overview'.
81. Ibid., 7.
82. Ibid.
83. Of particular note is the recent cross-country report by a student team from Boston University School of Law, led by Professor Susan Akram, a renowned refugee lawyer with expertise on the Middle East and Palestinians: *Protecting Syrian Refugees: Laws, Policies, and Global Responsibility Sharing*, http://www.bu.edu/law/central/jd/programs/clinics/international-human-rights/documents/FINALFullReport.pdf.
84. See for example, Dallal Stevens, 'Legal Status, Labelling and Protection: The Case of Iraqi "Refugees" in Jordan', *International Journal of Refugee Law* 25, no. 1 (2013): 1–38.
85. Law No. 24 of 1973 on Residence and Foreigners' Affairs (as amended) (Jordan); Liban: *Loi réglementant l'entrée et le séjour des étrangers au Liban ainsi que leur sortie de ce pays*, 10 July 1962 (Lebanon).
86. The issue of the numbers of Palestinians in Jordan is a sensitive one. Some estimates indicate that Palestinians comprise more than half the population of Jordan. Over 1.8 million have been granted Jordanian citizenship and there are more than two million registered Palestinian refugees already in Jordan.
87. Human Rights Watch, 'Lebanon: Palestinians Barred, Sent to Syria' (6 May 2014); Amnesty International, *Denied Refuge – Palestinians from Syria Seeking Safety in Lebanon* (2014). It should also be noted that in October 2014, Lebanon all but closed its border with Syria due to an inability to cope with the influx, and introduced new visa restrictions in January 2015.
88. Though not discussed in this article, Egypt has refused to recognise Palestinians as refugees and has been detaining as well as forcibly returning Palestinians to Syria. See for example, Human Rights Watch, *Egypt Don't Force Palestinians Back to Syria* (18 January 2013); Patrick Kingsley, 'A Syrian Palestinian Refugee in Egypt: 'If I Go Back to Syria I Will Die', *The Guardian* (online ed.), 14 January 2014, http://www.theguardian.com/world/2014/jan/14/syrian-palestinian-refugee-egypt-mahmoud.
89. See for further discussion of the situation regarding Iraqis in Jordan, Stevens, 'Legal Status, Labelling and Protection'.
90. Taylor Luck, 'For Syrian Refugees Fleeing Violence, Zaatari Camp "Another Hell"', *The Jordan Times*, 23 August 2012; Phoebe Greenwood, 'Rape and Domestic Violence Follow Syrian Women into Refugee Camps', *The Guardian*, 25 July 2013.
91. UNHCR/IRD, *Syrian Refugees Living Outside Camps in Jordan*, 18 March 2014, http://www.unhcr.org/urban/.

92.   Issam Abdallah, 'Lebanon Marks "Devastating" Milestone with Millionth Refugee', *Reuters* (online ed.), 3 April 2014,http://www.reuters.com/article/2014/04/03/us-syria-crisis-refugees-idUSBREA320T520140403.

93.   'Lebanese Burn Down Syrian Refugee Camp', *Alakhbar English* (online ed.), 2 December 2013, http://english.al-akhbar.com/node/17783; and in Turkey: 'Xenophobia against Syrian Refugees on Rise: Turkish Government, *Hurriyet Daily News* (online ed.), 25 August 2014, http://www.hurriyetdailynews.com/xenophobia-against-syrian-refugees-on-rise-turkish-government-.aspx?PageID=238&NID=70857&NewsCatID=341.

94.   'Freezing Conditions, Forgotten Camps – Refugees from Syria in Lebanon's Bekaa Valley', *Livewire* (online ed.), 20 December 2013,http://livewire.amnesty.org/2013/12/20/freezing-conditions-forgotten-camps-refugees-from-syria-in-lebanons-bekaa-valley/.

95.   UNHCR, 'UNHCR Warns of Dramatic Consequences if Funding Gaps for Syrian Refugees Continue', 3 July 2014, http://www.unhcr.org/53b518499.html.

96.   Though this is culturally acceptable in some areas of Syria, very young girls are being forced to marry in Jordan and Lebanon for fear of rape: Mark Anderson, 'Child Marriage Soars among Syrian Refugees in Jordan, *The Guardian* (online ed.), 16 July 2014,http://www.theguardian.com/global-development/2014/jul/16/child-marriage-syria-refugees-jordan; IRIN, 'Jordan: Early Marriage – A Coping Mechanism for Syrian Refugees?' (online ed.), 19 July 2012, http://www.irinnews.org/report/95902/jordan-early-marriage-a-coping-mechanism-for-syrian-refugees.

97.   *2014 Syria Regional Response Plan*; *Jordan Response Plan Overview*, 8–9; *Lebanon Response Plan Overview*, 6–7.

98.   IRIN, 'Jordan: Increased Domestic Violence among Iraqi Refugees – IOM Report' (online ed.), 29 April 2008, http://www.irinnews.org/report/77972/jordan-increased-domestic-violence-among-iraqi-refugees-iom-report; Karen Leigh, 'Domestic Violence on the Rise among Syrian Refugees', *The New York Times* (online ed.), 29 August 2014, http://kristof.blogs.nytimes.com/2014/08/29/domestic-violence-on-the-rise-among-syrian-refugees/?_r=0.

99.   However, the meaning of 'human dignity' is also a subject for further reflection. See for example, Christopher McCrudden, ed., *Understanding Human Dignity* (Oxford: Oxford University Press, 2014).

100.  See for example, UNHCR, 'UNHCR Policy on Refugee Protection and Solutions in Urban Areas' (UNHCR, September 2009), in which rights and needs are combined in a somewhat confusing manner in an attempt to articulate the concept of 'protection space'; see also Anne Evans Barnes, 'Realizing Protection Space for Iraqi Refugees: UNHCR in Syria, Jordan and Lebanon', Research Paper No. 67 (UNHCR, January 2009); Jeff Crisp et al., '"Surviving in the City": A Review of UNHCR's Operation for Iraqi Refugees in Urban Areas of Jordan, Lebanon and Syria' (UNHCR, July 2009). Crisp et al. define protection space as 'the extent to which there is a conducive environment for the internationally recognized rights of refugees to be respected and upheld', ibid., 4.

101.  See for example Marc Dubois, 'Protection: The New Humanitarian fig-Leaf', http://www.rsc.ox.ac.uk/files/publications/other/dp-protection-fig-leaf-2009.pdf.

102.  Ibid.

103.  'Humanity' is, for me, a call for compassion, humaneness, and empathy to alleviate suffering. For a discussion of humanity, human rights and refugees, see Colin Harvey, 'Is Humanity Enough? Refugees, Asylum Seekers and the Rights Regime', in *Contemporary Issues in Refugee Law*, ed. Satvinder Juss and Colin Harvey (Cheltenham: Edward Elgar, 2013), Ch. 3. Harvey discusses 'the interaction between the international legal regime that continues to place great store by the fact of a legally imagined status, and a globalized practice of human rights that underlines the centrality of inclusive guarantees', 68.

# Index

www.ingramcontent.com/pod-product-compliance
Ingram Content Group UK Ltd.
Pitfield, Milton Keynes, MK11 3LW, UK
UKHW010020280225
455677UK00023B/712